ISBN 978-3-409-12644-1   ISBN 978-3-322-90997-8 (eBook)
DOI 10.1007/978-3-322-90997-8

Journal of International Business

Special Issue
2/2004

Management International Review

Shirley J. Daniel/ Wolf D. Reitsperger (Guest Editors)
Challenges of Globalization
Guest Editors' Forward

Jonathan P. Doh/Terrence R. Guay
NGOs and Global Codes of Conduct

Michael N. Young/David Ahlstrom/Garry D. Bruton
The "Transnational Solution" for East Asian Corporate Governance

Björn Ambos/Wolf D. Reitsperger
Offshore Centers of Excellence

Steven S. Lui/Chung-Ming Lau/Hang-Yue Ngo
Globalization, HR Best Practices, and Firm Performance

Elizabeth Maitland/Stephen Nicholas/William Purcell/Tasman Smith
Regional Learning Networks

Mannsoo Shin
Cross-cultural Management and Work Values

William T. Stanbury/Ilan B. Vertinsky
Globalization: The Canadian Paradox

Mamduh Hanafi/S. Ghon Rhee
The Wealth Effect of Foreign Investor Presence

GABLER

EDITORIAL BOARD

Professor Raj Aggarwal, Kent State University, Kent – U.S.A.
Professor Jeffrey S. Arpan, University of South Carolina, Columbia – U.S.A.
Professor Daniel van Den Bulcke, Universiteit Antwerpen – Belgium
Professor John A. Cantwell, Rutgers University, Newark – U.S.A.
Professor S. Tamer Cavusgil, Michigan State University, East Lansing – U.S.A.
Professor Frederick D.S. Choi, New York University – U.S.A.
Professor Farok Contractor, Rutgers University, Newark – U.S.A.
Professor John D. Daniels, University of Miami, Coral Gables – U.S.A.
Professor Peter J. Dowling, University of Canberra – Australia
Professor Santiago García Echevarría, Universidad de Alcála de Henares, Madrid – Spain
Professor Lawrence A. Gordon, University of Maryland, College Park – U.S.A.
Professor Sidney J. Gray, University of Sydney – Australia
Professor Geir Gripsrud, Norwegian School of Management, Sandvika – Norway
Professor Jean-François Hennart, Tilburg University – The Netherlands
Professor Georges Hirsch, Centre Franco-Vietnamien de Formation à la gestion, Paris – France
Professor Andrew Inkpen, Thunderbird, The American Graduate School of International Management, Glendale – U.S.A.
Professor Eugene D. Jaffe, Bar-Ilan University, Ramat-Gan – Israel
Professor Erdener Kaynak, Pennsylvania State University, Middletown – U.S.A.
Professor Yui Kimura, University of Tsukuba, Tokyo – Japan
Professor Michael Kutschker, Katholische Universität Eichstätt, Ingolstadt – Germany
Professor Reijo Luostarinen, Helsinki School of Economics – Finland
Professor Klaus Macharzina, Universität Hohenheim, Stuttgart – Germany
Professor Roger Mansfield, Cardiff Business School – United Kingdom
Professor Mark Mendenhall, University of Tennessee, Chattanooga – U.S.A.
Professor Rolf Mirus, University of Alberta, Edmonton – Canada
Professor Michael H. Moffett, American Graduate School, Phoenix – U.S.A.
Professor Krzysztof Y. Obloj, University of Warsaw – Poland
Professor Lars Oxelheim, Göteborg and Lund University – Sweden
Professor Ki-An Park, Kyung Hee University, Seoul – Korea
Professor Robert D. Pearce, University of Reading – United Kingdom
Professor Lee Radebaugh, Brigham Young University, Provo – U.S.A.
Professor Edwin Rühli, Universität Zürich – Switzerland
Professor Alan M. Rugman, Indiana University, Bloomington, U.S.A.
Professor Rakesh B. Sambharya, Rutgers University, Camden, U.S.A.
Professor Reinhart Schmidt, Universität Halle-Wittenberg – Germany
Professor Hans Schöllhammer, University of California, Los Angeles – U.S.A.
Professor Oded Shenkar, The Ohio State University, Columbus – U.S.A.
Professor Vitor Corado Simoes, Universidade Técnica de Lisboa – Portugal
Professor John Stopford, 6 Chalcot Square, London NW1 8YB – United Kingdom
Professor Daniel P. Sullivan, University of Delaware, Newark – U.S.A.
Professor Norihiko Suzuki, International Christian University, Tokyo – Japan
Professor Stephen Bruce Tallmann, University of Utah, Salt Lake City – U.S.A.
Professor George Tesar, Umeå University, Umeå – Sweden
Professor José de la Torre, Florida International University, Miami – U.S.A.
Professor Rosalie L. Tung, Simon Fraser University, Burnaby, BC – Canada
Professor Jean-Claude Usunier, University of Lousanne, Lousanne – Dorigny – Switzerland
Professor Alain Charles Verbeke, Vrije Universiteit Brussel – Belgium
Professor Lawrence S. Welch, Mt Eliza Business School, Melbourne, Australia
Professor Martin K. Welge, Universität Dortmund – Germany
Professor Bernard Yin Yeung, New York University – U.S.A.
Professor Masaru Yoshimori, Yokohama National University – Japan

BOOK REVIEW EDITOR

Professor Dr. Johann Engelhard, Universität Bamberg – Germany

EDITOR

MANAGEMENT INTERNATIONAL REVIEW, *Professor Dr. Profs. h.c. Dr. h.c. Klaus Macharzina, Universität Hohenheim (510 E), Schloss-Osthof-Ost, D-70599 Stuttgart, Germany, Tel. (0711) 4 59-29 08, Fax (0711) 459-32 88, E-mail: klausmac@uni-hohenheim.de, Internet: http://www.uni-hohenheim.de/~mir Assistant Editors: Professor Dr. Michael-Jörg Oesterle, Universität Bremen, Germany, Professor Dr. Joachim Wolf, Universität Kiel, Germany, Editorial office: Mrs. Sylvia Ludwig*

VOLUME 44 · SPECIAL ISSUE · 2004/2

CONTENTS

Guest Editor's Forward 3

Jonathan P. Doh/Terrence R. Guay
Globalization and Corporate Social Responsibility:
How Non-Governmental Organizations Influence Labor
and Environmental Codes of Conduct 7

Michael N. Young/David Ahlstrom/Garry D. Bruton
The Globalization of Corporate Governance in East Asia:
The "Transnational" Solution 31

Björn Ambos/Wolf D. Reitsperger
Offshore Centers of Excellence: Social Control and Success 51

Steven S. Lui/Chung-Ming Lau/Hang-Yue Ngo
Global Convergence, Human Resources Best Practices, and Firm
Performance: A Paradox 67

Elizabeth Maitland/Stephen Nicholas/William Purcell/Tasman Smith
Regional Learning Networks: Evidence from Japanese MNEs
in Thailand and Australia 87

Mannsoo Shin
Convergence and Divergence of Work Values among Chinese,
Indonesian, and Korean Employees 105

William T. Stanbury/Ilan B. Vertinsky
Economics, Demography and Cultural Implications of Globalization:
The Canadian Paradox 131

Mamduh Hanafi/S. Ghon Rhee
The Wealth Effect of Foreign Investor Presence:
Evidence from the Indonesian Market 157

mir vol. 44 · Special Issue · 2004/2   1

GUIDELINE FOR AUTHORS

mir welcomes articles on original theoretical contributions, empirical research, state-of-the-art surveys or reports on recent developments in the areas of

a) International Business b) Transnational Corporations c) Intercultural Management d) Strategic Management e) Business Policy.

Manuscripts are reviewed with the understanding that they are substantially new, have not been previously published in whole (including book chapters) or in part (including exhibits), have not been previously accepted for publication, are not under consideration by any other publisher, and will not be submitted elsewhere until a decision is reached regarding their publication in **mir**. The only exception is papers in conference proceedings, which we treat as work-in-progress.

Contributions should be submitted in English language in a Microsoft or compatible format by e-mail to the Editor at klausmac@uni-hohenheim.de. The complete text including the references, tables and figures should as a rule not exceed 25 pages in a usual setting (approximately *7000 words*). Reply papers should normally not exceed 1500 words. The title page should include the following elements: Author(s) name, Heading of the article, Abstract (two sections of about 30 words each), Key Results (20 words), Author's line (author's name, academic title, position and affiliation) and on the bottom a proposal for an abbreviated heading on the front cover of the journal.

Submitted papers must be written according to mir's formal guidelines. Only those manuscripts can enter the reviewing process which adhere to our guidelines. Authors are requested to

– use *endnotes* for clarification sparingly. References to the literature are indicated in the text by author's name and year of publication in parentheses, e.g. (Reitsperger/Daniel 1990, p. 210, Eiteman 1989). The references should be listed in alphabetical order at the end of the text. They should include full bibliographical details and be cited in the following manner: e.g.

Reitsperger, W. D./Daniel, S. J., Dynamic Manufacturing: A Comparison of Attitudes in the U.S. and Japan, *Management International Review*, 30, 1990, pp. 203–216.

Eiteman, D. K., Financial Sourcing, in Macharzina, K./Welge, M. K. (eds.), *Handwörterbuch Export und Internationale Unternehmung*, Stuttgart: Poeschel 1989, pp. 602–621.

Stopford, J. M./Wells, L. T. Jr., *Managing the Multinational Enterprise*, New York: Basic Books 1972.

– avoid *terms* that may be interpreted denigrating to ethnic or other groups.
– be especially careful in dealing with gender. Traditional customs such as "... the manager wishes that **his** interest ..." can favor the acceptance of inequality were none exist. The use of plural pronouns is preferred. If this is impossible, the term "he or she" or "he/she" can be used.

In the case of publication authors are supplied one complimentary copy of the issue and 30 off-prints free of charge. Additional copies may be ordered *prior to printing*. Overseas shipment is by boat; air-delivery will be charged extra.

The author agrees, that his/her article is published not only in this journal but that it can also be reproduced by the publisher and his licensees through license agreement in other journals (also in translated versions), through reprint in omnibus volumes (i.e. for anniversary editions of the journal or the publisher or in subject volumes), through longer extracts in books of the publisher also for advertising purposes, through multiplication and distribution on CD ROM or other data media, through storage on data bases, their transmission and retrieval, during the time span of the copyright laws on the article at home and abroad.

Management
International Review
© Gabler Verlag 2004

Guest Editors' Forward

This special issue is devoted to the topic of globalization, one of the most emotionally charged terms in international business today. While globalization is not really a new phenomenon, advances in transportation and communications technology as well as decreasing trade barriers have increased the pace and magnitude of cross border interactions, bringing them to the forefront of discussion for scholars. In such discussions, the term "globalization" is sometimes used in a broader economic sense for capitalism or the market economy. However, globalization can be more rationally discussed in terms of 3 elements: 1) international trade, 2) foreign direct investment and 3) capital market flows.

Over the past 10 years, businesses have participated in an increasing level of international activity. For example, the level of international trade increased in developed countries from 27% to 39% of GDP and in developing countries from 10% to 17%. According to the World Bank, the share of foreign direct investment to GDP has also risen in both developed and developing countries and is now the largest form of private capital inflow to developing countries. These increases in trade and direct investment are generally seen by business as positive. However, there is less agreement about the issue of the globalization of capital flows, which have been more volatile than trade or FDI flows, and are sometimes blamed for the periodic economic crises that have occurred in the 1990s in Mexico, Thailand, Russia and Brazil. Capital markets and currency values are now much less under the control of national governments, particularly those with policies that are out of step with the free market.

One of the great driving forces behind globalization has always been technology. In the past, it was transportation technology, with steamships, railroads and finally air transportation allowing cheaper and faster movement of products across borders, thus making international trade more profitable. Today it is telecommunications technology that is making the flow of information, and more importantly, knowledge, available across great distances at a nominal cost. From the entrepreneur's perspective, the driving force behind globalization is market opportunity. In a way, new technology creates the opportunity for anytime, anywhere markets. From the geo-political perspective, better telecommunications

Guest Editors' Forward

technology now makes it harder for governments to control the flow of information and knowledge to citizens, and even people in remote areas may have access to a great deal of information about the outside world.

There are two issues often associated with globalization that are problematic to many scholars. The first is the effect of rapid economic growth on the environment. Once a country is past a certain level of development, environmental quality improves with economic development. However, for very poor countries striving to develop, compromises are sometimes made regarding the environment to satisfy short-term economic gains. The second problem often cited with regard to globalization is that it amplifies inequality within countries. The research actually reveals that there is no clear relationship between international trade and income inequality. In general, the more free and open the economy, the quicker it can adjust to the changes brought about by globalization, thus shortening the time frame for any inequalities created. It should be noted that both of these issues are related to economic development in general, and not to globalization per se.

This special issue began as an effort of the Pacific Asian Consortium for International Business Education and Research (PACIBER), founded in 1988 to establish linkages and promote international business education, research and exchange of information among faculty and students of its 29 member business schools in Asia, North America, and Oceania. With its secretariat at the crossroads of the Pacific in the University of Hawaii College of Business Administration Pacific Asian Management Institute, PACIBER strives to widen the scope of cooperation, facilitate communication and expand consciousness about international business in the Asia Pacific region. Through a broad solicitation of the call for papers, scholars from throughout the globe were invited to contribute papers, which were then subjected to a rigorous blind review process. This resulting volume reflects the breadth of issues that international business scholars may consider when exploring the impact of globalization on business.

The first three papers deal with organizational and structural issues that firms face in addressing the challenge of globalization. Doh and Guay focus on the influence of non-governmental organizations on MNC codes of conduct in a global environment, and the specific circumstances that allow NGOs to have more or less influence on the development and enforcement of these codes. In the next paper, drawing upon an Asian context, Young, Alstrom, and Bruton discuss the tensions between corporate governance systems that meet international investors' expectations versus practices embedded in local institutions and culture, and advocate a transnational solution to balance the expectations of various stakeholders. Ambos and Reitsperger move the discussion to the organization and control of offshore centers of excellence, relating modes of control to the technical success of these units, drawing on data from German MNCs.

The next set of papers deal with the issue of managing a global workforce. Lui, Lau, and Ngo explore the issue of whether there is global convergence in human resource practices or perhaps even a set of "best practices" that can be applied across borders. Their data from over 200 firms in Hong Kong find that full scale convergence of human resource practices is far from a reality. The issue of the global transfer of management practices and know how is further explored by Maitland, Nicholas, and Purcell. Their research tested for learning and the replication of human resource management capabilities in Australian- and Thai-based Japanese subsidiaries. Rather than explore corporate policies and practices, Shin explores the convergence and divergence of work values among workers in China, Indonesia, and Korea. The results provide some bases for both standardized and differentiated international human resource practices.

The last two papers, while very different in approach, address the impact of global forces on two countries – one developed and one developing. Stanbury and Vertinsky explore the effects of globalization on Canada's economy and on the political and cultural identities of Canadians. Despite the overwhelming flow of American cultural products, their data indicate that Canada remained distinct in the dimensions of culture that matter most. In contrast, Hannafi and Rhee investigate the wealth effect of foreign investor presence on the Indonesian domestic stock market before and after the announcement of lifting foreign stock ownership restrictions in Indonesia in 1997. While their study indicated positive wealth effects, the impact was modest and short-lived because of the Asian financial crisis, which some would blame on the impact of globalization on capital markets.

The primary conclusions that can be drawn from all of these studies are that there are many more questions than answers regarding the impact of globalization on international business, and that this topic will present a fertile field for international business research for years to come.

We would like to thank Professor Dr. Dr. h.c. Klaus Macharzina, Editor of Management International Review, for the opportunity to serve as guest editors for this issue. We also appreciate the help of dozens of reviewers who participated in this issue, and welcome the comments of scholars throughout the academy regarding their insights on the topic of globalization and particularly on the papers included herein.

SHIRLEY J. DANIEL
WOLF D. REITSPERGER

mir Edition

GABLER

Stefan Eckert

Aktionärsorientierung der Unternehmenspolitik?

Shareholder Value – Globalisierung – Internationalität

2004, XXXII, 518 pages, pb., € 64,00 (approx. US $ 64,00)
ISBN 3-409-12569-8

During the 1990s "shareholder value" has become a popular catchphrase for German companies. In his book the author examines whether this tendency is accompanied by a fundamental change in corporate attitudes towards shareholders. The argumentation is based on an in-depth case study, which stretches across a period of nearly 30 years. The author uncovers the ambiguity of the changes in corporate policy taking place and comes to the conclusion that the turn to shareholder value cannot just be seen as the consequence of competitive changes in a company's markets, but has to be interpreted as a cultural phenomenon.

This book is essential reading for students, lecturers, and researchers who are interested in topics such as International Management, Corparate Policy, and Corporate Governance. It should also be of special interest to corporate managers as well as decision makers working in investment funds or in shareholder associations.

Betriebswirtschaftlicher Verlag Dr. Th. Gabler GmbH, Abraham-Lincoln-Str. 46, 65189 Wiesbaden

Management
International Review
© Gabler Verlag 2004

Jonathan P. Doh/Terrence R. Guay

Globalization and Corporate Social Responsibility: How Non-Governmental Organizations Influence Labor and Environmental Codes of Conduct

Abstract

- Concerns over the potential negative spillovers from globalization have resulted in increasing demands for multinational corporations (MNCs) to adhere to international standards and codes of responsibility. Nongovernmental organizations (NGOs) have been important advocates for development and adoption of these standards and codes.

- In this paper, we provide a brief review of the emergence of NGOs and their influence on debates about globalization, and a specific assessment of NGO efforts to promote stronger labor and environmental policies of multinational corporations.

- We examine the role of NGOs in development and enforcement of twelve international agreements and codes of conduct addressing labor issues and environmental practices. We use findings from these cases and insights from international business and other managerial theory to develop propositions that explain the circumstances under which NGOs have more or less influence in developing and enforcing international codes.

Key Results

- We suggest NGOs will achieve the greatest impact on codes of conduct when: 1) they intervene early in the code development process; 2) they forge transnational coalitions with other organizations, including other NGOs, MNCs, and governments; 3) codes are devised outside of international organizations; and 4) the structure of the codes or agreements explicitly provides for involvement by non-business and non-state actors.

Authors

Jonathan P. Doh, assistant professor of management, College of Commerce and Finance, Villanova University, Villanova, PA, USA.
Terrence R. Guay, assistant professor of international relations and political science, Maxwell School, Syracuse University, Syracuse, NY, USA.

Introduction

The emergence of nongovernmental organizations (NGOs) as important institutional actors in the global political economy is a relatively recent phenomenon (Doh/Teegen 2002). The growing importance of NGOs in major global policy debates represents both a response to, and an element of, the globalization phenomenon. NGO influence has been felt in a range of major public policy debates, and NGO activism is responsible for major changes in corporate behavior and policy. Multinational corporations (MNCs) now are increasingly confronted by a range of international agreements and codes of conduct that attempt to govern their behavior, many of which are driven by NGO pressure. During the past decade, concerns over the downsides of economic globalization, particularly in the environmental and labor areas, have contributed to the growth of codes of conduct (Drezner 2000, Williams 2000, Kearney 1999). Such codes are viewed by many NGOs as a means to rein in the excesses of globalization. Codes may take the form of international agreements, or be sponsored by international organizations, the private sector, or non-profit organizations.

Until very recently, few research efforts have explored the influence NGOs have on corporate conduct. There have been some preliminary efforts to evaluate how the rise of NGOs may affect business-government relations (Doh 2003, Keim 2003) and on how codes of conduct affect a specific company or industry (van Tulder/Kolk 2001). However, these efforts have not sought specifically to examine the process through which NGOs influence the development and implementation of corporate codes. Drawing from research in international relations (IR), and management literature in international business (IB) and social issues in management (SIM), we construct a framework that classifies NGO influence on international codes and agreements. We identify four broad types of codes, classified by their principal sponsoring organizations: (1) international agreements signed by governments; (2) international codes sponsored by intergovernmental organizations (IGOs); (3) international codes sponsored by corporate groups and associations; and (4) international codes sponsored by not-for-profit NGOs. The main contributions of this paper are: (1) identification and specification of the connections between the rising influence and proliferation of NGOs and the propagation of codes of conduct; and (2) development of propositions, derived from our study of twelve codes and agreements and insights from international relations and management theory, to suggest when NGOs are likely to have greater influence in development, implementation, and monitoring of labor and environmental codes and agreements.

Our primary focus is on the processes and timing– rather than the outcome – of NGO involvement in codes and agreements. Through examination of how and when NGOs mobilize to affect codes, and evaluation of mechanisms provided for in agreements to permit NGO access, we believe our insights also have implications for the long-term viability of these increasingly pervasive mechanisms to influence and constrain MNC behavior around the world.

Globalization and the Influence of NGOs in Global Affairs

One of the most interesting phenomena of the post-Cold War era has been the rise in the number and influence of NGOs (The Economist 2000). The modern NGO advocacy movement emerged in mid-1984. Massive protests in South Africa, combined with escalating international pressure to force substantial capital flight through the process of "divestment" and the Sullivan Principles, created an intense challenge to the continuation of white minority rule. Since the mid 1980s, NGOs have had increasing and measurable influences on public policy, corporate strategy, and business-to-government relations.

NGOs: Definitions and Growth

NGOs can be defined as "self-governing, private, not-for-profit organizations that are geared to improving the quality of life of disadvantaged people" (Vakil 1997, p. 2060). Most would agree that common causes undertaken by NGOs include those related to environmental issues, as well as human rights, labor rights, and other areas. Another approach to the classification of NGOs is to distinguish between "operational" and "advocacy" NGOs (Gordenker/Weiss 1996, van Tuijl 1999). Operational NGOs provide social services such as education, health, or human relief, whereas advocacy NGOs lobby governments, MNCs, and IGOs. In this paper, we are primarily interested in advocacy NGOs, although we recognize that operational NGOs may be involved in code implementation, and that a given NGO may serve in both advocacy and operational roles.

The Internal Revenue Service (IRS) counted 819,008 not-for-profits in 2000 (Wall Street Journal 2001). In 1998 it was estimated that the total size of the "independent sector" in the United States, which includes the IRS figure as well as civic leagues, social welfare organizations, and religious congregations, reached 1.2 million organizations. These organizations employed an estimated 10.9 million individuals with revenues of nearly $680 billion (Independent Sector 2001). At the international level, a 1995 United Nations (UN) report suggested that there were nearly 29,000 international NGOs (The Economist 2000).

NGOs in Global Affairs

Recognition of NGOs as influential non-state actors is now widely accepted in the international relations (IR) field (Mathews 1997, Simmons 1998, Smith et al. 1997). Along with MNCs and IGOs, NGOs are the entities most frequently discussed as significant actors (and threats to the dominance of nation-states) in global affairs. Using their network of members, NGOs play an important role in collecting and disseminating information, as well as working with national governments, international organizations, and other non-state actors, including MNCs (Ottaway 2001). Keck and Sikkink (1998) argue that transnational advocacy networks are motivated primarily by principled ideas, and may influence not only the preferences of their own states, but also the preferences of individuals and groups elsewhere (including MNCs). However, defining and measuring NGO participation in international decision-making is an under-developed area of research (Clark 1995, Price 1998, Walter 2001). This paper contributes to the nascent literature directed toward defining, measuring, and understanding the NGO role in globalization.

Globalization, NGOs, and Corporate Social Responsibility: A Critical Stakeholder Perspective

Two streams of research in social issues in management (SIM) can inform and frame analysis of the role of NGOs in development of global corporate responsibility, especially in explaining the overall growth in NGO influence, and the increasing receptivity by governments and corporations to their involvement. Stakeholder theory helps in explaining the roles and influence of various actors, including NGOs, in development of labor and environment codes and agreements, while research in corporate social responsibility and performance provides instrumental insights as to the benefits and costs of adoption and implementation of these codes.

Stakeholder Theory

Since publication of Edward Freeman's Strategic Management: A Stakeholder Approach (1984), stakeholder management, stakeholder theory, and other variants of stakeholder analysis have occupied a great deal of managerial research. Freeman argued that business relationships should include all those who may "affect or be affected by" a corporation (Clarkson 1995, Freeman 1984, Freeman/Reed 1983). Much of the research in stakeholder theory has sought to systematically address the question of which stakeholders deserve or require management attention (Mitchell/Agle/Wood 1997). Approaches to this question have focused on relationships between organizations and stakeholders based on exchange transactions, power dependencies, legitimacy claims, or other claims (Cummings/Doh 2000, Donaldson/Preston 1995, Mitchell/Agle/Wood 1997). Researchers have attempted to integrate stakeholder theory with other managerial perspectives, particularly theories of governance and agency (Hill/Jones 1992, Jones 1995).

Stakeholder theory is useful as both an instrumental and normative frame for assessing the role of NGOs in the development and adoption of labor and environmental standards. Mitchell, Agle, and Wood's (1997) effort to develop a typology for classifying stakeholders is especially instructive. They proposed a theory of stakeholder identification and salience based on managerial assessments of stakeholders' possession of one or more of three relationship attributes: power, legitimacy, and urgency. When stakeholders possess all three of the stakeholder characteristics, managers should respond to their claims (Mitchell/Agle/Wood 1997, p. 878). Stakeholder management provides a natural theoretical base for understanding the general rationale for NGO involvement in codes, and the role of NGOs in defining, or at least influencing, development of international labor and environmental standards. Further, the role of NGOs may depend on their relative salience as stakeholders at a given point in time, and such a role may evolve as the relative salience of different stakeholders shifts and conditions change.

Corporate Social Responsibility and Performance

An additional variant of research related to the role of the corporation in modern society are those efforts designed to develop and test models of corporate social performance (CSP), corporate social responsibility (CSR1), and corporate social responsiveness (CSR2) (Carroll 1994, Carroll 1979, Wartick/Cochran 1985). Empirical studies and reviews of these efforts suggest a link between corporate *social* responsibility/performance and the *economic* performance of the corporation (Cochran/Wood 1984, Griffin/Mahon 1997, Preston/O'Bannon 1997, Preston/Sapienza 1990, Windsor/Preston 1988, Wood 1991). Such relationships suggest that incorporating NGOs into the strategy-making process may generate social benefits that yield higher financial returns. Prakash et al. (1996) suggest MNCs are not always opposed to environmental regulations. If the costs of implementing environmental agreements are diffuse, and the benefits concentrated, they will support such agreements. This insight suggests that when NGOs are successful in urging the widespread adoption of standards, corporations may support agreements if they are able to share the costs while preserving individual benefits. Nehrt (1998) contends that MNCs that conform to environmental regulations promulgated in one jurisdiction gain global first mover competitive advantages when other countries later adopt such standards. Hence, MNCs may willingly adopt international labor or environmental codes if they believe that such codes will eventually become standard in their industry.

In reviewing the emergent role of NGOs in developing international labor and environmental standards, research on CSP, CSR1, and CSR2 would suggest that firms experience benefits from improving their social and environmental performance. These benefits can result from competitive advantages that emanate from improved efficiency and performance, and also from reputation and goodwill that result from positive perceptions of the corporation. Further, returns may increase for those firms that adopt such standards because they receive protection or insulation from criticisms. Negative images and reputation will fall on those firms that do not subscribe to codes or agreements. In addition, as some firms adopt environmental management practices, others may follow, generating a dynamic, reflexive process (Deutsch 1998). Hence, we see motivation for business firms to seek collaborations and partnerships with NGOs under certain conditions. But what about the strategies of NGOs in influencing codes, and how do these strategies interact with participation by other actors, and the structure of the codes themselves? In the next section, we review these questions through construction of an organizing framework for classifying different types of codes, and specification of the roles of NGOs in code and agreement development, implementation, and monitoring.

NGOs and the Development of International Labor and Environmental Standards: An Organizing Framework

In this section, we propose a simple typology to classify NGO involvement in international labor and environmental standards. We identify four broad types of codes, classified by their principal sponsoring organizations: (1) international agreements signed by governments; (2) international codes sponsored by IGOs; (3) international codes sponsored by corporate groups; and (4) international codes sponsored by not-for-profit NGOs. We suggest that NGO participation may involve some combination of proposing, monitoring, and enforcing codes. The role of NGOs frequently evolves as these agreements and codes progress, often in the direction of increasing involvement and engagement. Table 1 summarizes the framework and findings.

Table 1. International Agreements and Codes of Conduct Governing Corporate Labor and Environmental Policies: Examples and NGO Role in Agreement Formulation and Compliance

	International Government-Government Agreements	International Codes Sponsored by IGOs	International Codes Sponsored by Industrial and Corporate Associations	International Codes Sponsored by Not-for-profit NGOs
Examples	North American Free Trade Agreement, World Trade Organization, Free Trade Agreement of the Americas	UN Global Compact, ILO Declaration of Principles concerning Multinational Enterprises and Social Policy, OECD Guidelines for MNEs	World Business Council for Sustainable Development (WBCSD), Global Environmental Management Institute (GEMI), ISO 14000	Social Accountability International SA8000, Rugmark, Forest Stewardship Council (FSC)
Representative List of NGOs Involved	Environmental (Sierra Club, World Wildlife Fund/Worldwide Fund for Nature – WWF), Labor (AFL-CIO, UAW), Corporate (US Chamber of Commerce, National Association of Manufacturers)	Labor (Trade Union Advisory Committee to the OECD, International Confederation of Free Trade Unions), Environmental (WWF, World Resources Institute, IUCN – the World Conservation Union), Human Rights (Amnesty, Human Rights Watch)	National chambers of commerce, national technical standards groups (American National Standards Institute), national industry associations, International Standards Organization	Labor (The International Textile, Garment and Leather Workers' Federation, Union Network Intl.), Development (Save the Children), Human Rights (Amnesty International), Environmental (National Resources Defense Council, National Wildlife Federation, WWF)
NGO Role in Agreement Formulation	Low	Low	High	High
NGO Role in Agreement Compliance	Moderate	Low/Moderate	Moderate	High

Many NGOs participate in the above codes on an *ad hoc* or informal basis.

International Government-to-Government Codes

Although "civil society" groups have been vocal on issues related to international labor and the environment for some time, NGO activism in the environmental arena, especially regarding concerns over the relationship between trade liberalization and environmental protection, accelerated in the early 1990s. Although a number of international agreements have opened up to receive NGO input and contributions directly, the primary mechanism for NGOs to influence is through the national governments that constitute the main participants to the agreements.

Pressure for inclusion of environment and labor issues in international government-to-government agreements received a strong push from the North American Free Trade Agreement (NAFTA). These efforts were a response to environmental NGOs and trade unions that expressed concerns over the agreement's potential to result in the lowering of standards, US loss of sovereignty over environmental and labor laws, and the perceived absence of public participation in environmental policies in Mexico. The Supplemental Agreement on Environmental Cooperation became a condition for US ratification of NAFTA, and allowed a country or NGO to file a dispute settlement case if a party exhibited a "persistent pattern of non-enforcement" of domestic environmental law (NAFTA 1993). The agreement also created a series of cooperative programs and established an administrative mechanism to oversee its operation. This mechanism includes a joint trilateral advisory committee made up mostly of members of environmental NGOs from all three countries (NAFTA 1993). Although NGOs did not participate directly in the drafting of the labor and environmental agreement, they did provide the catalyst for its negotiation, and their roles became codified as a result of the establishment of a formal place for NGOs in the proceedings of the administrative arms of the agreement (Johnson/Beaulieu 1996, Menz 1995).

At the conclusion of the Uruguay Round of multilateral trade negotiations under the auspices of the General Agreement on Tariffs and Trade (now the World Trade Organization or WTO), the WTO signatories agreed to create the Committee on Trade and Environment to study and oversee WTO-related work in the area of trade and the environment in order to promote sustainable development, and make recommendations on whether the WTO should be modified or revised to fulfill this objective (WTO 1995). In addition, The Uruguay Round agreements explicitly made provisions for cooperation and consultation with NGOs (Deslauriers et al. 2002, WTO 1996). One area in which NGOs expressed a great deal of interest was in the dispute settlement mechanism. After several cases and petitions the WTO established a mechanism for submission of NGO briefs, in which submitting parties must make clear their objectives, affiliation and financing (WTO 1996). NGOs must also provide a summary of their contribution to the issue at hand, and an explanation of why their material does not repeat material already received by the Body from countries, a channel that is still open to NGOs and remains the primary mechanism for WTO decision-making (Deslauriers et al. 2002, Charnovitz 2000, WTO 2001). In this case, as with NAFTA, NGOs were catalysts to the WTO's responses, and served primarily as outside advocates rather than internal champions.

The Free Trade Area of the Americas (FTAA) process is an ongoing negotiation designed to eliminate barriers to trade and investment among thirty-four countries, and is an example of an arena in which space is being created for the presentation of NGO views (FTAA 1998). In preparation for launching the negotiations, FTAA ministers acknowledged that a range of views existed regarding this initiative within their own countries. The first Open Invitation to Civil Society, issued in 1998, received 66 responses from civil society actors in 16 FTAA countries. Submissions included calls for the FTAA negotiators to consider labor standards or environmental protection (Deslauriers et al. 2002). A second Open Invitation was issued on April 10, 2000, and received 82 responses. The Committee on Civil Society will continue to receive input from civil society groups, and disseminate these views both to the FTAA negotiating groups and to the public. The Committee's mandate has also been strengthened and it has been instructed to consider mechanisms to "foster a process of increasing and sustained communication with civil society" (FTAA 2001). Through the FTAA/OAS (Organization of American States) consultative processes, NGOs are taking an increasingly active role in development of environmental and labor provisions linked to trade and investment agreements.

In general, the NGO role in the formulation of international codes sponsored by government can be characterized as relatively minimal (low), while their role in agreement compliance is moderate (Table 1). It should be clear, however, that as these government-to-government agreements increasingly institutionalize the role of civil society, and by extension, NGOs, the role of non-state non-firm actors in shaping agreements will undoubtedly grow.

International Codes Sponsored by Intergovernmental Organizations

Intergovernmental organizations (IGOs) are entities created by, and serving the interests of, their member states. The construction of IGOs requires member states to relinquish or pool some amount of national sovereignty to achieve certain objectives, including cooperation across policy areas, or establishing international rules and norms that guide and govern specific activities (such as trade). It is estimated that there were 6,115 IGOs in 1997 (Cusimano 2000, p. 218). IGOs have become increasingly relevant international actors during the second half of the twentieth century, and some have developed their own codes of conduct.

The International Labor Organization (ILO) addresses the conditions of workers. ILO labor standards come in the form of conventions (international treaties), non-binding recommendations, and, less formally, codes of conduct, resolutions, and declarations, of which the 1977 Tripartite Declaration of Principles concerning Multinational Enterprises and Social Policy (revised in 2000) is the best known (ILO 1977, ILO 2002). This declaration provides voluntary guidelines for MNCs, workers' and employers' organizations, and governments in such areas as development policy, rights at work, employment, training, conditions of work and life, and industrial relations. While neither MNCs nor governments are bound by this declaration to provide specific labor standards, there exists a procedure for disputes over the meaning and application of this declaration's provisions to be interpreted by the ILO. The ILO's institutional structure grants a formal role to trade unions and business organizations (along with member states) to set labor standards. NGOs that are not actual trade unions are limited to an indirect role of trying to influence the positions that these three groups bring to ILO negotiations. With this limited NGO role, the Declaration of Principles suffers from a lack of innovation and failure to address contemporary global labor concerns.

The principal Organization for Economic Cooperation and Development (OECD) code of conduct is the 1976 Guidelines for Multinational Enterprises (OECD 1976). The Guidelines are non-binding recommendations for MNCs operating in or from adhering countries. The Guidelines provide voluntary principles and standards for business conduct in such wide-ranging areas as employment and industrial relations, human rights, environment, information disclosure, competition, taxation, and science and technology. The Guidelines were revised in 2000, and now extend consultations to NGOs (OECD 2000). NGOs may request consultations with national governments on issues related to the Guidelines, and may participate in promotional activities organized by governments or the OECD. The 2000 Review also tried to address the perception that the 1976 Guidelines were toothless. While NGOs were closely consulted on the drafting of the 2000 Review, and an international coalition of 75 NGOs called it "a first step in the right direction of achieving true corporate accountability," many NGOs feel that, without binding international rules, the code is still too weak (de Jonquieres 2000).

One of the newest IGO-sponsored codes, the Global Compact, originated in an address by UN Secretary-General Kofi Annan to world business leaders at the 1999 World Economic Forum in Davos (UN 2000). The Compact encourages business self-regulation rather than legally binding regulations as the means to support nine core principles covering human rights, labor rights, and the environment. The Compact describes itself not as a regulatory instrument or code of conduct, but as a value-based platform designed to promote institutional learning. The response of NGOs to the Compact are mixed (Alden 2000, Cortese 2002). One view is that the initiative will require companies to post a yearly update on their progress on the Compact's principles, which will be subject to criticism. Yet the nonbinding nature of the Compact makes most NGOs skeptical of its likelihood of changing MNC behavior. The Compact's expectation that NGOs will monitor corporate performance and compliance assumes that NGOs have the resources to undertake a very wide-ranging function. NGOs have thus found it more productive to pressure MNCs directly rather than through the UN system.

It appears that NGOs have a very difficult time influencing codes sponsored by IGOs. IGOs are, by definition, formed by countries for purposes deemed relevant by their members. As such, there are fewer opportunities for non-state entities to influence the actions of IGOs than is the case for other codes. While we see signs that NGOs are being taken more seriously by IGOs, particularly the UN, IGOs will continue to serve the interests of their members, and take NGO views on codes into consideration only when the most influential countries agree that it is necessary and in their interests. Lobbying member countries prior to the establishment of IGO-sponsored codes appears to be a more promising avenue for NGO influence.

International Codes Sponsored by Industrial and Corporate Associations

A number of international codes and agreements have been developed under the auspices of industry associations, chambers of commerce, and other groups of companies and industrial sectors. In some instances, these agreements constitute efforts by industry groups to demonstrate to stakeholders that they are committed to global environmental responsibility thereby precluding pressure from NGOs or other groups. In others, they are full-fledged partnerships among corporations and NGOs.

The World Business Council for Sustainable Development (WBCSD) is a coalition of 150 international companies from more than 30 countries and 20 industrial sectors, united by a shared commitment to sustainable development (WBCSD 2002). The mission of the WBCSD is to provide business leadership as a catalyst for sustainable development, and to promote eco-efficiency, innovation, and corporate social responsibility. Although the WBCSD is itself organized as an NGO, the role of environmental NGOs in its development appears minimal.

The International Organization for Standardization (ISO) comprises a worldwide federation of national standards bodies from 100 countries. The organization seeks to facilitate the exchange of goods and services by establishing international standards and reconciling regulatory differences between countries (ISO 2002). The ISO 14000 series is a voluntary set of standards intended to encourage organizations to systematically address the environmental impacts of their activities. Stakeholder involvement is nominally supported by the ISO standards, but the influence of environmental NGOs in the standards-setting and implementation process varies by firm. The standard requires that firms must develop a process for dealing with external communication; however, the level of stakeholder involvement is discretionary. A business must have a plan for public disclosure, which could include active stakeholder participation.

The Global Environmental Management Initiative (GEMI) is a group of companies established to provide strategies for businesses to achieve Environmental

Health and Safety (EHS) excellence, economic success, and corporate citizenship (GEMI 1998). GEMI assists businesses in improving EHS performance, increasing shareholder value, and fostering corporate citizenship. GEMI's goals include identifying emerging issues vital to achieving a sustainable world while maintaining business growth, and developing options and approaches to solving the problems presented by these issues. GEMI seeks to foster an effective dialogue with stakeholders to help businesses understand concerns, share with those stakeholders the practices and results achieved by leadership companies, and create effective partnerships with other national and international groups (GEMI 2002). GEMI has taken a particularly active role in developing cooperative relationships with educational institutions and NGOs engaged in education activities.

The role of NGOs in the formulation of codes and agreements sponsored by corporate and industry associations is difficult to generalize. If we consider these associations themselves as NGOs, then the role is high. If we consider only non-corporate NGOs, the role is probably moderate. In either case, the NGO role in agreement compliance is, in many cases, moderate-to-high, since the role of advocacy NGOs is to serve as an oversight check on corporations' compliance with their own publicly-touted standards and commitments.

International Codes Sponsored by Not-for-profit NGOs

Finally, NGOs may be sponsors of corporate codes of conduct, either individually or collectively. Some NGOs focus on codes of conduct in specific industries, such as the Clean Clothes Campaign, while other codes are formed when NGOs combine with business groups to form a new NGO, such as the Forest Stewardship Council. It is significant that, in all of these instances, NGOs are sometimes regarded as replacing or supplanting the role of government, or modifying the way in which governments and business have traditionally interacted.

Social Accountability International (SAI), a human rights organization, established SA8000 in 1997 and revised it in 2001 (SAI 2001). SA8000 focuses on labor issues, and its principles are based on ILO conventions, the Universal Declaration of Human Rights, and the UN Convention on the Rights of the Child. The code addresses child labor, forced labor, health and safety, compensation and working hours, discrimination, discipline, free association, and collective bargaining. Certification of compliance with SA8000 means that a facility has been examined in accordance with SAI auditing procedures and found to be in conformance with the standard (SAI 2002). SAI has developed auditor training courses and a guidance document, and certifiers are required to consult with local NGOs and trade unions prior to each audit. Third parties, typically NGOs, trade unions, or workers, serve as independent auditors who verify whether companies meet SA8000 standards. NGOs have had a significant impact on the development of SA8000 and this code's implementation.

Rugmark is a non-profit organization seeking to end child labor in the carpet industries of India, Pakistan, and Nepal (Rugmark 2002). A partnership among development and human rights NGOs, companies exporting carpets from India, the Indo-German Export Promotion Council, and UNICEF-India set up a project to devise and regulate a special label for hand-knotted carpets made without the use of child labor. The Rugmark process includes loom and factory monitoring, consumer labeling, and running schools for former child workers. By agreeing to adhere to Rugmark's "no child labor" guidelines, and by permitting random inspections of carpet looms, manufacturers receive the right to put the Rugmark label on their carpets, which provides assurance that a carpet was not produced by children. As an NGO, Rugmark almost single-handedly developed and implemented this code.

One of the most significant agreements between NGOs and industry is in the area of forest products, where the Forest Stewardship Council (FSC) monitors forestry practices, and develops a global program combining public awareness, business collaboration, and green marketing (Carlton 2000, Domask 2003). In the early 1990s, the World Wide Fund for Nature and several other major NGOs began exploring the possibility of setting up a voluntary global certification and accreditation system that could be used to verify whether or not wood products were harvested in a socially and environmentally sound manner. Proponents of forest certification sought to show that forests can be managed in a manner that is viable economically without compromising conservation (FSC 2001). Through these means, the FSC convinced Home Depot, Wicke's, Lowe's, and Ikea to sell FSC-certified products. The FSC approach is somewhat unique because it relies on institutionalized cooperation between NGOs and businesses, but environmentally-oriented NGOs were pivotal in persuading retailers to apply pressure upstream on forestry companies.

It should be clear from this analysis that NGOs have more influence on NGO-sponsored codes than any other class of codes. While this may not, at first glance, appear surprising, it is significant that NGO-sponsored codes have been widely perceived to be successful, particularly those focused on specific industries (like carpet-making and forestry). Furthermore, NGO-sponsored codes have sought to form partnerships with industry, and this is perhaps the key to their acceptance by such a range of state and non-state actors.

NGOs, Codes of Conduct, and International Agreements: General Implications and Research Propositions

Our case analyses suggest a number of implications for evaluating the impact of NGOs on codes and agreements. In this section, we draw some conclusions from the case review, and link these conclusions to several related theoretical streams in international business, international relations, and social issues in management. We use this integration of empirical and theoretical insights to underpin several overarching propositions that form the basis of a theoretical framework to evaluate and predict NGO influence on corporate codes of conduct. While we do not claim that our observations will be universally applicable, we contend that the case analyses and insights from management theory provide solid grounding for our propositions. Further refinement based on additional empirical evidence is necessary to fully validate these assertions.

Implications from Cases Analyses

Brown et al. (2000) contend that NGOs are indeed helping to formulate and implement many international decisions and policies, and do so in seven ways. They include: identifying global problems that are not raised or resolved by existing international arrangements; helping to construct international values and norms that can guide future policies and practices; formulating and enforcing global public policies; reforming international institutions to respond to unmet needs; creating and disseminating social innovations that affect international governance processes; serving as catalysts or mediators for resolving conflicts at national and international levels; and mobilizing people and resources for international action on public problems.

In a recent paper, Christmann and Taylor (2002) analyze NGO impact on voluntary environmental initiatives (VEIs, similar to the codes of conduct discussed in this article), and conclude that NGOs put international pressure on business by monitoring corporate activities, publicly targeting firms, and influencing the behavior of customers in the marketplace by articulating environmental concerns and framing alternatives. The evidence from these 12 cases suggests that the role of NGOs on codes of conduct is mixed in terms of influence and outcomes, but that each of the activities described above is present in at least some of the codes. Although our sample is limited as a result of the relatively small number of cases reviewed, these representative examples do allow for some generalizations. Overall NGO influence appears to be greatest in codes sponsored by NGOs and weakest in codes sponsored by IGOs. Industry-sponsored codes and government-to-government agreements fall somewhere in between. It is logical that NGO-sponsored codes allow for the greatest degree of NGO involvement in formation and monitoring, but the relative success of these codes is nonetheless impressive.

It is somewhat surprising, however, that NGOs have been least effective penetrating the formative period of IGO-sponsored codes. One explanation may be that since the members of IGOs are nation-states, IGO-sponsored codes seek to reflect members' interests. This seems true of the OECD Guidelines and, to a lesser extent, the ILO Declaration. NGOs played a key role in pushing the UN to enlist MNC support in tackling labor, environmental, and human rights issues, and the Global Compact does allow for an NGO role in monitoring. However, a more influential role for NGOs is limited by a consensus among UN members to avoid a binding agreement covering these issues. In the case of industry-sponsored codes, NGOs actually play a more influential role than one would expect. This is due to the fact that industry-sponsored codes are often developed as a response to the need "to do something" to show private sector interest in labor or environmental issues. Industry-sponsored codes gain legitimacy by carving out some form of oversight or monitoring role for NGOs.

In terms of government-to-government agreements, the opportunity for NGOs to influence participating governments, and the potential for NGOs to pressure the collective of governments during the actual negotiations, presents a dual avenue for influence. Regarding the former, NGO influence depends heavily on the democratic and institutional arrangements within a given society that allow for NGOs to participate in the policy-making process. In the United States, Canada, and many European countries, governments have established formal mechanisms for NGO input. In the case of direct influence on the agreements, this process is still at an early stage, and the FTAA negotiations will be an interesting test case. One likely outcome is that, through the information sharing between and among NGOs that occurs in conjunction with government-to-government negotiations, countries that had not provided access for NGOs to influence policy within their national systems are likely to open up due to the combination of national, regional, and global pressure. This is particularly evident as NGOs themselves globalize through informal coalitions, more established alliances, or outright mergers.

The Dynamic Evolution of Codes and NGO Roles: The Example of GRI

The typology of codes of conduct presented here does not capture fully the dynamism of this phenomenon. In particular, there is an increasing incidence of multi-stakeholder agreements, such as the *Global Reporting Initiative* (GRI), that reflect significant participation by all of the major groups discussed here. The GRI was established in 1997 to develop globally applicable guidelines for reporting on the economic, environmental, and social performance, initially for corporations and eventually for any business, governmental, or non-governmental organization. Convened by the Coalition for Environmentally Responsible Economies (CERES) in partnership with the UN Environment Program, the GRI includes participation of corporations, NGOs, accountancy organizations, business associations, and other stakeholders from around the world (GRI 2002).

The GRI's 1999 draft Sustainability Reporting Guidelines represents the first global framework for comprehensive sustainability reporting, encompassing the "triple bottom line" of economic, environmental, and social issues.

In 2002, the GRI went a step further when it was established as a permanent, independent, international body with a multi-stakeholder governance structure. Its core mission will be maintenance, enhancement, and dissemination of the Guidelines through a process of ongoing consultation and stakeholder engagement (GRI 2002). The GRI is governed by a steering committee drawn from a diverse mix of stakeholders, including MNCs and NGOs. The GRI appears to represents a hybrid of the four types of codes we have described. The evolution of the GRI shows how codes may transition and progress in both obligations and participation.

Research Propositions

The case review above suggests a number of broad generalizations regarding the conditions that lead to greater NGO influence on codes and agreements. In addition, complementary theoretical insights provide additional support for the research propositions presented below.

Proposition 1. When NGOs are involved in initial development of codes and agreements, they will have more influence on both the initial shape and continuing evolution of agreements.

NGOs have more impact on codes when they intervene early in the code development process. Building on Vernon's conceptualization of an evolutionary product life cycle (Vernon 1966), more recent research has suggested that there are life cycles in which social issues emerge, evolve, and recede. Issues may follow a predictable evolutionary trajectory from policy to learning to commitment (Ackerman 1975). Mahon and Waddock (1992) identify four "zones" of classification for issues according to the position of pressure groups, public policy groups, and corporate groups with regard to their degree of rejection, indifference, or acceptance of the issues as relevant to their affairs. Their model suggests a linear progression in which public and pressure groups "lead" corporations in their earlier acceptance and action related to specific issues, and that such leading activity has the effect of shaping the impact on corporate adoptions of the issues in question. In addition, literature on "pioneering advantage" and order of entry suggests that early entrants have opportunities to shape market responses before the business environment has congealed (Lieberman/Montgomery 1988). Hence, where NGOs are involved in the *initial* development of codes and agreements, they will have the most influence on both the early shape and continuing evolution of agreements.

NGOs' influence, however, is neither static nor linear: NGO influence may ebb and flow as the relative salience of different stakeholders shift as issues considered by codes evolve (Mitchell/Agle/Wood 1997).

Proposition 2. When NGOs align with other organizations – public, private, and not-for-profit – they will have more influence on both the initial shape and continuing evolution of agreements.

NGOs are more successful in shaping codes of conduct when they have formed coalitions of numerous like-minded groups. In some cases, international NGOs have allied with national and local partners (a "top-down" approach), while in other "bottom-up" cases national NGO and social movements have built coalitions with international allies to influence national and international policymakers (Brown et al. 2000). Research in network strategies and collaborative strategy in international business has identified the many benefits of alliances and joint ventures (Buckley/Casson 1996, Contractor/Lorange 1988). Black and Boal (1994) argued that resources gained through alliances include "system-wide" resources generated by a complex network of firms. Dyer and Singh (1998) have identified four potential sources of interorganizational competitive advantage from alliances: relation-specific assets, knowledge-sharing routines, complementary resources and capabilities, and effective governance.

As our case analyses demonstrate, government-to-government agreements provide a dual avenue for NGO influence, as national NGOs are presented with opportunities to influence their home government directly, and multinational NGOs or networks of national NGOs can advocate to administrative and institutional entities that emerge from such organizations. This creates a dynamic and multi-level process for NGO involvement, especially as NGOs themselves take advantage of the Internet and other technologies to extend their global networks and influence.

Proposition 3. When IGOs are the principal architects of codes and agreements, NGOs will have less influence than when NGOs themselves or corporate associations are the sponsors or drivers.

NGOs have limited success influencing codes sponsored by IGOs and international government-to-government agreements. This is partly because IGOs look to their constituent governments as legitimate representatives of societal stakeholders, obviating the perceived need for NGOs (either local or international) as intermediaries between civil society and governmental representatives. Moreover, IGOs appear to view NGOs as a complicating force in what is already a difficult and complex set of negotiations and interactions.

Realism (or more specifically, neorealism), the dominant paradigm of the international relations literature, places nation-states as the central and most powerful actors in global affairs (Keohane 1986, Waltz 1979). Most realists accept that there are circumstances under which states choose to create international organizations or regimes, but contend that such structures are designed to serve the interests of the state (Grieco 1990, Keohane 1984, Krasner 1983). Notwithstanding the observations presented earlier in our discussion that emphasized the increasing influence of NGOs in international affairs, non-state actors still have difficulty penetrating the decision-making structure of IGOs and interstate negotiations. This proposition is supported by our study of IGO-sponsored codes.

Proposition 4. When the agreement or code expressly provides for input from non-state, non-business actors, for example, when industry- or government-sponsored codes provide for NGO involvement, NGOs will have greater influence.

NGOs will have greater influence when the structure of the negotiations requires input from non-state and non-business actors. So, for example, where industry associations are the principal architects of codes, NGOs can have a substantial influence because such corporate associations must secure NGO support in order to demonstrate the legitimacy of their commitment to the principles of the codes. Such commitments by corporate and NGO stakeholders may allow for a cooperative evolution of the codes, and potentially, forestall direct government intervention. In such situations, both business and NGOs "win" – the business or industry in question avoids regulation by the state and the participating NGOs can claim influence over corporate actions in the labor and/or environmental realm. In addition, some international agreements (WTO, FTAA) increasingly provide explicit access for NGOs, a development that is supported by the critical stakeholder perspective presented above. NGO stakeholders are increasingly demonstrating power, legitimacy, and urgency, and as such, government and corporate code sponsors "have a clear and immediate mandate to attend to and give priority to that stakeholder's claim" (Mitchell/Agle/Wood 1997, p. 878).

Conclusion: Implications for Policy, Practice, and Research

There are a number of potential implications of NGO involvement in codes of conduct and international labor and environmental agreements. While we have not expressly examined the "success" of the agreements – we leave that to future research – we have detailed some interesting and potentially important implications of efforts by NGOs to gain access to the process by which these agreements are developed and implemented. First, there may be risks of "privatizing" public policies that deal with environmental, labor, and social issues, which leads to a loss in democratic accountability (Gereffi et al. 2001, Henderson 2001, Kapstein 2001). A related concern is that voluntary (rather than regulatory-based) approaches permit non-participating companies to shirk responsibilities, allowing only firms with resources and commitment to bear initial compliance costs. As noted above, however, there may be benefits to being "first movers" in adhering to new standards that later become pervasive (Nehrt 1998).

In addition, NGOs are not equipped to be comprehensive code monitors (Mayne 1999). Hence, codes in which NGOs constitute the only oversight may lack rigor and enforcement. In one critic's view, codes and other agreements promoting corporate social responsibility are "the product of an undemocratic collaboration between multinationals and campaigning organizations, the former buying peace and acceptability by succumbing to the demands of the latter" (Tomkins 2001). In a similar vein Haufler (2001, p. 122) argues, "International industry self-regulation [including codes of conduct] has the potential to encourage significant improvements but only in concert with traditional political processes."

From the perspective of multinational corporations, and their response to globalization pressures, the emergence of NGOs as important actors presents both challenges and opportunities. A number of individual corporations and representative associations have embraced NGOs as partners in forging a new alliance that meets both economic objectives, and goals of social and environmental development. The GRI described above is a clear example of the potential dual benefits from these partnerships. At the same time, however, the insertion of NGOs into a set of exchanges that had previously been the exclusive domain of governments and business places MNCs in a confusing and sometimes contradictory situation in which they must meet government requirements and obligations, as well as respond to NGO pressures and demands (Doh/Teegen 2002). This situation presents MNCs with a potential double jeopardy in which responding to government regulation may sour relations with NGOs and vice versa. On the other hand, it may also offer the possibility of satisfying governmental requirements through demonstration of responsiveness to NGOs, a potentially productive development for the future of business-government-NGO deliberations over globalization (Doh 2003).

The role of NGOs in development and implementation of international environmental and labor codes is evolving rapidly. Once viewed as "outsiders" who serve to frustrate or interfere with the operation of governments and corporations internationally, NGOs are becoming more integral to the process and outcome of global discussions over important social and environmental issues. Governments and corporations must respond to the increasing interest of NGOs and the broader civil society groups they represent. The initial insights presented in this paper provide an ample agenda for future research directions, especially consideration of the timing of NGO intervention, and the evolutionary nature of NGO involvement in these codes and agreements. Careful consideration by all relevant stakeholders of how best to include NGOs in the policymaking process will have a substantial influence not only on the evolution of multilateral approaches to environmental and labor codes, but also on the very nature of global governance and the future role of multinational enterprise in the global economy.

References

Ackerman R. W., *The Social Challenge to Business*, Cambridge, MA: Harvard University Press 1975.
Alden, E., Multinationals in Labour Pledge: Trade Liberalisation Voluntary Plan Will Hold Companies to Account, *Financial Times*, 28 July 2000, p. 12.
Black, J. A./Boal, K. B., Strategic Resources: Traits, Configurations and Paths to Sustainable Competitive Advantage, *Strategic Management Journal*, 15, 1994, pp.131–148.
Brown, L. D./Khagram, S./Moore, M. H./Frumkin, P., Globalization, NGOs, and Multisectoral Relations, in Nye Jr., J. S./Donahue, J. D. (eds.), *Governance in a Globalizing World*, Washington, DC: Brookings Institution Press 2000, pp. 271–296.
Buckley, P. J./Casson, M., An Economic Model of International Joint Venture Strategy, *Journal of International Business Studies*, 27, 1996, pp. 849–876.
Carlton, J., How Home Depot and Activists Joined to Cut Logging Abuse, *The Wall Street Journal*, 26 September 2000, p. 1.
Carroll, A. B., A Three-dimensional Conceptual Model of Corporate Performance, *Academy of Management Review*, 4, 1979, pp. 497–505.
Carroll, A. B., Social Issues in Management Research: Experts' Views, Analysis and Commentary, *Business and Society*, 33, 1, 1994, pp. 5–29.
Charnovitz, S., Opening the WTO to Nongovernmental Interests, *Fordham International Law Journal*, 24, 2000, pp. 173–216.
Christmann, P./Taylor, G., Globalization and the Environment: Strategies for International Voluntary Environmental Initiatives, *Academy of Management Executive*, 16, 30, 2002, pp. 121–135.
Clark, A. M., Non-governmental Organizations and Their Influence on International Society, *Journal of International Affairs*, 48, 2, 1995, pp. 507–525.
Clarkson, M. B. E., A Stakeholder Framework for Analyzing and Evaluating Corporate Social Performance, *Academy of Management Review*, 20, 1, 1995, pp. 92–106.
Cochran, P. L./Wood, R. A., Corporate Social Responsibility and Financial Performance, *Academy of Management Journal*, 27, 1984, pp. 42–56.
Contractor, F. J./Lorange, P., Why Should Firms Cooperate? The Strategy and Economics Basis for Cooperative Ventures, in Contractor, F./Lorange, P. (eds.), *Cooperative Strategies In International Business*, Lexington, MA: Lexington Books, 1988, pp. 3–30.
Cortese, A., The New Accountability: Tracking the Social Costs, *New York Times*, 24 March 2002, Sect. 3, p. 4.
Cummings, J. L./Doh, J. P., Identifying Who Matters: Mapping Key Players in Multiple Environments, *California Management Review*, 42, 2000, pp. 83–104.
Cusimano, M.K., Editor's Preface to Chapter Nine: Intergovernmental Organizations, in Cusimano, M.K. (ed.), *Beyond Sovereignty: Issues for a Global Agenda*, Boston: Bedford/St. Martin's 2000, pp. 217–220.
de Jonquieres, G., OECD Agrees Global Company Code, *Financial Times*, 28 June 2000, p. 17.

Deslauriers, J./Kotschwar, B./Teegen, H./Doh, J., Nongovernmental Organizations and Economic and Geographic Integration in the Americas, paper presented at the *Academy of International Business Annual Meeting*, San Juan Puerto Rico, July 1, 2002.
Deutsch, C., For Wall Street, Increasing Evidence That Green Begets Green, *New York Times*, 19 July 1998, p. 7.
Doh, J. P./Teegen, H., Nongovernmental Organizations as Institutional Actors in International Business: Theory and Implications, *International Business Review*, 11, 2002, pp. 665–684.
Doh, J. P., Nongovernmental Organizations, Corporate Strategy, and Public Policy: NGOs as Agents of Change, in Doh, J. P./Teegen, H. J. (eds.), *Globalization and NGOs: Transforming Business, Governments, and Society*, Westport, CT: Praeger 2003, pp. 1–18.
Domask, J., From Boycotts to Partnership: NGOs, the Private Sector, and the World's Forests, in Doh, J. P./Teegen, H. J. (eds.), *Globalization and NGOs: Transforming Business, Government, and Society*, Westport, CT: Praeger 2003, pp. 157–186.
Donaldson, T./Preston, L. E., The Stakeholder Theory of the Corporation: Concepts, Evidence, and Implications, *Academy of Management Review*, 20, 1995, pp. 65–91.
Drezner, D. W., Bottom Feeders, *Foreign Policy*, 121, 2000, pp. 64–70.
Dyer, J. H./Singh, H., The Relational View: Cooperative Strategy and Sources of Interorganizational Competitive Advantage, *Academy of Management Review*, 23, 1998, pp. 660–679.
The Economist, NGOs: Sins of Secular Missionaries, 29 January 2000, pp. 25–27.
Forest Stewardship Council (FSC) – U.S., *Status of FSC-Endorsed Certification in the United States*, Washington, DC: FSC-US 2001.
Freeman, R. E., *Strategic Management: A Stakeholder Approach*, Boston: Pitman 1984.
Freeman, R. E./Reed, D. L., Stockholders and Stakeholders: A New Perspective on Corporate Governance, *California Management Review*, 25, 3, 1983, pp. 88–106.
Free Trade Agreement of the Americas (FTTA), *Fourth Trade Ministerial: Joint Declaration of Ministers*, San José, Costa Rica, 19 March 1998, www.ftaa-alca.org/ministerials/costa_e.asp.
Free Trade Agreement of the Americas (FTAA), *Sixth Trade Ministerial: Joint Declaration of Ministers*, Buenos Aires, Argentina, 7 April 2001, www.ftaa-alca.org/ministerials/BAmin_e.asp.
Gereffi, G./Garcia-Johnson, R./Sasser, E., The NGO-Industrial Complex, *Foreign Policy*, 125, 2001, pp. 56–65.
Global Environmental Management Institute (GEMI), *Survey of MNC Environmental Practices Abroad*, 1998.
Global Environmental Management Institute (GEMI), *About*, 2002, www.gemi.org/docs/about/about.htm.
Global Reporting Initiative (GRI), 2002, http://globalreporting.org/AboutGRI/Overview.htm
Gordenker, L./Weiss, T., *NGOs, the UN, and Global Governance*, Boulder, CO: Lynne Rienner 1996.
Grieco, J., *Cooperation Among Nations*, Ithaca, NY: Cornell University Press 1990.
Griffin, J. J./Mahon, J. F., The Corporate Social Performance and Corporate Financial Performance Debate: Twenty-Five Years of Incomparable Research, *Business and Society*, 36, 1, 1997, pp. 5–15.
Haufler, V., *A Public Role for the Private Sector: Industry Self-Regulation in a Global Economy*, Washington: Carnegie Endowment for International Peace 2001.
Henderson, D., *Misguided Virtue: False Notions of Corporate Social Responsibility*, Wellington: New Zealand Business Roundtable 2001.
Hill, C. W. L./Jones, T. M., Stakeholder-Agency Theory, *Journal of Management Studies*, 29, 1992, pp. 131–154.
Independent Sector, The New Nonprofit Almanac, 2001.
International Labor Organization (ILO), *Tripartite Declaration of Principles concerning Multinational Enterprises and Social Policy*, adopted by the Governing Body of the International Labor Office at its 204th Session, 1977, http://www.ilo.org/public/english/standards/norm/sources/mne.htm#added.
International Labor Organization (ILO), *Codes of Practice*, 2002, http://www.ilo.org/public/english/standards/norm/sources/codes.htm.
International Standards Organization (ISO), ISO Information Center 2002, http://www.iso14000.com.
Johnson, P. M./Beaulieu, A., *The Environment and NAFTA: Understanding and Implementing The New Continental Law*, Washington: Island Press and Toronto: Broadview Press 1996.

Jones, T. M., Instrumental Stakeholder Theory: A Synthesis of Ethics and Economics, *Academy of Management Review*, 20, 2, 1995, pp. 404.
Kapstein, E. B., The Corporate Ethics Crusade, *Foreign Affairs*, 80, 5, 2001, pp. 105–119.
Kearney, N., Corporate Codes of Conduct: The Privatized Application of Labour Standards, in Picciotto, S./Mayne, R.(eds.), *Regulating International Business: Beyond Liberalization*, Basingstoke, UK: Macmillan 1999, pp. 205–234.
Keck, M.E./Sikkink, K., *Activists Beyond Borders: Advocacy Networks in International Politics*, Ithaca, NY: Cornell University Press 1998.
Keim, G., Non-governmental Organizations and Business-government Relations: The Importance of Institutions, in Doh, J. P./Teegen, H. J. (eds.), *Globalization and NGOs: Transforming Business, Government, and Society*, Westport, CT: Praeger 2003, pp. 19–39.
Keohane, R. O. (ed.), *Neorealism and its Critics*, New York: Columbia University Press 1986.
Keohane, R. O., *After Hegemony: Cooperation and Discord in the World Political Economy*, Princeton, NJ: Princeton University Press 1984.
Krasner, S., *International Regimes*, Ithaca, NY: Cornell University Press 1983.
Lieberman, M./Montgomery, D., First Mover Advantages. *Strategic Management Journal*, 9, 1988, pp. 41–58.
Mahon, J. F./Waddock, S. A., Strategic Issues Management: An Integration of Issue Life Cycle Perspectives, *Business & Society*, 31, 1992, pp. 19–32.
Mathews, J. T., Power Shift, *Foreign Affairs*, 76, 1997, pp. 50–66.
Mayne, R., Regulating TNCs: The Role of Voluntary and Governmental Approaches, in Picciotto, S./Mayne, R. (eds.), *Regulating International Business: Beyond Liberalization*, Basingstoke, UK: Macmillan 1999, pp. 235–254.
Menz, F., An Environmental Policy for North America post-NAFTA, *North American Outlook*, 4, 3, 1995, pp. 1–15.
Mitchell, R. K./Agle, B. R./Wood, D. J., Toward a Theory of Stakeholder Identification and Salience: Defining the Principle of Who and What Really Counts, *Academy of Management Review*, 22, 4, 1997, pp. 853–886.
Nehrt, C., Maintainability of First Mover Advantages when Environmental Regulations Differ Between Countries, *Academy of Management Review*, 23, 1, 1998, pp. 77–97.
The North American Free Trade Agreement, Texts of the Agreement, Implementing Bill, Statement of Administrative Action, and Required Supporting Statements (NAFTA), Washington, DC: US Government Printing Office 1993.
Organization for Economic Cooperation and Development (OECD), *Declaration on International Investment and Multinational Enterprises*, June 1976, http://www.oecd.org/oecd/pages/document/displaywithoutnav/0,3376,EN-document-notheme-1-no-no-9259-0,00.html.
Organization for Economic Cooperation and Development (OECD), *Declaration on International Investment and Multinational Enterprises*, June 2000. http://www.oecd.org/EN/document/0,,EN-document-93-3-no-6-19737-93,00.html.
Ottaway, M., Corporatism Goes Global: International Organizations, Nongovernmental Organization Networks, and Transnational Business, *Global Governance*, 7, 2001, pp. 265–292.
Prakash, A./Krutilla, K./Karamanos, P., Multinational Corporations and International Environmental Policy, *Business and the Contemporary World*, 8, 3/4, 1996, pp. 119–144.
Preston, L.E./O'Bannon, D. P., The Corporate Social-financial Performance Relationship: A Typology, *Business and Society*, 36, 4, 1997, pp. 419–429.
Preston, L.E./Sapienza, H. J., Stakeholder Management and Corporate Performance, *Journal of Behavioral Economics*, 19, 1990, pp. 361–375.
Price, R., Reversing the Gun Sights: Transnational Civil Society Targets Land Mines, *International Organization*, 52, 3, 1998, pp. 613–644.
Rugmark, 2002, http://www.rugmark.org/.
Simmons, P. J., Learning to Live with NGOs, *Foreign Policy*, 112, 1998, pp. 82–96.
Smith, J./Chatfield, C./Ron Pagnucco, R. (eds), *Transnational Social Movements and Global Politics: Solidarity Beyond the State*, Syracuse, NY: Syracuse University Press 1997.
Social Accountability International (SAI), *Social Accountability 8000*, 2001, http://www.cepaa.org/Standard%20English.doc.
Social Accountability International (SAI), 2002, http://www.sa8000.org/certification.htm.

Tomkins, R., When Caring is a Good Investment, *Financial Times*, 5 October 2001, p. 10.
United Nations (UN), *Global Compact*, 2000, http://unglobalcompact.org/un/gc/unweb.nsf/.
Vakil, A. C., Confronting the Classification Problem: Toward a Taxonomy of NGOs, *World Development*, 25, 12, 1997, pp. 2057–2070.
van Tuijl, P., NGOs and Human Rights: Sources of Justice and Democracy, *Journal of International Affairs*, 52, 2, 1999, pp. 493–512.
van Tulder, R./Kolk, A., Multinationality and Corporate Ethics: Codes of Conduct in the Sporting Goods Industry, *Journal of International Business Studies*, 32, 2, 2001, pp. 267–283.
Vernon, R., International Investment and International Trade in the Product Cycle, *Quarterly Journal of Economics*, 80, 1966, pp. 190–207.
Wall Street Journal, Tax Report, September 26, 2001, p. A1.
Walter, A., NGOs, Business, and International Investment: The Multilateral Agreement on Investment, Seattle, and Beyond, *Global Governance*, 7, 1, 2001, pp. 51–76.
Waltz, K., *Theory of International Politics*, New York: McGraw Hill/Addison Wesley 1979.
Wartick, S. L./Cochran, P. L., The Evolution of the Corporate Social Performance Model, *Academy of Management Review*, 10, 1985, pp. 758–769.
Williams, O.F., *Global Codes of Conduct: An Idea Whose Time Has Come*, Notre Dame, IN: University of Notre Dame Press 2000.
Windsor, D./Preston, L.E., Corporate Governance and Social Performance in the Multinational Corporation, in Preston, L.E. (ed.), *Research in Corporate Social Performance and Policy*, Greenwich, CT: JAI Press 1988, pp. 45–58.
Wood, D. J., Corporate Social Performance Revisited, *Academy of Management Review*, 16, 1991, pp. 691–718.
World Business Council for Sustainable Development (WBCSD), 2002, http://www.basd-action.net/about/wbcsd.shtml.
World Trade Organization (WTO), *Uruguay Round Agreement Establishing the World Trade Organization*, Geneva: WTO 1995.
World Trade Organization (WTO), *Guidelines for Arrangements on Relations with Non-Governmental Organizations Decision adopted by the General Council*, WTO/L/162,18, Geneva: WTO, July 1996.
World Trade Organization (WTO), *International Trade Statistics 2001*, Geneva: WTO 2001.

Management International Review

Neuerscheinungen

Doris Lindner
**Einflussfaktoren
des erfolgreichen
Auslandseinsatzes**
Konzeptionelle Grundlagen –
Bestimmungsgrößen – Ansatzpunkte
zur Verbesserung
2002
XX, 341 S. mit 38 Abb., 21 Tab.,
(mir-Edition),
Br. € 59,–
ISBN 3-409-11952-3

Tobias Specker
**Postmerger-Management in den
ost- und mitteleuropäischen
Transformationsstaaten**
2002
XX, 431 S. mit 60 Abb., 28 Tab.,
(mir-Edition),
Br. € 64,–
ISBN 3-409-12010-6

Jörg Frehse
**Internationale
Dienstleistungskompetenzen**
Erfolgsstrategien für die europäische
Hotellerie
2002
XXVI, 353 S. mit 48 Abb.,
(mir-Edition),
Br. € 59,–
ISBN 3-409-12349-0

Anja Schulte
**Das Phänomen
der Rückverlagerung**
Internationale Standortent-
scheidungen kleiner und mittlerer
Unternehmen
2002
XXII, 315 S. mit 17 Abb., 2 Tab.,
(mir-Edition),
Br. € 59,–
ISBN 3-409-12375-X

Andreas Wald
**Netzwerkstrukturen und
-effekte in Organisationen**
Eine Netzwerkanalyse
in internationalen Unternehmen
2003
XVIII, 238 S. mit 19 Abb., 61 Tab.,
(mir-Edition),
Br. € 49,90
ISBN 3-409-12395-4

Nicola Berg
Public Affairs Management
Ergebnisse einer empirischen
Untersuchung in Multinationalen
Unternehmungen
2003
XXXIV, 471 S. mit 20 Abb., 67 Tab.
(mir-Edition),
Br. € 64,–
ISBN 3-409-12387-3

Betriebswirtschaftlicher Verlag Dr. Th. Gabler, Abraham-Lincoln-Str. 46, 65189 Wiesbaden

Management International Review
© Gabler Verlag 2004

Michael N. Young/David Ahlstrom/Garry D. Bruton

The Globalization of Corporate Governance in East Asia: The "Transnational" Solution

Abstract

- Corporate governance is one of the primary mechanisms by which an organization interfaces with its environment. As globalization proceeds, firms must effectively manage corporate governance practices to reap the promised benefits of the new integrated global economy.

- In East Asia, firms face increasing pressure to provide governance systems that meet international investors' expectations. Yet this creates tension as corporate governance practices are embedded in local institutions and culture. As a result, firms are frequently torn between providing what global investors expect and what the local culture will support.

- Rather than focusing on an "either/or" solution to this dilemma, we draw on the multinational business metaphor (Bartlett/Ghoshal 1989) to advocate a "transnational solution" that balances the expectations of global investors against those of local stakeholders. We interview several corporate governance experts and participants in East Asia to further develop this position.

Key Results

- We essentially find that change is coming slowly to East Asian corporate governance practices. Firms are indeed adopting corporate governance practices that balance demands from the global and the local environments. The pressure for global convergence is greatest where there is interface with the global economy (e.g., investor relations, financial reporting, etc.) while pressures for uniqueness is greatest in those areas that are more embedded in a local institutional context (e.g., TMT compensation and incentive systems, board structures, etc.).

Authors

Michael N. Young, Assistant Professor of Management, Faculty of Business Administration, The Chinese University of Hong Kong, Hong Kong.
David Ahlstrom, Associate Professor of Management, Faculty of Business Administration, The Chinese University of Hong Kong, Hong Kong.
Garry D. Bruton, Associate Professor of Management, M.J. Neely School of Business, Texas Christian University, Fort Worth, TX, USA.

Introduction

In recent years East Asia[1] has evolved from a commodity agriculture-based economy to a world-class competitive economy in several sophisticated industries (Rohwer 2001). While many business practices have changed and adapted to global standards during this economic transformation, the region has failed to adequately reform corporate governance practices in line with what many consider to be global standards (Faccio/Lang/Young 2001). Problems with corporate governance practices could ultimately prove to be an obstacle for the smooth globalization of firms in the region (Brancato 1999). As the recognition of corporate governance problems has grown, a general agreement has formed that reform is needed (Johnson et al. 2000, Serapio/ Shenkar 1999). However, there is continuing disagreement as to the direction that those potential reforms should take. Two primary positions dominate the debate on corporate reform in East Asia. One argues that East Asian firms should adopt global standards of corporate governance based largely on the Anglo-American model (Allen 2000, Rubach/Sebora 1998). The second position advocates that East Asian firms develop systems that are unique to their particular institutional environment (Guillen 2000, Choi et al. 1999).

However, both of these positions fail to capture the full complexity of corporate governance in the often rough and tumble business world of East Asia's emerging economies. In response, we seek to strike a balance between these two positions, with the underlying belief that each position contains some validity in its arguments. We argue that, over the foreseeable future, it is likely that East Asian corporate governance practices will come to resemble global practices in certain ways – particularly those that are critical for interfacing with the global economy (e.g., factors such as investor relations and financial reporting). At the same time, it is likely that East Asian firms will retain or further develop unique corporate governance practices in other areas – especially those areas that are more embedded in a local institutional context (e.g., factors such as TMT compensation, incentive systems & board structures).

To examine this position and build support for the analysis, we explore the theoretical underpinnings of corporate governance in the East Asian region using the *transnational strategy* metaphor from international business (Bartlett/ Ghoshal 1989) to describe the global/local paradox inherent in corporate governance reform. We build these insights through interviews with managers and corporate governance experts in the region to further ground the understanding of current corporate governance practice and the inherent tensions created by globalization.

Corporate Governance and Globalization

Corporate governance is "the relationship among various participants in determining the direction and performance of corporations" (Monks/Minow 2001, p. 1). Given its position as the strategic rudder of the corporate ship, corporate governance plays a pivotal role as the interface between an organization and its environment (Bluedorn et al. 1994, Boyd/Carroll/Howard 1996). In particular, corporate governance processes and mechanisms are a means by which an organization interfaces with outside investors and stakeholders. From an economy-wide perspective, if organizations are governed effectively, then capital will flow to those sectors of the economy where the rewards are highest (Wurgler 2000). From an organizational perspective, those organizations that effectively align with their environments are more likely to obtain a competitive advantage (Powell 1992). This suggests that unless firms in East Asia effectively reform corporate governance, they may lose out on the benefits promised by globalization (Backman 1999, Young et al. 2001).

If corporate governance in East Asia is to change, what should be the direction of change? It is known that there are differences in corporate governance practices across various countries in the world (Sundaram et al. 2000), and there is disagreement as to the extent to which these practices are converging (Guillen 2000). One argument contends that there will ultimately be convergence with the global standards, which are dominated by the Anglo-American model (Rubach/Sebora 1998) while another argument is that different geographic and cultural regions should emphasize corporate governance practices unique to their cultural heritage (Guillen 2000). That is, any changes should be those that are consistent with the area's culture. We review each of these opposing positions to show contrasts and similarities before building the case for "transnational corporate governance."

The Case for Convergence of Corporate Governance Practices

The belief that corporate governance practices around the world will converge toward similar standards (Cadbury 1999, Rubach/Sebora 1998) originated with classical economic growth theory. From this perspective every nation goes through similar "stages of growth" as it moves from a traditional society to a modern, mass consumption society (Rostow 1960). The process involves several preconditions: a stable government, improved education, a group of innovators and businessmen to utilize the savings and expanded trade. Eventually the country will reach the "take off" stage (Rostow 1960) after which economic progress will dominate and the process would be self-sustaining (Fusfeld 1994).

Contemporary versions of the corporate governance convergence argument rely less on the inexorable "stages of growth" argument, and more on the view that globalization will initiate a "survival-of-the-fittest" process by which firms will be forced to adopt best practices in use (Rubach/Sebora 1998). These best practices are arguably exemplified by the corporate governance practices of the United States (US) and the United Kingdom (UK). This model has already spread to other countries, particularly those that employ a common law framework (La Porta/Lopez-de-Salines 1998).

Proponents of the convergence view of corporate governance point out that pressure from international investors and other stakeholders, all of whom have a stake in promoting transparent corporate governance, are encouraging the expansion of the Anglo-American model. They note that investors are willing to pay a premium for stock in firms with transparent governance practices. The result is that firms that adhere to the Anglo-American model of corporate governance should obtain a cost of capital advantage that, in the long run, will give them an advantage over firms that do not conform to international norms (Rubach/Sebora 1998, Wurgler 2000). For example, the California Public Employees' Retirement System (CALPERS) recently developed a list of emerging market economies, including many East Asian countries, in which they *would not* invest in because of factors such as financial transparency, market liquidity, poor and unenforced regulation, and favorative legal regimes (CALPERS 2002, Ahlstrom et al. 2003). Therefore, there are powerful incentives for the convergence of East Asian corporate governance practices and global standards.

There is evidence to support the increasing convergence of certain corporate governance practices around the world. For example, in many countries, proponents of reform agree on the centrality of certain principles and practices (Allen 2000). These global standards are based largely on Anglo-American concepts of corporate governance, reflecting both the strength of the US economy, and the leadership of the US and the UK in developing and refining standards of corporate governance and regulation (e.g., see the UK's Cadbury Report on corporate governance guidelines).

These standards include factors such as enhancing shareholders value; the need for independent nonexecutive directors; institutional investors and financial intermediaries to act as a check against management and a lever for enhancing board independence; the importance of higher levels of financial disclosure and transparency, and improved auditing practices and enforcement of regulations (Allen 2000). Most reformers would agree that, although not perfect, the above standards form the groundwork for the most robust and workable system of corporate governance yet available and that it is a worthwhile goal toward which transitional economies should strive (World Bank 1997).

The Case for Uniqueness of Corporate Governance Practices

Not all observers agree with the convergence hypothesis, instead maintaining that corporate governance systems would best remain unique, corresponding to the institutional environment in which they are embedded (Guillen 2000). This view draws from the belief that firms perform best when they match their strategic actions to their environmental setting (Dess/Origer 1987). In this view, successful firms will be those that understand the local environment and create corporate governance mechanisms that match that environment with their corporate governance (Choi et al. 1999). Thus, changes in corporate governance would require a better understanding of the culture and institutions of East Asia and the creation of systems that better reflect the existing culture and institutions, as opposed to adopting corporate governance systems developed in places with very different cultures and institutional systems, such as the US and the UK.

As part of this argument against convergence and for uniqueness in corporate governance, researchers argue further that it is futile to attempt to identify best corporate governance practices or model in the abstract for a worldwide setting because the firms of different countries are socially and institutionally equipped to follow different competitive strategies (Porter 1990). For example, Monks and Minow (2001, p. 296) ask: "What chance is there for convergence [in governance] among markets that are wildly different?" Guillen (2000, pp. 198–199) adds that "The three arguments against convergence in corporate governance – legal, institutional, and political – provide enough reason to cast serious doubt on the idea that there is convergence in corporate governance" and that scholars have "found very little evidence suggesting convergence."

In total, these various factors lead researchers to believe each institutional environment will likely encourage different systems of corporate governance that will, in turn, facilitate different types of competitive strategies and temporal considerations (Guillen 2000, Porter 1990). This leads Faccio, Lang, and Young (2001) to imply that rather than converging, East Asian corporate governance systems may actually be *diverging*. The implication of which is market forces that reward performance are rewarding those firms that best match their corporate governance to their environments.

"Transnational" Corporate Governance

As can be seen above, both the arguments for convergence and uniqueness can be compelling. Both positions appear to have valid points; the result is that rather than a dichotomous perspective on corporate governance a combination of the two views may be most appropriate (Lewis 2000). The competing objectives in corporate governance reform in the face of globalization can be viewed as analogous to the dilemma faced by multinational firms (Bartlett/Ghoshal 1989, Ghoshal 1987). Ghoshal (1987) noted that multinational firms face a dilemma balancing the need for standardizationfor sharing of resources and economies of scaleagainst the need for local responsiveness to local tastes and requirements. According to Ghoshal, a *multidomestic strategy* is one that maximizes local responsiveness, while a *global strategy* is one that maximizes standardization. Bartlett and Ghoshal (1989) use the term *transnational strategy* to describe the situation whereby a multinational firm balances both standardization and local responsiveness, and contend that this is superior to either of the other strategies alone.

As East Asian firms face continuing globalization, they encounter a similar set of circumstances with regard to corporate governance. They must standardize corporate governance to pacify global investors, while at the same time maintain traditional elements to satisfy local stakeholders. Thus firms are caught between internal alignment and external alignment (Huff/Huff/Thomas 1992). There is little doubt that continuing globalization is pressuring organizations to present corporate governance structures that are understandable to global investors. However, firms have to balance this pressure against the need to have control structures that are compatible with the local culture. If firms fail to push reforms they will lose opportunities from global investors, but if they change existing governance structures too dramatically, they will alienate employees, suppliers and other local stakeholders, which can negatively impact firm performance.

Just as it is difficult for firms to implement transnational corporate strategy because of inherent paradox, it is difficult for firms to implement transnational corporate governance for similar reasons. Policy makers and organizations need to identify those practices where convergence is necessary to facilitate a smooth interface with the global economy, while also identifying those aspects of corporate governance that are best tailored to the local environment. For example, it is going to be critical for firms to improve transparency and disclosure to make financial statements and corporate structures understandable to global investors (Allen 2000, Iskander et al. 1999). However, a firm's incentive systems for top executives should also be constructed so that they are in line with local norms and systems of suppliers based on relationships (Chen 2001, Khanna/Palepu 2000, Xin/Pearce 1996).

Of course, balancing these objectives will be difficult, yet many East Asian firms, which are dominated by the Overseas Chinese Diaspora, should be able to achieve this task even better than some other regions of the world. While Western thinking conventionally views the world as consisting of exclusive opposites, Chinese thinking is more likely to foster reconciliation of apparent polarities in what Chen (2002) refers to as paradoxical integration. For East Asian organizations, balancing the external demands from the global economy with the internal demands of the local culture in a unified system of corporate governance can be an example of the Chinese "middle way" of transcending paradox (Chen 2001, 2002).

Corporate Governance in East Asia

When analyzing East Asian corporate governance, it needs to be recognized that firms in the region tend to be controlled by the Overseas Chinese Diaspora (Backman 1999), and are dominated by the Chinese family structure (Chen 2001). These factors, in turn, impact the corporate governance process (Young et al. 2001). For example, although nearly all publicly listed Asian corporations have shareholders, boards of directors, and "professional" managers like their counterparts in North American and Europe, these similarities in reality are often more in form than in substance. In practice, informal constraints, such as relational ties, family connections, and government contacts, play a greater role in shaping corporate governance in East Asia, leading to outcomes often at odds with what is expected in the West (Peng 2000, Low 2002). For example, of the three primary functions performed by boards of directors – service, control and resource dependence (Johnson/Daily/Ellstrand 1996) – the service and control functions are less pronounced while the resource dependence role is more pronounced in East Asia (Young et al. 2001). Put simply, while firms in East Asian countries may have adopted the formal corporate governance frameworks of developed economies, the outcomes often are different.

The reason for the similarity in appearance but not in practice can partly be attributed to the institutional environment faced by firms in East Asia. The regulatory framework for East Asian equity markets is less developed than that of the West. This lack of development increases transaction costs, slows information flow, and encourages commercial transactions to be with related firms or well-established business partners (Boisot/Child 1996). East Asian corporations are also more likely to be family controlled and owned (Carney 1998, Chen 2001). The controlling family provides the management with no separation of ownership from control (Backman 1999). Thus, rather than a misalignment of interests between shareholders and managers as the major concern of corporate governance, the misalignment of interests with minority shareholders and majority shareholders is more prevalent in East Asian corporate governance (Young et al. 2002). It is also likely that a firm is associated with a particular "business group" and this allows for distortion in how governance is conducted in East Asia (Keister 2000). For example, "related transactions" or asset swapping may take place between business group members in an attempt to fleece minority shareholders (Backman 1999, Claessens et al. 2000, Faccio/Lang/Young 2001). These factors formed the backdrop for our qualitative examination of corporate governance practices in East Asia, to which we turn next.

Methodology

To examine the issues discussed above, a qualitative research design was employed. It has been argued that when initially investigating a domain, qualitative investigations are needed to ensure the right questions are asked in order to ground later quantitative investigations (Daft/Lewin 1990). Therefore, to build a solid grounding of actual corporate governance practice in East Asia, and to help predict future changes, we conducted in-depth semi structured interviews with individuals actively engaged in corporate governance in East Asia.

We did this by first examining the extant literature on corporate governance, family business and Asian business practices. This revealed five basic dimensions around which we based our investigation: (1) transparency and disclosure (Allen 2000); (2) board of director oversight (Young et al. 2001); (3) institutional structures for minority shareholders' voice (Faccio/Lang/Young 2001); (4) financing issues (Rhee/Chang 1993); and (5) ethnic networks (Backman 1999, Chen 2001, Kao 1993, Xin/Pearce 1996). We then interviewed a senior venture capitalist from the region to structure the initial interview questions. This individual was chosen based on his or her familiarity with global corporate governance practices as well as the practices specific to East Asia. Additionally, that individual had participated in funding a variety of firms and served on several boards of directors. These firms represented both family firms – where the venture capitalist was a minority shareholder, and new ventures – where the venture capitalist was a dominant shareholder. Venture capitalists provided information on the current situation and the general state of corporate governance in East Asian firms. From this initial interview and the extant corporate governance literature, the basic questions to be investigated and asked of participants were determined.

From the initial interview, it became clear that Hong Kong and Singapore essentially set the agenda for corporate governance issues in East Asia. These two areas have a legal environment that is more fully developed and thus others in the region often look to Hong Kong and Singapore in determining their corporate governance practices and regulations. Many venture capitalists and consultants may live in these cities, but have business interests across the region. Therefore, the focus of the remaining interviews came from these two areas.

With the aid of the Asian Corporate Governance Association in Hong Kong and other venture capitalists, we next identified four individuals who sat on corporate boards and were familiar with corporate governance in East Asia. We followed a purposive sampling approach to the sample selection and subsequent follow up (Lincoln/Guba 1985). Purposive sampling calls for selecting participants with specific characteristics, such as those cases displaying certain unusual patterns (Lincoln/Guba 1985).

After four initial interviews, changes in the interview protocol were made and the sample was then further extended to 21 more individuals in Hong Kong and Singapore with extensive experience in corporate governance. In total, 25 individuals closely involved in corporate governance in East Asia were interviewed. These included six top managers of East Asian firms, ten outside board members (seven of whom were venture capitalists, and three of whom were private equity and developmental capital specialists), four consultants based in Hong Kong and Singapore who advise on corporate governance issues, two government officials from Hong Kong and Singapore, one banker based in the region and active in turnaround, and two officials from nonprofit corporate governance associations based in Hong Kong. These individuals were selected for their knowledge of the function and governance of firms in East Asia. Additionally, the sample was selected to gain insight into two types of firms in East Asia that many knowledgeable observers feel may be increasingly employing different types of governance approaches, consistent with theoretical contrast sampling (Lincoln/Guba 1985, Yin 1994).

Everyone in the sample was asked the same base set of questions, modifying them necessarily for the different reference point in the case of the firm founders. In addition, as we learned more from the interviews, we asked subsequent subjects to respond to the tentative conclusions drawn from the early groups of interviews and our review of the relevant literature. This approach is broadly consistent with a replication logic approach to data gathering and analysis, and is particularly effective in studying variations of a model especially in a new research site or area (Eisenhardt 1989, Yin 1994).

The result is that multiple subjects involved in corporate governance, from both the insider (firm founders) and outsider (outside board members) points of view, were interviewed. In addition, we interviewed several outside observers such as consultants and individuals in nonprofit corporate governance associations (Asian Corporate Governance Association and Hong Kong Association of Company Secretaries). Interviewing both insiders and outsiders allows for a fuller understanding of the key issues involved (Headland/Pike/Harris 1990). In addition to our interview data, we supplement the findings with examples from periodicals and popular books written on corporate governance in East Asia.

Findings

As is often recounted in the extant governance literature (Low 2002), East Asian corporate governance still has relatively less transparency, information flow, outside board members, and rights for minority shareholders compared with that of most Western firms. Yet we also found that firms in East Asia are indeed being pressured to adopt practices consistent with global standards from global investors and global institutions as well as from a new, reform-minded generation of young managers. The results are presented below along the five dimensions previously identified. The discussion identifies both the current status of corporate governance in the region and changes that are occurring.

Transparency and Disclosure

Disclosure requirements in East Asia continue to be less strict and harder to enforce than those in the US or UK. For example, one banker closely involved in the turnaround of a firm on which he served on the board of directors commented:

> Disclosure, or giving a greater say to minority shareholders in the running of the business, is usually unheard of for the more traditional firms run by [Overseas Chinese] people with traditional backgrounds. Auditors are not there to provide much input; they are stonewalled when possible.

However, things are gradually changing in the area of information disclosure. A few of the interview subjects noted that although East Asian firms in general provide less information than would be expected by global standards, some of them are actually voluntarily increasing the amount of information disclosed as a result of outside pressure.

Board of Director Independence

In general, boards are less independent of management in East Asia than would normally be expected in other parts of the world (Young et al. 2002). Previous research indicates that a typical measure of an effective structure is whether individual board members are able to make decisions without undue influence from management (Phan 2000). However, boards of directors in East Asian firms rarely exercise true independence from management (Phan 1998, Au et al. 2000). Even in cases where a board member owns a large number of firm shares, they still often are given little say. Stated one Singapore based financier who had taken large stakes in several Asian firms:

Usually we get a board seat in exchange for our investment. Sometimes we have a lot of input [into firm strategy], but in some cases top management gives us little say in important matters. They tend to be tight-lipped about their plans and do not seek much input from the board or anyone outside of their inner circle for that matter. This [input seeking] does happen sometimes, but we are encouraging firm founders to be more open so we can help them.

At the same time, some innovative firms see the advantages of having an independent board and are beginning to change the relationship between boards of directors and shareholders. While these changes are in part due to the pressure of capital market regulators, they are also coming from managers who recognize the value of board independence. Some of the structural changes pursued have included separating the positions of Chairman and CEO (or Managing Director), appointing a majority of non-executive directors, encouraging regular CEO evaluation by the board and strategic auditing with active board involvement (Phan 1998, McGuinness 1999). Yet, similarities in board structure may be more symbolic than substantive and therefore may not translate to board independence for East Asian firms (Young et al. 2002). In summary, while East Asian boards are beginning to make moves toward independence due to outside pressure and internal advantage, the changes are more in form than in substance.

Minority Shareholder Rights

Closely related to the lack of independence in boards of directors is the dominance of majority shareholders. In East Asia, either the founder or their families control most locally listed companies (Faccio/Lang/Young 2001). In addition, the controlling shareholders are often politically well connected with local government officials. In this setting, the personal preferences of large individual shareholders or the political exigencies of government-linked corporations can result in minority shareholders being excluded from decision-making. This has set the stage for what has been called minority shareholder expropriation (Young et al. 2002), something that was discussed recently in *The Economist* (2000, p. 68):

> Foreign minority shareholders have often had little rights in East Asia. Robert Kuok, from Malaysia, initially made money trading oil, flour and sugar. Mr. Kuok controls the Shangri-La chain of luxury hotels, Hong Kong's main English language newspaper and much else. He recently had to merge the privately held but profitable subsidiary that managed his hotels into the publicly listed but less profitable arm that owned them analysts say that he was moved by minority shareholders who disliked

being fleeced. Pressures such as these are one reason why Mr. Kuok privately talks of delisting again.

Compared to the improvements in transparency and disclosure pointed out earlier, the trend of giving minority shareholders a greater voice appears to be moving more slowly. Despite the best efforts of minority shareholder activists, the region is slow to change in this regard. As *Business Week* columnist Mark Clifford recently pointed out:

> Minority shareholders have a long tradition of getting shafted by controlling families in Hong Kong – indeed, throughout much of Asia. Over the years, Hong Kong regulators have tried to stop the worst of the abuses, but to no avail. It's still "buyer beware." That's the hard lesson just learned anew by independent shareholders in Hong Kong (*BusinessWeek Online* 2002).

In spite of the recognized need for change, institutional norms in East Asia, even in Hong Kong, which is better than other places, do not support the notion of minority shareholders' interests (Gomes 2000, Young et al. 2002).

Financing Issues

Family firms in Asia seek outside equity reluctantly, often using stock market listings to get cash out of a business or to exit altogether (Chen 2001). For this reason, it is common for firms in their business portfolios to have profitable businesses privately held while less profitable firms are publicly traded (Backman 1999, Faccio/Lang/Young 2001). Some firms in Asia commonly seek financing through private equity sources and other outside equity financing. These investors may learn that corporate governance mechanisms do not automatically incorporate their voice into management of the firm. However, over time, as the depth of their relationship with the management and major shareholders increases, investor input also increases. One East Asian venture capitalist based in Singapore commented:

> [We give some] marketing advice ... [and] we certainly give a lot of input. This is a business that we understand quite a lot, a simple business. I think what we brought to the table is the financial language, the management of the growth of the company and helping the CEO to pick some of his key executives. The other is really to work with which markets to explore ... They are usually receptive because they know we can help them.

Several Asian venture capitalists mentioned that they felt the newer breed of entrepreneurs in East Asia did value their input and stonewalled less. This allowed the venture capitalists a more active role from the very beginning of the relationship. They felt this also gave them the opportunity to provide advice not only on the financial side but also regarding strategic issues, such as where to source materials or locate offices internationally. As these firms seek out more sources of outside funding, the managers in these firms may be forced to share control and provide more information to venture capitalists and other investors. This suggests that corporate governance style will move toward globally accepted best practices.

Ethnic Networks and Affiliates

Traditionally, East Asian businesspeople have dealt with members of their ethnic network when possible (Fallows 1995, Kao 1993). This is particularly true among the more traditional businesspeople. Most East Asian business is still controlled by the Diaspora of Chinese emigrants (Backman 1999, Chen 2001, Faccio/Lang/Young 2001). Creditors, suppliers and contractors often speak the same Chinese dialect as the owner-manager, whether they are based in Malaysia, Indonesia, the Philippines, Thailand, or even Hong Kong and Singapore. Some still work through the Chiu Chow (Teochiu), Hokkien (Fukkien), Hakka, Cantonese, and Shanghainese business associations. Transactions within this network are traditionally underwritten with handshakes and trust rather than with signatures and contracts. These associations and informal networks enforce behavior and agreements using sanctions, norms and peer pressure. Commented a former head of the ASEAN banking association:

> In much of East Asia, business is still done in the traditional way. People still like to work with others from their language or dialect group. Businesspeople are taught that you buy from "Uncle" even if he doesn't have the best price or best terms. Some of that is changing now, partly because there is standardization on English among businesspeople in this area or sometimes on Malay in Malaysia and Indonesia. The young people are speaking the old dialects less and less these days. And that could be driving some of the change in business practice here.

Most of the bankers, financiers and executives in our sample admitted that in spite of the change in East Asia, much of the dealing was still out of view and the close networks of family and dialect are still there and continue to influence. Similarly, more traditional East Asian firms continue to raise money from within the networks and from affiliated banks. In Thailand, for example, several banking families control much of the local banking industry and regulate access to larger loans and capital markets, often staying within their friends and family network and dialect group when possible. Backman (1999, p. 75) provides the following illustration:

Table 1. Summary of Findings

Aspect of Corporate Governance	Globally Accepted Best Practices of Corporate Governance	"Traditional" East Asian Corporate Governance Practices	Transnational Corporate Governance in East Asia
Transparency and Disclosure	More openness in firm management processes; Information disclosure is encouraged; firms are held to accounting standards modelled after GAAP.	Opaque business practices; "closed door" meetings between power brokers; Ceremonial general shareholders' meetings; No voluntary information disclosure; little regard for accounting practices	Increased reliance on outside equity has made firms more open in their financial transparency and disclosure. For example, in order to list on NYSE, firms must adhere to US GAAP.
Board of Director Independence	Push for board of director independence	Boards of directors have little or no independence	Firms have followed the Western trend of separating the Chairman and CEO function and other changes to give the appearance of more board independence, but old ways die hard and the degree of real change is questionable.
Minority Shareholders' Rights	Minority shareholders are afforded legal protection	Minority shareholders have little say and are subject to expropriation	There is pressure on many fronts to protect minority shareholders, but complaints and expropriation continue.
Financing Issues	Organizations often use outside equity for expansion, particularly in new, risky areas	Organizations rarely use outside financing	Many organizations have reluctantly sought outside financing as a result of the Asian financial crisis.
Ethnic Networks & Affiliates	Suppliers and associates are selected based more on business terms	Suppliers and associates are chosen on political or family connections	The information revolution is decreasing the value of privileged information and networks. A new generation of managers, often educated in North America or the UK, are encouraging more openness and access for outside investors.

Even so, there may be only so many family members to go round. Not so long ago, many overseas Chinese firms only recruited managers from the same Chinese dialect group as the founding family when they had to go outside the family. Some firms still do this. When Thailand's enormous Charoen Pokphand Group expanded to Indonesia, the group's Chearavanont family entrusted the management of its new Indonesia branch only to Teochiu speakers – the same Chinese dialect as themselves. However, the vast majority of Indonesia's Chinese population ancestrally are not Teochiu but Hokkien speakers. The Chearavanonts looked all around Indonesia for Teochius. One of the few significant pockets of them exists in Pontianak, a city in the Indonesian province of West Kalimantan on the island of Borneo. This was a rather obscure place to source senior management, but that is exactly what the Chearavanonts did. Not surprisingly, selecting from such a small pool put a significant constraint on the management talent available to the company, and its fortunes in Indonesia suffered accordingly.

The performance implications of this focus on ethnic networks are becoming clearer to many firms and investors in the region and the emphasis on ethnic networks likely will decline – albeit slowly – in the future. Table 1 summarizes the findings.

Discussion

Several composite points can be derived from the above findings and are summarized in Table 1. First, the generation of overseas Chinese businessmen that built huge empires is now preparing to hand those empires over to their sons or daughters, most of whom were educated in Western universities, far away from Asia's "bamboo network." This new generation has spent time overseas, or has had Western type business training[2] and thus is more likely to emphasize notions of shareholder value as opposed to the family's interests. Observed a Singapore private equity specialist:

> The younger generation seems to be more willing to change. Many of them have been educated overseas and received a Western business education. They are open to new approaches to governance. They will listen to outsiders and not mistrust their intentions.

Another individual who has director experience both on new economy high technology firms and on traditional economy firms commented on the topic of generational attitudes toward outsiders:

> I think it is their [Overseas Chinese business owners] feeling that they have run that construction company or plantation pretty well for 20 years, and who are you coming in now to tell them what to do. The younger generation seems more willing to give outsiders some say in their business. They even do not worry about giving us controlling interest in their firms sometimes.

Second, corporate governance standards are feeling pressure to change from globalization of capital markets. The Asian financial crisis made big Asian businesses more reliant on overseas capital. The financial crisis devastated the balance sheets not only of most Asian companies, but also of their banks. This means that firms have had to rely in large part on equity injections from western institutional investors to recapitalize themselves.

Third, the Internet poses a threat to traditional, backroom business practices. The recent financial crisis has been has forced the change that might occur over a generation into a time period of a few years. It has forced the business leaders to reluctantly seek outside help with management and finance. As one of the interview subjects commented: "[During the Asian boom years] you could run a large empire with very few people making few decisions. Now you need a large number of small decisions." As a result, the East Asian tycoons may not be able to rely simply on their own extended families to run their businesses, but will have to recruit outside professionals (Clifford 2002). The global availability of information, particularly financial information, may prove to be a key change agent by undermining business models that are based on networks of Chinese around the world, on privileged information and secret backroom dealing (Backman 1999). As such, it lowers barriers to entry, and allows for the rapid rise of new competitors; as information becomes more abundant, instantaneous and accessible to all, the value of well-connected intermediaries and networks is reduced.

Conclusion

As globalization continues, East Asian firms find themselves torn between embracing the new economy while attempting to maintain traditional practices embedded in their rich and varied cultures. This dilemma is reflected in the ongoing reform of corporate governance practices in East Asia. Change is coming slowly to East Asian firms, where the dominant Chinese Diaspora still controls most businesses and follow traditional practices. Our research finds support for the position that, like the search for global efficiency and local responsiveness pursued by multinational firms, successful corporate governance practices embrace aspects of global corporate governance complemented with local practices.

East Asian firms still have a strong sense of family and hierarchical organizational structures. Yet it was not so long ago that other parts of the world, including Europe and North America, experienced a family business period before corporate forms and governance practices with which are familiar today emerged

(Chandler 1990, *The Economist* 2003). Some of today's industrial icons, such as Ford, started as family businesses and have become, over time, modem, transparent, shareholder-friendly companies with rule of law and contracts becoming more important. East Asia may follow a similar, but not identical, path. It is likely that certain aspects of corporate governance and control will retain a distinctly Asian flavor. This can be felt in corporate boardrooms and other mechanisms across the region where change is occurring, albeit slowly and with resistance. Nonetheless there is genuine change. Exhibit 1 describes the case of a new breed of Asian corporate governance that maintains a balance between the local and the global.

Exhibit 1. The New Asian Corporate Governance – VTech Holdings.

> As the old network passes, so will the world that bred East Asia's patriarchs – whether they run huge empires or smaller corporate fiefdoms. This may condemn some of today's tycoons to further substantiating the Chinese proverb that wealth is made and lost within three generations. A more likely evolution is that the heirs of Asia's tycoons will gradually become modern managers alongside other entrepreneurs. They would no longer be "tycoons" in the old sense but managers running world-class corporations that happen to be based in East Asia. Today, VTech is one of the more prominent examples. VTech is a market leader in educational toys and other handheld consumer electronics such as cordless telephones. From the beginning the chairman and founder of Vtech, Allan Wong, has tried to build his company differently from many other firms in East Asia, paying particular attention to corporate governance. He aims to increase shareholder value; he discloses more than is required by law; VTech avoids arbitrary placement of family members in high positions while seeking research and development talent all around the world (Wingrove 1996). VTech takes pains to point out that it is not a family company. Its performance during the Asian financial crisis was exemplary as the stock price actually rose during the downturn (Tanzer 1998). VTech continues to win praise from analysts for its focused corporate strategy in of its core businesses and transparent corporate governance.

Much of the pressure to raise standards of governance is coming from international institutions such as the World Bank and the Organization for Economic Cooperation and Development, which have issued guidelines for government action. But changing the system of shareholder control, and the tradition of minimum disclosure, is likely to prove harder than simply introducing some outside business school graduates into the group, warn critics of the traditional pyramid system. The lack of transparency afforded to shareholders still makes it difficult to end such practices. It is likely that the immediate future will bring a period of change, but not a governance revolution. Over the next decade, the region's economies will likely retain many of the structural features that have allowed traditional family firms to flourish. Yet, the rise of the Internet, increased (and speedy) financial information, and the disintermediation of traditional middlemen will mean that those companies that adjust to new markets are most likely to prosper in the long term (Evans/Wurster 2000).

Many East Asian firms are attempting to figure out ways of meeting demands imposed by the new global economy and outside investors while staying consistent with the demands of local stakeholders and their institutional environment. In the process of doing this, they are developing alternative corporate governance structures that are in some ways similar to those of firms in other parts of the world yet at the same time unique in other ways. The *transnational corporate governance* solution, while difficult and at times paradoxical, is likely the best alternative course for the foreseeable future.

Endnotes

1 By East Asia, we are referring to the countries in which the Chinese Diaspora play a prominent role in the business community, including regions such as Hong Kong and Taiwan as well as the Southeast Asian countries of Indonesia, Malaysia, the Philippines, Singapore and Thailand (Backman 1999, Rohwer 2001).
2 Virtually all of the major universities in East Asia have a curriculum and teaching materials similar to those in the West. Asian universities have started seeking accreditation from the American Association of Schools of Business (AACSB).

References

Ahlstrom, D./Young, M. N./Nair, A./Law, P., Managing the Institutional Environment: Challenges for Foreign Firms in Post-WTO China, *SAM Advanced Management Journal*, 68, 2, 2003, pp. 41–49.
Allen, J., Code Convergence in Asia: Smoke or Fire?, *Corporate Governance International*, 3, 1, 2000, pp. 23–37.
Au, K./Peng, M. W./Wang, D., Interlocking Directorates, Firm Strategies, and Performance in Hong Kong: Towards a Research Agenda, *Asia Pacific Journal of Management*, 17, 1, 2000, pp. 29–47.
Backman, M., *Asian Eclipse: Exposing the Dark Side of Business in Asia*, Singapore: John Wiley & Sons (Asia) 1999.
Bartlett, C. A./Ghoshal, S., *Managing Across Borders: The Transnational Solution*, Boston: Harvard Business School Press 1989.
Bluedorn, A. C./Johnson, R. A./Cartwright, D. K./Barringer, B. R., The Interface and Convergence of the Strategic Management and Organizational Environment Domains, *Journal of Management*, 20, 2, 1994, pp. 201–262.
Boisot, M./Child, J., From Fiefs to Clans and Network Capitalism: Explaining China's Emerging Economic Order, *Administrative Science Quarterly*, 41, 4, 1996, pp. 600–628.
Boyd, B. K./Carroll, O./Howard, M., International Corporate Governance Research: A Review and Agenda for Future Research, in: Cheng, J. L. C./Peterson, R. B. (eds.), *Advances in International Comparative Management*, Vol. 11, Stamford, CT: JAI Press 1996, pp. 191–215.
Brancato, C. K., Building on Sand, *Asian Business*, 35, 8, 1999, pp. 8–9.
Cadbury, A., What are the Trends in Corporate Governance? How Will They Impact Your Company? *Long Range Planning*, 32, 1, 1999, pp. 12–19.

CALPERS, *Permissible Equity Markets Investment Analysis and Recommendations*, prepared and published by Wilshire Associates, 1299 Ocean Avenue, Suite 700, Santa Monica, CA 2002.
Carney, M., A Management Capacity Constraint? Obstacles to the Development of the Overseas Chinese Family Business, *Asia Pacific Journal of Management*, 15, 2, 1998, pp. 137-162.
Chandler, A. D., *Scale and Scope: The Dynamics of Industrial Capitalism*, Cambridge, MA: Belknap Press 1990.
Chen, M. J., Transcending Paradox: The Chinese "Middle Way" Perspective, *Asia Pacific Journal of Management*, 19, 2002, pp.179-199.
Chen, M. J., *Inside Chinese Business: A Guide for Managers World Wide*, Boston: Harvard Business School Press 2001.
Choi, C. J./Raman, M./Usoltseva, O./Lee, S. H., Political Embeddedness in the New Triad: Implications for Emerging Economies, *Management International Review*, 39, 1999, pp. 257-275.
Clifford, M., Hong Kong's Cautionary Christmas Carol, *Business Week Online*, August 23, 2002, http://www.businessweekasia.com/magazine/content/2_36/online.htm.
Claessens, S./Djankov, S./Lang, L. H. P., The Separation of Ownership and Control in East Asian Corporations, *Journal of Financial Economics*, 58, 2000, pp. 81-112.
Daft, R. L./Lewin, A. Y., Can Organization Studies Begin to Break out of the Normal Science Straightjacket? An Editorial Essay, *Organization Science*, 1, 1990, pp. 1-10.
Dess, G. G./Origer, N. K., Environment, Structure, and Consensus in Strategy Formulation: A Conceptual Integration, *Academy of Management Review*, 12, 2, 1987, pp. 313-330.
Eisenhardt, K. M., Building Theories from Case Study Research, *Academy of Management Review*, 14, 4, 1989, pp. 532-550.
Evans, P./Wurster, T. S., Blown to Bits: How the New Economics of Information Transforms Strategy, Boston, MA: Harvard Business School Press 2000.
Faccio, M./Lang, L./Young, L., Dividends and Expropriation, *American Economic Review*, 91, 2001, pp. 54-78.
Fallows, J. M., Looking at the Sun: The Rise of the New East Asian Economic and Political System, New York: Vintage Books 1995.
Fusfeld, D. R., *The Age of the Economist* 7th edition, New York: Harper Collins 1994.
Ghoshal, S., Global Strategy: An Organizing Framework, *Strategic Management Journal*, 8, 5, 1987, pp. 425-440.
Gomes, A., Going Public Without Governance: Managerial Reputation Effects, *Journal of Finance*, 55, 2000, pp. 615-46.
Guillen, M., Corporate Governance and Globalization: Is There Convergence Across Countries?, *Advances in International Comparative Management*, 13, 2000, pp. 175-204.
Headland, T. N./Pike, K. L./Harris, M. (eds.), *Emics and Etics: The Insider/Outsider Debate*, Newbury Park, CA: Sage Publications 1990.
Hitt, M./Gimeno, J./Hoskisson, R., Current and Future Research Methods in Strategic Management, *Organizational Research Methods*, 1, 1998, pp. 6-44.
Huff, J. O./Huff, A. S./Thomas, H., Strategic Renewal and the Interaction of Cumulative Stress and Inertia, *Strategic Management Journal*, 13, 1992, pp. 55-75.
Iskander, M./Meyerman, G./Gray, D. F./Hagan, S., Corporate Restructuring and Governance in East Asia, *Finance & Development*, 36, 1, 1999, pp. 42-45.
Johnson, J. L./Daily, C. M./Ellstrand, A. E., Boards of Directors: A Review and Research Agenda, *Journal of Management*, 22, 3, 1996, pp. 409-438.
Johnson, S./Boone, P./Breach, A./Friedman, E., Corporate Governance in the Asian Financial Crisis, *Journal of Financial Economics*, 58, 2000, pp. 141-186.
Kao J., The Worldwide Web of Chinese Business, *Harvard Business Review*, 71, 2, March-April 1993, pp. 24-36.
Keister, L. A., *Chinese Business Groups: The Structure and Impact of Interfirm Relations During Economic Development*, Hong Kong: Oxford University Press (China) Ltd. 2000.
Khanna, T./Palepu, K., The Future of Business Groups in Emerging Markets: Long-run Evidence from Chile, *Academy of Management Journal*, 43, 3, 2000, pp. 268-285.
La Porta, R./Lopez-de-Silanes, F., Law and Finance, *Journal of Political Economy*, 106, 6, 1998, p. 1113.

Lewis, M. W., Exploring Paradox: Toward a More Comprehensive Guide, *The Academy of Management Review*, 25, 4, 2000, pp. 760–776.
Lincoln, Y. S./Guba, G. G., *Naturalistic Inquiry*, Beverly Hills, CA: Sage 1985.
Low, C. K. (ed.), *Corporate Governance: An Asia-Pacific Critique*, Hong Kong: Sweet & Maxwell Asia 2002.
McGuinness, P. B., *A Guide to the Equity Markets of Hong Kong*, New York: Oxford University Press 1999.
Monks, R. A. G./Minnow, N., *Corporate Governance* 2nd edition, Oxford, UK: Blackwell 2001.
Peng, M. W., *Business Strategies in Transition Economies*, Thousand Oaks, CA: Sage 2000.
Phan, P. H., Effective Corporate Governance in Singapore: Another Look, *Singapore Management Review*, 20, 2, 1998, pp. 43–61.
Phan, P., *Taking Back the Boardroom*, Singapore: McGraw-Hill 2000.
Powell, T. C., Organizational Alignment as Competitive Advantage, *Strategic Management Journal*, 13, 2, 1992, pp. 119–134.
Porter, M. E., *The Competitive Advantage of Nations*, New York: Free Press 1990.
Rhee, S. G./Chang, R. P., The Microstructure of Asian Equity Markets, *Journal of Financial Services Research*, 6, 4, 1993, pp. 437–454.
Rohwer, J., *Remade in America: How Asia Will Change Because America Boomed*, Singapore: John Wiley & Sons (Asia) Pte Ltd. 2001.
Rostow, W. W., *Stages of Economic Growth: A Non-communist Manifesto*, Cambridge: Cambridge University Press 1960.
Rubach, M. J./Sebora, T. C., Comparative Corporate Governance: Competitive Implication of an Emerging Convergence, *Journal of World Business*, 33, 2, 1998, pp. 167–184.
Serapio, M. G./Shenkar, O., Reflections on the Asian Crisis: Introduction to the Special Issue, *Management International Review*, 39 Special Issue 1999/4, pp. 3–12.
Sundaram, A. K./Bradley, M./Schipani, C. A./Walsh, J. P., Comparative Corporate Governance and Global Strategy, in: Grosse, R. E. (ed.), *Thunderbird on Global Business Strategy*, New York: John Wiley & Sons, Inc. 2000, pp. 110–150.
Tanzer, A., The VTech Phenomenon, *Forbes*, 162 (88), October 19, 1998, pp. 88–90.
The Economist, The End of Tycoons, 355, April 29, 2000, pp. 67–69.
The Economist, The Way We Govern Now, 366 (8306), January 11, 2003, p. 62.
Wingrove, N., Hong Kong's VTech Blends East, West R&D Management, *Research Technology Management*, 39, 4 July/August 1996, pp. 6–7.
World Bank, *China's Management of Enterprise Assets: The State as Shareholder* (Country Study), Washington DC: The World Bank 1997.
Wurgler, J., Financial Markets and the Allocation of Capital, *Journal of Financial Economics*, 58, 2000, pp. 187–214.
Xin, K. R./Pearce, J. L., Guanxi: Connections as Substitutes for Formal Institutional Support, *Academy of Management Journal*, 39, 6, 1996, pp. 1641.
Yin, R. K., *Case Study Research: Design and Methods* 2nd edition, Beverly Hills, CA: Sage Publications 1994.
Young, M. N./Ahlstrom, D./Bruton, G. D./Chan, E. S., The Resource Dependence, Service and Control Functions of Boards of Directors in Hong Kong and Taiwanese Firms, *Asia Pacific Journal of Management*, 18, 2, 2001, pp. 223–244.
Young, M. N./Peng, M. W./Ahlstrom, D./Bruton, G. D., Governing the Corporation in Emerging Economies: A Principal-Principal Perspective, *Best Paper Proceedings of the Academy of Management Annual Meeting* 2002.

Management
International Review
© Gabler Verlag 2004

Björn Ambos/Wolf D. Reitsperger

Offshore Centers of Excellence: Social Control and Success

Abstract

- The global dispersion of knowledge and technological capabilities has moved MNCs to assign lead responsibilities to offshore units in order to take advantage of this phenomenon.

- Moving core competencies to the periphery enables the firm to take advantage of resources not present in its home country, posing at the same time issues of integration and control.

- This paper challenges common suggestions of the superiority of social control to best utilize Centers of Excellence (CoEs) established abroad. Utilizing a sample of German national origin, we test propositions grounded in social network theory.

Key Results

- Our sample confirms that German MNCs abstain from high socialization to attain strategic goals in their Centers of Excellence abroad. Moreover, high socialization as a means of control is negatively correlated with the technical success of CoEs abroad.

Authors

Björn Ambos, Senior Lecturer in Marketing, Management School, The University of Edinburgh, Edinburgh, UK.
Wolf D. Reitsperger, Professor em., Honolulu, HI, USA.

Introduction

Ever since organizations started to disperse their value creating activities, research has tried to answer the question of how to organize and coordinate these activities (Pugh et al. 1968, Macharzina 1993). Numerous publications have addressed this issue (Stopford/Wells 1972, Egelhoff 1982, Franko 1973, Daniels et al. 1984) and perhaps Bartlett and Ghoshal (1989) have made the most prominent attempt in this respect. In their book the authors conclude that MNCs are increasingly faced with complex environments. Specialized, often network-based structures are the answers to deal effectively with these increasingly complex environments and the challenges they present for MNCs' coordinating and control activities. The authors suggest that in these networks subsidiaries fulfill clearly defined, albeit differing, roles and that headquarters need to adjust coordination and control activities to reflect these differentiated roles. In particular, Bartlett and Ghoshal (1989) propose that using social control should coordinate units holding a strategically important mandate. The argument rests in part on the assumption that for these units other more traditional control instruments fail to function. This notion has been repeatedly treated in the literature (Macharzina 1992, Wolf 1994, Evans et al. 1989, Baliga/Jaeger 1984).

While these notions seem to be commonly accepted in the literature, empirical research fails to support them. Gupta and Govindarajan (1994), studying control in MNCs for example, fall short of finding support for their hypothesis that globally innovating subsidiaries were exposed to high social control. Similarly, Asakawa (1996), in a study of Japanese R&D units in Europe, discovered that, contrary to common belief, these companies did abstain from the use of socialization as coordinating and control mechanisms. While the explanations of the authors vary, they culminate in a common suggestion: socialization as the *sine qua non* instrument to control strategic lead units in complex environments may not be a viable tool to achieve desired results. Hence, our current thinking on social control may be ill-suited to guide MNCs' coordination and control decisions by preventing subsidiaries in foreign countries from acquiring or creating the desired technologies and know-how commensurate with the strategic needs of the MNC. This paper attempts to shed light on this issue by building on the existing literature to develop a theoretical argument for low socialization between centers of excellence. Subsequently, propositions developed from these arguments are empirically tested using a sample of German R&D centers in foreign countries.

Presenting our arguments and ideas we will proceed as follows: first, we briefly review the literature focusing on different subsidiary roles and the use of social control by MNCs. Subsequently we develop propositions concentrating on differentiated subsidiary roles, which may fit high or low social control patterns.

Second, a methodology guiding the research will be presented. The third section is concerned with statistical analysis, which is followed by a discussion of the results of the empirical tests. The final section discusses the findings and their implications for theory and practice.

Theoretical Background

Subsidiary Roles and Centers of Excellence

There have been various attempts to conceptualize the roles of foreign subsidiaries (see Schmid et al. 1998 for an overview). Various writers (e.g., Ghoshal/Bartlett 1990, Martinez/Jarillo 1991, Ghoshal/Nohria 1989, Nohria/Ghoshal 1994, Gupta/Govindarajan 1991, Forsgren/Pedersen 1997, 1998, White/Poynter 1984, Taggert 1997, Birkinshaw/Morrison 1995) acknowledge that MNCs assign different missions and roles to their subsidiaries abroad. The theoretical foundations, which are the bases of their arguments, vary as much as the derived implications. This is partly a result of the different criteria used by the authors to build their respective typologies, which are developed to capture and define a variety of different subsidiary roles. While some authors use market-based criteria, others use company criteria related to subsidiary competence, autonomy or the inflow and outflow of knowledge. This paper concentrates on one particular MNC subsidiary type: The Center of Excellence (CoE). Other terms specifying the same phenomenon are strategic leader, competence center, global innovator, capability center or simply strategic center.

Defining CoE is apparently more difficult than it first seems (Paterson/Brock 2002, Schmid 1999). While a formal definition on how we operationalize the construct will follow in the methods section, we briefly summarize commonly shared assumptions about them. One characteristic shared by most studies is the CoE's strategic position or mandate inside the firms' networks (Bartlett/Ghoshal 1986, Gupta/Govindarajan 1994, Moore/Birkinshaw 1998, Andersson/Forsgren 2000, Schmid 1999). Thus, CoEs are usually defined as corporate leaders mandated to *create* or *augment* firm capabilities in order to secure its survival (Bartlett/Ghoshal 1986, Gupta/Govindarajan 1991, Hedlund/Ridderstråle 1997, Kuemmerle 1997, 1999, Kuemmerle/Roosenbloom 1999, Chiesa 1996). As part of their mandate, CoEs usually acquire the sole responsibility for an area of excellence (Hood/Young 1982, Pearce 1989, White/Poynter 1984, Brockhoff 1998). Other factors commonly mentioned are the CoEs' responsibility for a larger geographical area (White/Poynter 1984, D'Cruz 1986, Bartlett/Ghoshal 1989, Gupta/Govindarajan 1991) and a high degree of local embeddedness (Andersson/Forsgren 1996, 2000, Kuemmerle 1999, Asakawa 1996). The latter particularly characterizes technology-oriented CoEs, since knowledge creation usually takes place in localized knowledge clusters (Porter 1990, Chiesa 1996, Frost et al. 2002).

Social Control

Van Maanen and Schein (1979) define socialization as the process by which an individual learns which behaviors and perspectives are acceptable inside an organization. In this respect, social control provides the power associated with implicit norms to guide the behavior of organizational members. In this way MNCs ascertain that the behavior of subsidiary managers is in the company's best interest, without requiring any direct intervention on the part of headquarters. Mainly for this reason, social control has such an overwhelming appeal by providing the means of control, without the obvious and negative connotations associated with autocracy or the creativity stifling consequences of bureaucracy.

Companies eager to achieve social control emphasize the creation of shared norms and values. The mechanisms used to reach this goal are multiple and vary by MNCs' national origin. Japanese firms, for example, send managers overseas to establish control by acting as agents promoting headquarter culture. Unilever, a UK firm, uses a different approach to socialization by grouping top managers in international training camps in order to homogenize corporate culture throughout its subsidiaries (Bartlett/Ghoshal 1989).

Social control in foreign subsidiaries is not an undisputed matter (Welch/ Welch 1997). One simple albeit strong argument against social control is put forward by Egelhoff (1999). In an attempt to contrast traditional models of MNCs to new, e.g., network structures, Egelhoff criticizes the use of social control by imposing a "company centric" culture on all subsidiaries. He argues that a company centric culture will hamper integration and assimilation into the local community. In the case of CoEs whose aim is to engage in the creation and acquisition of new knowledge, a company centric culture may inhibit their success rather than enhance it. Research shows that integration into the local research community is of utmost importance in helping to acquire and process newfound knowledge, which will benefit the MNC (Porter 1990, Kuemmerle 1999, Frost et al. 2002). As a consequence, MNCs may be inclined to give CoEs some leeway, or to try to establish control by less invasive means than socialization.

A second stream of research leads to a similar insight. Building on social network theory (e.g., Nelson 1989, Podolny/Baron 1997), Hansen (1999) examines conditions facilitating or inhibiting the search *vis à vis* the transfer of knowledge in organizations. His research leads to the conclusion that in cases where the search of new knowledge is prevalent, weak interunit ties are advantageous. This argument rests on the observation that weak ties between units reduce the risk of acquiring redundant knowledge (Granovetter 1973, Burt 1992). We expect that social control, which demands a strong normative integration of values and perspectives throughout the network, would require strong rather than weak ties. Thus, strong social control would negatively impact the acquisition of new knowledge by fostering the likelihood of acquiring redundant knowledge. In reference to Weick (1976), Hansen (1999) puts forward yet another argument for the benefits of weak interunit ties in knowledge search. As argued by Weick (1976), organizational entities that are loosely bound into the corporate network are more adaptive, simply because they are less constrained by the organization of which they are a part. Relating this to our particular case of CoEs, we deduce that these units, when endowed with a clear mandate to search for new knowledge and to augment the MNCs existing capabilities, will be better able to fulfill their missions when the ties between units are weak, or stated differently, when social control is low. Based on the discussion above, we propose two hypotheses:

Hypothesis 1. MNCs will refrain from imposing strong social control on their Offshore Centers of Excellence.

Hypothesis 2. Imposing strong social control on Offshore Centers of Excellence will negatively affect subsidiary performance.

Methodology

Sample

To test these propositions, we used primary data from 134 foreign R&D units of German MNCs. Data were collected via a standardized questionnaire mailed to all firms listed in the German top 500, of which 106 are known to operate overseas R&D facilities. Forty-nine firms agreed to participate, leading to an overall response rate of 46%. We limited our study to subsidiaries of German firms, since prior research showed that national origin might influence the use of coordination instruments (Bartlett/Ghoshal 1989, Harzing 1999, Cantwell/Janne 1999). The responding firms spend 66% of all privately funded R&D in Germany, and provide a representative picture of German technological activities. Targeting vice presidents of R&D at the headquarter level as respondents, we faced both theoretical and practical challenges. While it would have been advantageous to obtain some of our measures at the subsidiary level, we felt that our key measures, "subsidiary mandate" and "unit performance", might be biased when taken at the subsidiary level. We therefore decided to follow the suggestion of Ghoshal and Nohria (1989) and Roth et al. (1991) obtaining data from headquarters only, because subsidiary managers might be partial when providing an assessment of their own CoE's performance (Roth et al. 1991).

Data and Measures

Data were obtained on the strategic mission of the subsidiary, its external embeddedness and market scope, as well as on the degree of social control applied to the unit under investigation. In addition we collected data on unit success. (For a detailed description of the measures see appendix.)

To isolate Centers of Excellence from other overseas R&D investments, we decided to use a traditional approach. Qualifying units would have a clear mandate to augment the firm's capabilities, and would need to be sufficiently equipped with resources to be able to do so. The questionnaire items used to assess these two dimensions are provided in the appendix. As in prior studies, our technological mandate variable appeared to be bi-modal (Kuemmerle 1999), and was subsequently split at the 50% mark, resulting in two distinct categories: one being "augmenting" (creating) firm capabilities and the other "exploiting" existing capabilities. Using our second measure, "task interdependence", which we dichotomized by using a median split, we obtained a total of four strategic mandates: Local adaptors, Integrated Research Units, Global Development Units and Centers of Excellence. Only those units which had low task-related interdependencies (i.e., were in the possession of all critical resources), and had a clear focus on enhancing (augmenting) the firms' capabilities were classified as CoE (see Exhibit 1).

We also obtained some data on the *external embeddedness* of the unit and its *market scope* to validate our CoE measure. External embeddedness was assessed following von Boehmer's (1995) approach, using a graphical presentation of the subsidiary and all possible cooperation partners. Managers were asked to indicate partners, and in a second step rate the importance of the existing cooperation. (For a detailed description see appendix). According to our arguments above, we expected CoEs to be highly embedded into the local research community. A second measure asked managers to indicate the market scope of the subsidiary by categorizing it as local, regional or global. In relation to all other subsidiaries we expected CoEs to be globally oriented.

The other central variable, *socialization*, was assessed by using a three-item scale similar to the one used by Harzing (1999) and Martinez and Jarillo (1991). Managers were to indicate the degree to which values are shared, the use of expatriates as a means of control, and the frequency of R&D personnel exchange

Figure 1. Identifying Centers of Excellence

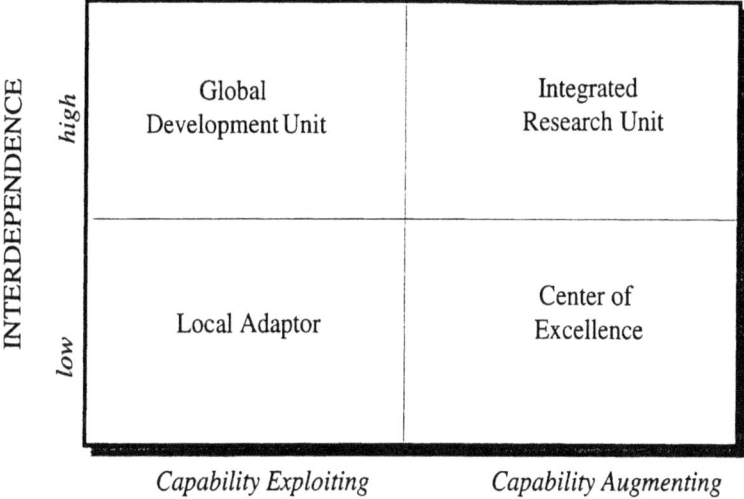

between units. The items were measured on a five-point scale originally used by Martinez and Jarillo (1991) which was slightly modified to suit the specific purpose of our study. Cronbach's alpha for our scale was 0.67.

Measuring subsidiary success in an international setting is an unresolved issue in international business research (Venkatraman/Ramanujam 1986, Brockhoff 1998). R&D success was measured directly, and in relation to predefined goals. The performance scale was adapted from Schmaul (1995) and encompassed two categories: meeting predefined technical goals (technical success), and meeting time as well as budgetary goals (economic success). The same approach was used in several studies and is considered a valid instrument (Hauschildt 1991, Brockhoff 1998, Schmaul 1995). In addition we collected profitability and return on sales data.

Results

Preliminary tests were used to determine the validity of the study. First, using cross-tabulation we examined the market scope and compared it to the sample as a whole. Ninety-five percent of our CoEs were global in focus, as compared to

Table 1. One way ANOVA – Network Partner and Mission of the R&D Unit

Network partners	Strategic Mission[a] Mean scores				F-Value
	1 (n = 47)	2 (n = 19)	3 (n = 46)	4 (n = 20)	
external partners:					
Competitors	0,44	0,24	0,25	0,18	0,131
Suppliers	1,71	**1,82**	0,80	1,16	3,755*
Customers	2,33	1,94	1,40	1,83	3,656*
Other Firms	0,49	0,88	0,35	0,67	1,345
Private Research Institutions	0,60	**0,88**	**1,25**	0,40	3,491*
Universities	0,97	**1,47**	**1,30**	0,65	2,917*
Governmental Agencies	0,51	0,71	0,45	0,44	0,440
internal partners:					
Central R&D	1,82	1,41	**2,55**	**2,45**	6,101**
other (internal) R&D Unit	1,36	1,24	**1,85**	**1,86**	2,199*
local Production/Marketing	**2,24**	1,64	0,95	1,88	4,314*
other (internal) Production/Marketing	1,09	0,94	0,65	1,00	0,771

[a] (1) Local Adaptors, (2) Center of Excellence, (3) Integrated Research Unit, (4) Global Development Unit
* $p < 0,01$.
** $p < 0,001$.

54% for the sample as a whole. The remaining CoEs had at least a regional scope, providing support for our measure. Second, we were interested if, as stated, these centers were integrated into the local research community. To that end we conducted a one-way ANOVA. Results are reported in Table 1. The first column identifies the cooperation partner, the following columns reflect the meanscores, while the last reports the F-value. In case of significantly higher cooperation intensity, our findings are highlighted in bold. Significantly lower cooperation intensities we marked with a dash. The results show that CoEs are heavily embedded in the local research community, particularly private research institutions, universities, and government. Interestingly, CoEs not only possess strong ties to the respective research communities, but also to suppliers and customers. This may be an indication that CoEs are not only striving to obtain technology driven innovations but also to seek market driven innovations.

As a second step a one-way ANOVA was used to compare socialization intensity in CoEs with the whole population. The results are presented in Table 2. The exhibit shows that social control is lower in CoEs than in all other units. By utilizing a Sheffé test, we subsequently tested for significant differences among the individual groups. The results confirm that CoEs are subject to significantly less socialization than two of the three other types (global development units and integrated research units). With respect to the local adaptor role, no signifi-

Table 2. One way ANOVA - Use of Socialization as a Means of Control in CoE

	Strategic Mission[a]				F-Value
	1 (n = 47)	2 (n = 19)	3 (n = 46)	4 (n = 20)	
Use of Social Control	2,61	2,14	3,37	3,04	8,49*

[a] (1) Local Adaptors, (2) Center of Excellence, (3) Integrated Research Unit, (4) Global Development Unit
* $p < 0,001$.

cant relationship was observed and socialization was relatively low. The issue will be discussed in greater depth later on. Overall, the results confirm our argument. As predicted, the degree of social control in CoEs is much lower as compared to other units. This is support for *Hypothesis 1*.

In a final step we correlated the success measures with the social control variable. First, we conducted a factor analysis using varimax rotation obtaining two factors, economical and technical success, with all variables loading on one of them. Using the regression scores of these two factors, we subsequently performed a correlation analysis. The results of this analysis are reported in Table 3. Negative correlation would provide support for our second hypothesis, since a higher degree of social control should result in less success of a CoE.

The results of the statistical analysis provide partial support for *Hypothesis 2*, since only the correlations with technical success are significant, as well as negative. Our economic indicators, time goals and budgetary goals, were not found to be related to the degree of social control. Neither was it found that higher socialization would lead to significantly lower profits or returns on sale. We will return to this issue, as well as to other results in the concluding section.

Finally, in the spirit of exploratory research, we applied the same analysis to the remaining three subsidiary types. Although we did not set out to develop a theoretical framework for dealing with these units, we felt that investigating the relationship between socialization and performance for these units would enrich the presentation of results and lead to further research. The results reveal an interesting pattern. While no significant relationships with respect to technical success were found, both integrated research units and local adaptors show sig-

Table 3. Social Control and Success in German CoE

	Technical Success	Economic Success	Profit 1999	Return on Sales
Social Control	–0.624	0.356	–0.284	–0.211
Sig. level	0.072	0.347	0.347	0.534

nificant positive correlations with respect to our economic success criterion ($r = 0,822$, $p = 0,004$ and $r = 0,535$; $p = 0,001$ respectively). These results seem to indicate that in subsidiaries that are not self-sufficient units or subsidiaries that are mandated to locally exploit firms' capabilities, high degrees of social control may enhance efficiency.

Discussion and Conclusion

In this paper we advanced an argument challenging the appropriateness of high social control in offshore centers of excellence. Social control has been advocated by various authors as the superior means of control for strategic lead units. Prior studies often failed, however, to confirm this notion. Building on social network theory, and recognizing the CoE as a highly embedded unit with the mandate to innovate, we expected a negative link between high social control and CoE performance. The MNCs in our study refrain from imposing strong social control on their CoE. If they do, we find that strong social control is negatively related to technical performance. These results are well in support of Hansen (1999), who argues that social control, or strong ties among CoEs, may inhibit effective search processes by impeding effective knowledge acquisition. Our empirical findings also support Egelhoff's (1999) suggestion that social control tends to counteract the integration of the CoE into the local research community, thereby inhibiting the acquisition and creation of new knowledge and as a consequence technical performance.

While we found a negative impact of social control on technical performance, the results do not allow similar conclusions for economic performance. This may be primarily due to noise in the economic performance data. One reviewer suggested that technical success is probably the area where the limitations caused by corporate socialization would be most noticeable, since economic success will most probably reflect a large number of confounding factors. Statistically significant results with respect to economic success and socialization for two of the other roles lead us to speculate in yet another direction. In granting the CoE some leeway to pursue technical goals, the MNC may allow the CoE to trade technical for short-term economic success. This is plausible for two reasons. First, researchers and scientists have a natural inclination to disregard the constraints of economic imperatives, and tend to regard creative freedom as a basic right in the pursuit of technical and scientific advances. Second, the MNC may willingly trade economic success recognizing synergistic benefits at the systems level or down the road. Significant and positive correlations between socialization and economic performance for local adaptors seem to lend support to this argument, since in units aiming to implement existing knowledge, strong ties or high degrees of socialization have positive performance effects. Extending this line of reasoning, we foresee an interesting research agenda: In this paper the theoretical argument developed focused on the creation and augmentation of corporate capabilities abroad. Yet, dissemination, or dispersion of the gain associated with them, seems to be just as important for CoEs (Frost et al. 2002, Paterson/Brock 2002). Unfortunately, this issue could not be addressed with our research design, since it would have required measuring performance as a function of transmitted knowledge. Yet, as argued, evidence from our local adaptors tells us that knowledge dissemination might be facilitated through high degrees of socialization. In this sense organizations might ultimately be faced with a paradox: On one hand, headquarters may be well advised to retain low socialization to enhance CoE capability to innovate, on the other hand sharing innovations and newfound know-how may increase pressures to establish high levels of socialization. Asakawa (2001), studying Japanese R&D investments abroad, noticed a breakdown of social control. His research showed that subsidiaries' roles evolved over time, and suggested that headquarters should adapt control accordingly (Asakawa 2001). This is an indication that the right dose of socialization may be a matter of timing as well as the nature of the tasks performed.

As a note of caution, our sample contains only Centers of Excellence of German national origin and the results may vary by MNC national origin. Secondly, our research design assumes a dyadic headquarter subsidiary relationship. While our own field research revealed that this assumption holds in R&D, this may not be the case in other areas. Finally, the design of the study does not allow interpretations concerning cause-effect relationships. Perhaps qualitative research could enrich the presented results.

Appendix

Measurement of Variables

Socialization

Based on Martinez/Jarillo (1991) and Harzing (1999) we measured socialization on a three-item Likert type scale (ranging from 1 "used rarely" to 5 "used very frequently") that asked respondents to indicate the extent to which the headquarters used (i) transfer of managers, (ii) transfer of R&D personnel, and (iii) the degree to which the local managers share the common values of the headquarter managers (ranging from 1 "no common values" to 5 "identical values"), to coordinate and control the respective subsidiary. Cronbach's alpha for our scale was 0.67.

Technological Mandate

Based on Kuemmerle (1997, 1999) the technological mandate was assessed as a constant sum scale. Managers were asked to indicate the percentage of personnel in the laboratory working on capability augmenting as compared to capability exploiting projects. Definitions of the constructs were provided in the questionnaire. The resulting variable was strongly bi-modal, and was subsequently split at the 50% mark for subsequent analysis.

Task-related Interdependence

Following Harzing (1999) and Conger (1992), task-related interdependence was operationalized on a six point scale, asking for the percentage of work that was received from other units versus the percentage of work that was passed forward to other units respectively. Our final measure was a composite index of these two aspects.

R&D Laboratory Success

Following Brockhoff (1990, 1998) and Schmaul (1995) performance was measured directly at the R&D function by asking respondents to indicate the degree to which the focal R&D unit achieved or failed to adhere to pre-specified technical, time and budget goals. Sample items included: "What is the average time overrun?" and "Indicate the average share of projects completed successfully?"

Market Scope

This construct was measured as a categorical variable. Respondents were asked to indicate whether the unit predominantly focused on local, regional, or global markets.

External Embeddedness

Based on von Boehmer (1995) we used a graphical scale to obtain information on a total of seven external, as well as four internal cooperation partners. For the exact wording see below:

The chart below shows the local R&D lab and a number of organizational units internal and external to the company.

Example:

- Please *identify its cooperation partners* by drawing a line.
- Indicate the intensity of the cooperation by assigning them a number from 1 (low) to 3 (high)

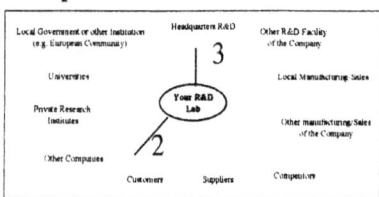

1 = low   2 = medium   3 = high

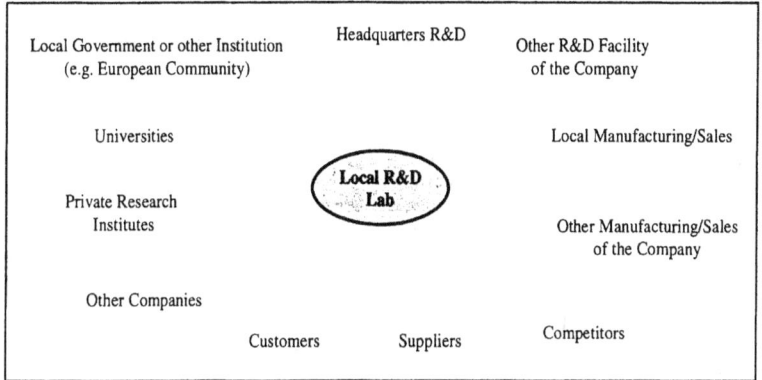

References

Andersson, U./Forsgren, M., Subsidiary Embeddedness and Control in the Multinational Corporation, *International Business Review*, 5, 1996, pp. 487–508.

Andersson, U./Forsgren, M., In Search of Centre on Excellence: Network Embeddedness and Subsidiary Roles in Multinational Corporations, *Management International Review*, 40, 2000, pp. 329–350.

Asakawa, K., *The Multinational Tension in R&D Internationalization: Strategic Linkage Mechanisms of Distant Contextual Knowledge in Japanese Multinational Companies*, unpublished dissertation, INSEAD, Fontainebleau 1996.

Asakawa, K., Evolving Headquarters-Subsidiary Dynamics in International R&D: The Case of Japanese Multinationals, *R&D Management*, 31, 2001, pp. 1–14.

Baliga, B. R./Jaeger, A. M., Multinational Corporations: Control Systems and Delegation Issues, *Journal of International Business Studies*, 15, 1984, pp. 25–40.

Bartlett, Ch. A./Ghoshal, S., Tab Your Subsidiaries for Global Reach, *Harvard Business Review*, 1986, pp. 87-94.
Bartlett, Ch. A./Ghoshal, S., *Managing Across Borders: The Transnational Solution*, Boston: Harvard Business School Press 1989.
Birkinshaw, J./Morrison, A. J., Configurations of Strategy and Structure in Subsidiaries of Multinational Corporations, *Journal of International Business Studies*, 26, 1995, pp. 729-754.
Boehmer, A. von, *Internationalisierung von Forschung und Entwicklung – Typen, Bestimmungsgründe und Erfolgsbeurteilungen*, Wiesbaden: Gabler 1995.
Brockhoff, K., *Stärken und Schwächen Industrieller Forschung und Entwicklung*, Stuttgart 1990.
Brockhoff, K., *Internationalization of Research and Development*, Berlin: Springer 1998.
Burt, R. S., *Structural Holes: The Social Structure of Competition*, Cambridge, MA: Harvard University Press 1992.
Cantwell, J./Janne, O., Technological Globalization and Innovative Centers: The Role of Corporate Technological Leadership and Locational Hierarchy, *Research Policy*, 28, 1999, pp. 119-120.
Chiesa, V., Managing the Internationalization of R&D Activities, *IEEE Transactions on Engineering Management*, 1996, pp. 7-23.
Conger, S., An Exploration of the Use of Information Technologies for Inter-Unit Coordination, in Gattinger, U., *Technology Mediated Communication*, 1992, pp. 63-117.
Daniels, J. D./Pitts, R. A./Tretter, M. J., Strategy and Structure of U.S. Multinationals: An Exploratory Study, *Academy of Management Journal*, 27, 1984, pp. 292-307.
D'Cruz, J., Strategic Management of Subsidiaries in Etemand, H./Dulude, L.S. (eds.), *Managing the Multinational Subsidiary: Response to Environmental Changes and to Host Nation R&D Policies*, London: Croom Helm 1986.
Egelhoff, W. G., Strategy and Structure in MNC: An Information Processing Approach, *Administrative Science Quarterly*, 37, 1982, pp. 435-458.
Egelhoff, W. G., Organizational Equilibrium and Organizational Change: Two Different Perspectives of the Multinational Enterprise, *Journal of International Management*, 1999, pp. 15-33.
Evans, P./Lank, E./Farquhar, A., Managing Human Resources in the International Firm – Lessons From Practice, in Evans, P./Doz, Y./Laurent, A. (eds.), *Human Resource Management in International Firms – Change, Globalization, Innovation*, London, 1989, pp. 113-143.
Forsgren, M./Pedersen, T., Centres of Excellence in Multinational Companies: The Case of Denmark, Working Paper, Institute of International Economics and Management, Copenhagen Business School 1997.
Forsgren, M./Pedersen, T., Centres of Excellence in Multinational Companies: The Case of Denmark, in: Birkinshaw, J./Hood, N. (eds.), *Multinational Corporate Evolution and Subsidiary Development*, London: Macmillan 1998.
Franko, L. G., *The European Multinationals*, London: Harper and Row 1973.
Frost, T. C./Birkinshaw, J. M./Ensign, P. C., Centers of Excellence in Multinational Corporations, *Strategic Management Journal*, 23, 2002, pp. 997-1018.
Ghoshal, S./Bartlett, Ch. A., The Multinational Corporation as an Interorganizational Network, *Academy of Management Review*, 15, 1990, pp. 603-625.
Ghoshal, S./Nohria, N., Internal Differentiation within MNCs, *Strategic Management Journal*, 1989, pp. 323-337.
Granovetter, M. S., The Strength of Weak Ties, *American Journal of Sociology*, 6, 1973, pp. 1360-1380.
Gupta, A. K./Govindarajan, V., Knowledge Flows and the Structure of Control Within MNCs, *Academy of Management Review*, 1991, pp. 768-792.
Gupta, A. K./Govindarajan, V., Organizing for Knowledge Flows Within MNCs, *International Business Review*, 3, 1994, pp. 443-457.
Hansen, M. T., The Search-Transfer Problem: The Role of Weak Ties in Sharing Knowledge across Organization Subunits, *Administrative Science Quarterly*, 44, 1999, pp. 82-111.
Harzing, A.-W. K., *Managing the Multinationals*, Northhampton: Elgar Publishing 1999.
Hauschildt, J., Towards Measuring the Success of Innovation, *Proceedings of Portland International Conference on Management of Engineering and Technology*, Portland, Oregon, USA, 1991, pp. 605-608.

Hedlund, G./Ridderstråle, J., Toward a Theory of the Self-Renewing MNC, in Toyne, B./Nigh, D., *International Business*: An Emerging Vision Columbia, SC: University of South Carolina Press, 1997, pp. 329-354.
Hood, N./Young, S., US Multinational R&D, *Multinational Business*, 2, 1982, pp. 10-23.
Kuemmerle, W., Building Effective R&D Capabilities Abroad, *Harvard Business Review*, March-April, 1997, pp. 61-69.
Kuemmerle, W., The Drivers of Foreign Direct Investment into Research and Development: An Empirical Investigation, *Journal of International Business Studies*, 30, 1999, pp. 1-24.
Kuemmerle, W./Rosenbloom, R., Functional Versus Capability-oriented Innovation Management in Multinational Firms, Working Paper, Harvard Business School 1999.
Macharzina, K., Rahmenbedingungen und Gestaltungsmöglichkeiten bei Umsetzung von globalen Strategieansätzen, *Deutsche Gesellschaft für BWL e.V.*, 1992, pp. 29-55.
Macharzina, K., Steuerung von Auslandsgesellschaften bei Internationalisierungsstrategien, in Haller, M. et al. (ed.), *Globalisierung der Wirtschaft*, 1993, pp. 79-109.
Martinez, J. I./Jarillo, J. C., Coordination Demands of International Strategies, *Journal of International Business Studies*, 22, 1991, pp. 429-444.
Moore, K./Birkinshaw, J. M., Managing Knowledge in Global Service Firms: Centers of Excellence, *Academy of Management Executive*, 12, 1998, pp. 81-92.
Nelson, R. R., The Strength of Strong Ties: Social Networks and Intergroup Conflict in Organizations, *Academy of Management Journal*, 32, 1989, pp. 377-401.
Nohria, N./Ghoshal, S., Differentiated Fit and Shared Values: Alternatives for Managing Headquarters-Subsidiary Relations, *Strategic Management Journal*, 1994, pp. 491-502.
Paterson, S. L./Brock, D. M., The Development of Subsidiary-Management Research: A Review and Theoretical Analysis, *International Business Review*, 11, 2002, pp. 139-163.
Pearce, R. D., *The Internationalization of Research and Development by Multinational Enterprises*, New York: St. Martin's Press 1989.
Podolny, J. M./Baron, J. N., Relationships and Resources: Social Networks and Mobility in the Workplace, *American Sociological Review*, 62, 1997, pp. 673-693.
Porter, M. E., *The Competitive Advantage of Nations*, London: Macmillan 1990.
Pugh, D. Y./Hickson, D. J./Hinings, C. R./Turner, C., Dimensions of Organization Structure, *Administrative Science Quarterly*, 13, 1968, pp. 65-105.
Roth, K./Schweiger, D./Morrison, A., Global Strategy Implementation at the Business Unit Level: Operational Capabilities and Administrative Mechanisms, *Journal of International Business Studies*, 22, 1991, pp. 369-402.
Schmaul, B., *Organisation und Erfolg internationaler Forschungs- und Entwicklungseinheiten*, Wiesbaden: Gabler 1995.
Schmid, S., *Centers of Competence in MNCs: Do Japanese MNCs Differ from German MNCs?*, Working Paper, Universität Eichstätt, Ingolstadt 1999.
Schmid, S./Bäurle, I./Kutschker, M., *Tochtergesellschaften in int. tätigen Unernehmen – Ein "State-of-the-Art" unterschiedlicher Rollentypologien*, Working Paper, Universität Eichstätt, Ingolstadt 1998.
Stopford, J. M./Wells, L. T., *Managing the Multinational Enterprise*: Organization of the Firm and Ownership of the Subsidiaries, New York: Basic Books 1972.
Taggert, J. H., An Evaluation of the Integration-Responsiveness Framework: MNC Manufacturing Subsidiaries in the UK, *Management International Review*, 37, 1997, pp. 295-318.
Van Maanen, J./Schein, E. H., Towards a Theory of Organizational Socialization, in: Staw, B. M. (ed.), *Research in Organizational Behavior*, 1, 1979, pp. 209-264, Greenwich, CT: JAI Press.
Venkatraman, N./Ramanujam, V., Measurement of Business Performance in Strategy Research: A Comparison of Approaches, *Academy of Management Review*, 1986, pp. 801-814.
Weick, K. E., Educational Organizations as Loosely Coupled Systems, *Administrative Science Quarterly*, 21, 1976, pp. 1-19.
Welch, L./Welch, D., Being Flexible and Accommodating Diversity: The Challenge for Multinational Management, *European Management Journal*, 15, 1997, pp. 677-685.
White, R. E./Poynter, T. A., Strategies for Foreign-Owned Subsidiaries in Canada, *Business Quarterly*, Summer, 1984, pp. 59-69.
Wolf, J., *Internationales Personalmanagement, Kontext, Koordination, Erfolg*, Wiesbaden: Gabler 1994.

mir *Edition*

Heiko Hamann

Informationsversorgung in Transnationalen Unternehmungen

Konzeptionelle Grundlagen – Anforderungen – Technologien

2003, XXXIV, 404 pages, pb., € 64,00 (approx. US $ 64,–)
ISBN 3-409-12464-0

Corporations that operate globally have special requirements with respect to their information supply. The author has constructed a model from which he derives suitable criteria for those requirements. The theoretical study is supplemented by an empirical case study conducted at Siemens AG. Current information technologies are described and analysed.

This book is addressed to researchers and students of Strategic Management, especially of International Management, Controlling and Economical Informatics. It ist equally interesting for management consultants and managers in international corporations and IT-departments.

Betriebswirtschaftlicher Verlag Dr. Th. Gabler GmbH, Abraham-Lincoln-Str. 46, 65189 Wiesbaden

Management
International Review
© Gabler Verlag 2004

Steven S. Lui/Chung-Ming Lau/Hang-Yue Ngo

Global Convergence, Human Resources Best Practices, and Firm Performance: A Paradox

Abstract

- In view of rapid globalization and the subsequent heightened competitive pressure, it is imperative to investigate whether, as the convergence thesis has suggested, globalization is leading towards a universal adoption of Human Resource best practices (HRBP).

- Based on Barney's (1991) argument that a firm's competence needs to be unique, rare, and hard to imitate, if firms are increasingly adopting the same set of HRBP, these practices can no longer provide the competitive advantage for them.

- In this paper, we integrate the globalization argument with institutional theory and resourced-based view to formulate several hypotheses to test the extent of convergence in HRBP and the subsequent effect on firm performance on a sample of 248 firms operating in Hong Kong.

Key Results

- While our results find some support for firms' convergence in adopting HRBP, a full-scale convergence effect due to globalization is not found. The practices also have minimal effect on firm performance.

Authors

Steven S. Lui, Visiting Assistant Professor, Department of Management, City University of Hong Kong.
Chung-Ming Lau, Professor, Department of Management, The Chinese University of Hong Kong.
Hang-Yue Ngo, Professor, Department of Management, The Chinese University of Hong Kong.

Introduction

Globalization is having a tremendous influence on various aspects of business. It is accelerating the flow of resources and information, and hence values, practices, and technology can be easily diffused. In particular, new management ideas and practices are disseminated among firms at a very fast pace. This is even more the case when multinational corporations (MNCs) play a relatively more important role in many economies. A growing body of literature has examined the impact of globalization on the management system and practices of firms (Eden/Lenway 2001, Guillen 2001, Warner 2002). Recent studies have found that MNCs have a significant impact on human resource management practices (De Cieri/Dowling 1997). However, less is known about the effectiveness of global human resources policies and practices. This is not a desirable situation as human resources policies and practices are the keys to workforce productivity and the competitive advantage of firms (Pfeffer 1994). This is particularly the case for firms under great pressure to make rapid and constant changes in the global competitive environment. Such a knowledge gap, therefore, needs to be filled.

In view of rapid globalization and the subsequent heightened competitive pressure, a key research question for the field is: Will globalization lead to the universal adoption of HR best practices? And if so, what are the implications for firm performance? This question is especially relevant to Asian countries because of the increasing globalization of firms in this area which means they are now competing globally with firms all over the world. The answer to this question has important implications for HRM. According to the convergence view of globalization, organizations are structured similarly in form and perhaps have similar outcomes (Guillen 2001). Based on Barney's (1991) argument that a firm's competence needs to be unique, rare, and costly to imitate, if firms are increasingly adopting the same set of HR best practices, these practices can no longer provide competitive advantages to them. This presents a paradox for globalization research. On the one hand, globalization leads to more similarity, and on the other, these similarities do not allow firms to compete more effectively. In addition, although globalization is theoretically closely related to legitimization and institutionalization (Meyer et al. 1997), there is a lack of empirical support for the notion of global culture (Guillen 2001).

In this paper, we first introduce the convergence argument of globalization. By integrating this argument with institutional theory and the resource-based view, we develop our hypotheses regarding the possible convergence of HR best practices. We then empirically examine the extent of convergence of these HR best practices and their effects on firm performance. Different from other studies which have focused on whether firms operating across different countries are adopting a universal set of HR practices, we chose to study the HR practices of firms operating in one single area, thus controlling for specific institutional and cultural factors that may mitigate the effect of globalization (Lau/Ngo 2001). Hong Kong was chosen as the research setting because it is relatively open to globalization, contains many foreign firms, and has a global reach.

Theoretical Framework

Globalization highlights the integration of today's economies in terms of a number of aspects. Globalization is often understood as a progressive integration of financial, product, and labor markets across national boundaries (Jones 2002). Guillen (2001) defines globalization as "a process leading to greater interdependence and mutual awareness (reflexivity) among economic, political, and social units in the world, among actors in general" (p. 236). Since globalization has created a borderless world (Ohmae 1990), one of its effects is convergence. The convergence argument was first discussed in Kerr et al. (1973). The contention is that as industrialization and technology become more widespread, common problems occur and similar reactions are adopted to deal with these problems. This leads to a convergence in ways of living around the world.

Most supporters of the convergence argument have provided comprehensive data to show the convergence of various aspects of people's life styles under the condition of globalization. Ritzer (1993) documents how different societies have assimilated the fast food culture exemplified by McDonald's. Some economists and sociologists have argued that modernization has caused societies to converge (Guillen 2001). Based on the rationale behind the convergence standpoint, some HR researchers have declared that there are a set of universal human resource best practices (HRBP) which, if used by firms, would lead to better firm performance (Huselid 1995, Pfeffer 1994). Delery and Doty (1996) argue that best practices are always better than other practices and should be applied everywhere, regardless of industry or geography.

However, it is well recognized in strategic management and marketing literature that there is a tension between global integration and local responsiveness (Ghoshal 1987, Yip 1995). Much discussion has been focused on the convergence and divergence debate (McGaughey/De Cieri 1999, Rowley/Benson 2002). Supporters of the divergence argument claim that economic entities remain distinguishable because of government intervention and cultural heritage. Ngo et al. (1998) find significant differences in the HRM practices of MNCs from different countries operating in Hong Kong. In a similar vein, Bae and Rowley (2001) examine the cultural limitations of bringing high performance work systems to

Korea. Shaw et al. (1993), on the other hand, attribute the differences in the HR practices of Hong Kong and Singaporean firms to the different government policies of the two Asian cities.

Warner (2002), in his study of Asia-Pacific economies, contends that it is too simplistic to treat the whole region as a homogeneous terrain, and suggests a soft convergence scenario in which the common features across the regions are only *prima facie*. Hence, it is suggested that there is some degree of convergence at the macro level even while organizations have specific practices that are locally adapted. McGaughey and De Cieri (1999) further theorize the complexity of convergence and divergence of international human resource management. They suggest that there are four modes of convergence-divergence dynamics, and hence similarities and dissimilarities may arise depending on different variables and processes, and evolutionary changes in the organization and environment.

Von Glinow, Drost, and Teagarden (2002) report the results of a search by a research consortium for whether there is a convergence of international human resource management practices. They find both epic and emic practices. Though there is a converging trend in some HR practices across cultures, industries, and organizations, there is also a concern with the polycontextuality of international HR practices.

Following the best practices argument, we would expect to see all firms converging towards a similar set of HRBPs (Bae/Rowley 2001, Delery/Doty 1996, Rowley/Bae 2002). Paradoxically, convergence could reduce the competitiveness of firms as their HR systems will no longer be distinctive from those of other firms. Marchington and Grugulis (2000) also question the meaning of specific best practices as well as their consistency with each other. If a firm has to compete strategically in a global market, it should possess differentiated HR practices in order to sustain its own competitive advantage. This paradox has prompted us to examine the validity of a universal set of best practices. The next section gives details of how we formulate the hypotheses to test this assertion.

Hypotheses Development

Globalization requires organizations to move people, ideas, products, and information around the world. It leads to "universalism" and places substantial pressure on firms to standardize practices and policies (Rowley/Benson 2002). While it is reasonable to expect globalization to affect HRBPs, the argument "globalization, then convergence" is too general to guide this study. The following hypotheses are developed by integrating the general thrust of globalization with institutional theory and the resource-based view.

Institutional theory explains the convergence of firm practices with the concept of legitimacy (DiMaggio/Powell 1983, Scott 1995). Meyer et al. (1997) contend that many world models are organized similarly in terms of their structures. They conclude that nation-states are "more isomorphic than most theorists would predict and change more uniformly than is commonly recognized" (p. 173). It has been argued that when firms of different country origins operate in a local environment, they face similar legal, social, and economic factors. In response to institutional pressure, they adopt similar management practices in order to gain legitimacy and acceptance (Lau/Ngo 2001, Rowley/Benson 2002). This is known as local isomorphism. Rosenzweig and Nohria (1994) studied the effect of local isomorphism on different HRM practices. They conclude that firms have to adopt similar practices in the face of similar political and economic environments.

Globalization creates yet another institutional environment that firms have to respond to. This is the environment composed of their key competitors in the international market (Ferner/Quintanilla 1998). This environment is immediately related to HRBP adoption. For example, Japanese business is being restructured for low growth and globalization. Japanese firms have already changed their traditional HR practices (such as life-time employment and a seniority promotion system) to conform to modern employment practices (Harukiyo/Hook 1998). As HRBPs are well accepted by researchers and practitioners as the best way of organizing human resources, managers are more likely to follow the norms and practices of major competitors in the international market who have been adopting HRBPs in order to gain legitimacy. In addition, the flow of managers is facilitated by MNCs and internationalized operations. These managers bring similar practices to different operations (De Cieri/Dowling 1997). Institutional theory, therefore, predicts a convergence towards HRBP adoption, not because these practices are more effective, but because of the mimetic intention to gain legitimacy in the institutional environment (Gooderham et al. 1999, Shaw et al. 1993). Thus, when firms are oriented towards mimicking other firms' HR practices, they would tend to adopt more best practices in order to gain legitimacy. A mimetic orientation would mean firms have the mindset of following industry norms as well as those of their major competitors. Based on the above argument, we put forward the following hypothesis:

Hypothesis 1. A higher level of mimetic orientation in HRM will lead to a higher level of adoption of HRBPs.

On the other hand, the resource-based view considers the adoption of HRBPs as a means of building up the resources of a firm (Wright/McMahan 1992). As firms need to compete globally, they realize that they have to follow HRBPs in order to successfully implement their strategic plans. They then adopt more HR practices, such as performance-based compensation and employee development, which are in line with their increasingly strategic orientation. The strategic orientation of HRM thus represents a managerial mindset of aligning a firm's HR practices and its strategy (Gomez-Mejia et al. 1995, Huang 2000). Fey and Bjorkman (2001) argue that even Russian firms actively align their HRM practices with their firm strategy in order to improve their performance.

Wright et al. (1998) empirically examine the impact of strategy and the involvement of HR executives in strategic decision-making on HR effectiveness, and find a strong relationship exists. Similarly, Harris and Ogbonna (2001) find strong relationships between strategic human resource management, market orientation, and organizational performance. Harvey, Buckley, and Novicevic (2000) even go as far as suggesting that the ability to develop strategic global HRM is critical for doing business in emerging markets. It follows from extant theory and empirical studies that firms with a stronger strategic orientation in HRM would be more likely to employ HR practices that would lead to a higher level of firm performance. Hence, these firms would adopt HR best practices. We therefore put forward the following hypothesis:

Hypothesis 2. A higher level of strategic orientation in HRM will lead to a higher level of adoption of HRBPs.

The globalization argument further suggests that the adoption of HRBPs would increase in an environment of increasing globalization. Zivnuska, Ketchen, and Snow (2001) argue that in the present converging economy with a strong trend towards globalization, firms face a new set of similar HR challenges such as eliciting employee creativity, managing diversity, conducting international business, and competing for the best employees. As firms' operations become more international, managers become more aware of a universal standard that is being applied everywhere as the best standard (Bae/Rowley 2001). In addition, due to global competition, they have to behave and perform in a similar fashion to their counterparts. As noted earlier, it has been suggested that the Japanese employment system has changed as a result of globalization (Harukiyo/Hook 1998). Similarly, Rowley and Bae (2002) have reported some convergence of HRBPs in Korea, also as a result of globalization.

As firms need to deal with the high level of uncertainty and intense competition of the global market, transferring HRBPs from country to country is becoming increasingly common. This trend has been facilitated by advancements in information and communication technologies, the proliferation of MNCs, and the frequent flow of people and ideas across borders. According to the institutional argument, firms need to converge in order to gain legitimacy in both the industry and the country in which they operate (Meyer et al. 1997, Scott 1995). Under the influence of mimetic forces, firms will behave similarly if they are more globalized. Hence, when they intend to be, and are, more globalized, they have to organize themselves and instigate practices that are in accordance with international standards. Studies have already suggested that multinational firms follow similar practices because of strategic reasons as well as lower transaction costs (Rondinelli/Rosen/Drori 2001), especially when there is a greater reliance on the parent's resources and tighter organizational interdependence (Hannon/Huang/Jaw 1995). Child and Tse (2001) note that a transitional economy like China is also moving towards international best practices because of global institutional forces. Accordingly, we expect that under increasing globalization, firms with a higher level of mimetic orientation and a higher level of strategic orientation in HRM would adopt more HRBPs than those with a lower level of globalization. Hence, we put forward two other hypotheses about the possible interaction effects between level of globalization and HR orientations:

Hypothesis 3a. The effect of strategic orientation in HRM on HRBPs will be stronger in firms with a higher level of globalization.

Hypothesis 3b. The effect of mimetic orientation in HRM on HRBPs will be stronger in firms with a higher level of globalization.

The above hypotheses are exclusively related to the adoption of HRBPs. Firms that adopt these best practices have the intention of enhancing their competitive advantages and performing better than their competitors (Delery/Doty 1996, Dyer/Reeves 1995, Pfeffer 1994). However, adopting best practices with an expectation of reaching a high level of performance is one thing, but performing well after adopting these orientations and best practices is another matter altogether. According to the resource-based view of a firm, competitive advantages only come from unique and valuable resources (Barney 1991). When all firms behave similarly, no competitive advantages will exist. HRBPs could be regarded as valuable resources; however, they are not unique to a specific firm. When resources are valuable but not rare or inimitable, a firm can only achieve competitive parity at best, but not competitive advantage (Barney 1991). Hence, regardless of what kind of orientation a firm adopts, HRBPs would not lead to superior firm performance.

We hypothesize that the extent of the adoption of HRBPs does not lead to higher firm performance. In contrast to the findings of strategic human resource management studies (e.g., Harris/Ogbonna 2001), we would not expect a firm with mimetic HR orientation and strategic HR orientation to be able to perform well if they follow HRBPs. Therefore, the effects of the interactions between HRBPs and orientations on firm performance would be minimal. Similarly, when a firm is more globalized, the extent of its adoption of HRBPs would be higher, as predicted earlier, and hence the effect on firm performance would be minimal.

Hypothesis 4a. The adoption of HRBPs will not be associated with firm performance.

Hypothesis 4b. The effect of HRBPs on firm performance will be insignificant in firms that adopt both strategic orientation in HRM and mimetic orientation in HRM.

Hypothesis 4c. The effect of HRBPs on firm performance will be insignificant in firms with a higher level of globalization.

Method

Sample

The data was collected from a questionnaire survey of 2,000 Hong Kong firms of different sizes and belonging to different industries that were in a database of a local media agency specializing in recruitment. These firms are actively operating in Hong Kong and hence are a more representative sample than those found in the trade directory or chamber of commerce memberships. The respondents were human resource managers who are the appropriate people in their company to provide HR information.

The questionnaire, together with an invitation letter, was sent to the respondents by e-mail and by post in 2001. Incentives were offered to the respondents to complete and return the questionnaire. Follow-up calls were also made. Two hundred and forty-eight responses were received, representing a response rate of 12.4%. The sample contained a good variation of firms of different country ownership and from different industries. A comparison of the respondents' profiles indicated that they were quite representative, according to other studies, of firms operating in Hong Kong (Lau/Ngo 2001, Ngo et al. 1998).

For the firms that responded, the average number of employees was 154. With regard to country of ownership, 57.2% ($n = 139$) of them were local Chinese firms; American firms were the second largest group (13.2%, $n = 32$), followed by joint ventures (6.2%), Japanese firms (4.5%), British firms (4.1%), and foreign firms from various parts of the world. The firms were engaged in different businesses. Twenty-nine percent of them ($n = 72$) were in the IT and telecommunications industry, 20.2% were in manufacturing, 19.8% were in trading and marketing, and 9.3% were in banking, insurance, and finance.

Measures

HR Best Practices

Based on an extensive literature search of HR best practices (e.g., Arthur 1994, Huselid 1995, Huselid et al. 1997, Koch/McGrath 1996, Lee/Miller 1999, Mac-Duffie 1995, Ngo et al. 1998), a 25-item instrument of HRBPs was developed. The respondents were asked to describe the extent to which their firms had adopted the practices on a 5-point Likert scale, ranging from "not at all" to "very extensive". Similar perceptual scales have been commonly used in studies of HRM practices (e.g., Delery/Doty 1996, Fey/Bjorkman 2001). A factor analysis with varimax rotation was conducted to identify the underlying dimensions of these items. The analysis yielded five acceptable factors with an eigenvalue above 1, explaining 56.3% of the original variance. We assigned items to scales only when the item had a factor loading of 0.4 or higher on a single factor. Six items were excluded based on the result of the factor analysis. The five dimensions and their respective items are shown in Table 1.

Table 1. Factor Structure of HRM Best Practices

	Factor 1	Factor 2	Factor 3	Factor 4	Factor 5
Factor 1 Employee development (α = 0.85)					
Training and orientation for new hires	**0.47**	0.33	0.14	0.32	0.27
Management training for executives	**0.73**	0.27	0.15	0.04	0.19
Training needs analysis	**0.78**	0.26	0.13	0.02	0.17
Cost-benefits analysis to assess training effectiveness	**0.76**	0.16	0.05	−0.07	0.21
Employee involvement programs; e.g., quality circle, JCC	**0.67**	0.31	0.01	0.18	0.05
Regular staff attitude surveys	**0.52**	0.04	−0.01	0.22	0.26
Factor 2 Career development (α = 0.85)					
Promotion from within the organization	0.20	**0.70**	0.26	0.22	−0.03
Well-defined career ladders	0.31	**0.65**	0.09	0.14	0.16
Merit-based promotion	0.15	**0.68**	0.38	0.25	0.09
Adoption of formal grievance procedure	0.23	**0.61**	0.22	0.16	0.28
Adoption of formal disciplinary procedure	0.24	**0.62**	0.11	0.20	0.38
Factor 3 Performance-based compensation (α = 0.76)					
Compensation tied to performance appraisals	0.33	0.18	**0.67**	0.32	0.00
Bonus and profit sharing	0.00	0.15	**0.73**	−0.05	0.32
Pay for performance compensation	−0.00	0.21	**0.78**	0.15	0.13
Factor 4 Selective hiring (α = 0.67)					
Gathering a large pool of applicants before hiring	−0.16	0.18	0.06	**0.67**	0.09
Employment testing prior to hiring	0.18	0.15	0.04	**0.77**	−0.04
Structured and standardized interviews for hiring	0.17	0.09	0.15	**0.72**	0.25
Factor 5 Strategic HR planning (α = 0.72)					
Manpower planning	0.28	0.16	0.27	0.11	**0.68**
Formal job analysis	0.23	0.15	0.12	0.12	**0.78**

The grouping of these five factors is very similar to that of the best practices reported in the literature. The first factor, which included items that measure a firm's development practices and employee feedback mechanism, was labeled *employee development* (six items, alpha = 0.85). The second factor, labeled *career development* (five items, alpha = 0.85), included items that measure systematic promotion and grievance procedures. The third factor was labeled *performance-based compensation* (three items, alpha = 0.76) and included items that measure how performance is linked to compensation. The fourth factor, *selective hiring* (three items, alpha = 0.67), included items relating to structured hiring practices such as employment testing and standardized interviews. The last factor, *strategic HR planning*, included two items (alpha = 0.72) that measure the extent of manpower planning and the formal job analysis of a firm. These five factors formed the dependent variables of our regression models of HRBPs.

Globalization

As there is no one single measure that can reflect the extent of globalization, we used three proxies to measure the extent of globalization of a firm. First, we used the ownership (capital origin) of a firm as a proxy. It is customarily believed that firms with a foreign origin, especially from western countries, will adopt more international practices. Local Chinese firms, on the other hand, are more conservative when it comes to employing new management practices. Moreover, non-local firms in Hong Kong are subsidiaries of foreign firms, and so tend to adopt practices in accordance with international standards. A dummy variable (i.e., country origin) was thus created, with 0 for a local firm and 1 for a non-local firm. Second, we grouped firms according to whether they belonged to the IT industry or a non-IT industry. We expected IT-based firms to have a higher level of globalization since the IT industry tends to operate within a global setting with international sourcing and operations. As there is no national boundary, firms in this industry have to meet certain international standards. A dummy variable of industry (IT industry = 1) was created.

Finally, we measured the intention of firms to become a world-class organization by adopting the most current management techniques. We created an index to measure the intention of a firm to implement five types of global management practices (i.e., forming new teams, business process re-engineering, total quality management, outsourcing and subcontracting, and exploring new markets). These practices have been identified as global practices in a number of areas, including technology, quality management, and strategic management (Anakwe/Igbaria/Anandarajan 2000, Christmann/Taylor 2001, Rondinelli/Rosen/Drori 2001). We expected that globalization would pressure a firm to adopt these practices, thus a firm's intention to follow such techniques reflects its level of globalization. A firm would score 0 if it did not intend to adopt any of these practices, and 5 if it intended to adopt them all.

Mimetic HR Orientation (mHR)

We developed a 2-item scale to measure mimetic HR orientation. The respondents were asked, using a 5-point scale, to indicate to what extent their firms adopted HR practices that were similar to those of major competitors in the same industry, and followed industry norms. The reliability of this scale was 0.72 in this study.

Strategic HR Orientation (sHR)

We used a 3-item scale to measure strategic HR orientation adapted from Huang (2000). The respondents were asked to indicate on a 5-point scale to what extent the HR function was involved in the major strategic decisions, how closely it was linked to business strategy, and whether it was influenced by long-term rather than short-term considerations. The reliability of this scale was 0.73 in this study.

Firm Performance

This was measured by a 3-item scale measuring the respondents' own assessments of their firm's performance relative to the industry. It included indicators such as sales and turnover, net profit, and new product development. The alpha was 0.76 for the scale. Perceptual measures of performance have been used in many studies, particularly human resource studies, and are found to be reliable (Delaney/Huselid 1996, Lau/Ngo 2001).

Firm size

This was controlled in our analysis as firm size has been found to be related to the adoption of HR practices (Fields/Chan/Akhtar 2000, Gooderham/Nordhaug/Ringdal 1999). We used the natural log of employee size to measure firm size.

Results

Table 2 presents the means, standard deviations, and correlations among the variables included in the analysis. Initial examination of the correlations revealed some interesting relationships. The correlations among the five types of HRBPs were quite high (rs ranged from 0.30 to 0.65), implying that the firms tended to

Table 2. Means, Standard Deviations, and Correlations Among Study Variables

	Mean	S.D.	1	2	3	4	5	6	7	8	9	10	11
1 Firm size (ln employee no.)	3.75	1.54											
2 Ownership (non-local = 1)	0.45	0.50	0.08										
3 Industry (IT = 1)	0.31	0.46	−0.21***	−0.07									
4 Global practice	1.45	1.34	0.14	0.03	0.06								
5 mHR	3.03	0.87	0.19**	0.07	−0.13*	0.19**							
6 sHR	2.92	0.86	0.12	0.04	−0.12	0.23***	0.39***						
7 Employee development	3.14	1.07	0.28***	0.13*	−0.13*	0.27***	0.40***	0.44***					
8 Career development	3.55	1.01	0.39***	0.07	−0.12	0.17**	0.45***	0.39***	0.65***				
9 Performance-based compensation	3.81	1.16	0.18**	0.07	−0.13*	0.26***	0.26***	0.33***	0.40***	0.53***			
10 Selective hiring	3.95	1.01	0.33***	0.00	−0.22***	0.07	0.34***	0.28***	0.36***	0.47***	0.35***		
11 Strategic HR planning	3.65	1.14	0.14*	0.04	−0.05	0.23***	0.32***	0.44***	0.56***	0.50***	0.43***	0.30***	
12 Firm performance	3.27	0.61	0.17**	0.11	−0.16*	0.16*	0.12	0.14*	0.16*	0.19**	0.10	0.12	0.16*

Note: N = 220
* $p < 0.05$
** $p < 0.01$
*** $p < 0.001$

Table 3. ANOVA Results for the Five HRBPs Across Country Origin and Industry

	Ownership (Country origin)				Industry				
	Local	Asia	Non-Asia	F ratio	Manufacturing & construction	Trading & marketing	Banking	IT	F ratio
Employee development	3.00 (1.08)	3.42 (1.03)	3.30 (1.06)	2.74	3.22 (1.04)	3.04 (1.02)	3.35 (1.17)	2.91 (1.04)	1.99
Career development	3.51 (1.04)	3.76 (0.89)	3.69 (1.01)	1.21	3.68[a] (0.89)	3.46[b] (0.87)	3.86[b c] (1.09)	3.32[a c] (1.08)	3.52**
Performance-based compensation	3.76 (1.18)	4.14 (1.10)	3.88 (1.18)	2.61	3.97[a] (1.06)	3.55[b] (1.32)	4.22[b c] (1.00)	3.52[a c] (1.25)	4.81**
Selective hiring	3.97 (0.99)	4.08 (0.99)	3.99 (1.09)	0.59	4.17[a] (0.93)	4.00[b] (1.12)	4.16[c] (0.96)	3.31[a b c] (0.96)	4.69**
Strategic HR planning	3.64 (1.09)	3.81 (1.21)	3.72 (1.20)	0.66	3.64 (1.16)	3.53 (1.15)	4.00 (1.06)	3.52 (1.18)	2.13

Note: Numbers in table are mean values with standard deviations in parentheses.
Means with the same superscript letter are significantly different at 0.05 by the LSD test.
$n = 222-242$; ** $p < 0.01$

adopt these practices simultaneously. The three globalization indices were related to HRBPs in different ways. Intention to adopt global management practices was positively related to all HRBPs except selective hiring ($r = 0.07$, $p > 0.10$). A non-local ownership was significantly and positively related to employee development only ($r = 0.13$, $p < 0.05$), whereas being in the IT industry was significantly and negatively related to employee development, selective hiring, and performance-based compensation (rs ranged from -0.13 to -0.22).

In order to have a better understanding of the extent of HRBP adoption by firms from different countries and different industries, several ANOVA analyses were performed to examine the possible differences. Table 3 reports the results of the ANOVA analyses. No significant differences in HRBP adoption were found among firms of different origins. This confirms the convergence proposition. When HRBP adoption was examined across industries, three of the five practices showed significant differences. In most cases, the IT industry was found to be significantly different from other industries. However, the extent of the adoption of HRBPs was lower in the IT industry.

We ran five separate sets of moderated regression analyses to test *Hypothesis 1* to *Hypothesis 3*. For the first step, firm size was entered into the regression. For the second step, mHR, sHR, and the globalization indices were entered into the model. For the final step, the interaction terms between globalization indices, mHR, and sHR were entered. A significant increase in the R^2 of the regression model would indicate a significant moderating effect of globalization. The regression results are shown in Table 4.

The effects of both mHR and sHR on the five types of HRBPs were found to be significant (except for the effect of mHR on performance-based compensation), as revealed in Models 2, 5, 8, 11, and 14. These two variables contributed to the substantial increase in the R^2 of the models. Thus, *Hypothesis 1* and *Hypothesis 2* gained empirical support. On the other hand, the globalization measures had different impacts on the five dependent variables. Industry and ownership were insignificant for all five types of HRBPs. A firm's intention to adopt global practices did, however, have a significant effect on employee development and performance-based compensation, but not on the other three types. It is worth noting that the interaction terms entered for the final step were insignificant, failing to add any significant explanatory power to the models, as shown in Models 3, 6, 9, 12, and 15. The only significant term was mHR with ownership on selective hiring. In other words, *Hypothesis 3a* and *Hypothesis 3b* were not supported.

The performance implications of HRBPs were examined in several regression analyses. Table 5 reports the results. Model 1 indicated that the control variable, the three globalization measures, and strategic and mimetic orientations had no significant impact on firm performance, though the equation was significant and some coefficients were marginally significant at the 0.1 level. When the

Table 4. Regression Results for the Five HRBPs

	Employee development			Career development			Performance-based compensation			Selective hiring			Strategic HR planning		
	Model 1	Model 2	Model 3	Model 4	Model 5	Model 6	Model 7	Model 8	Model 9	Model 10	Model 11	Model 12	Model 13	Model 14	Model 15
Firm size	0.25***	0.15**	0.15**	0.35***	0.27***	0.26***	0.17**	0.08	0.08	0.33***	0.26***	0.26***	0.15**	0.08	0.08
Direct effects															
Industry (IT = 1)		-0.03	-0.17		-0.04	-0.04		-0.12	-0.08		-0.13	0.05		-0.02	-0.22
Ownership (non-local = 1)		0.09	0.18		0.01	0.03		0.04	-0.26		-0.04	-0.49		0.02	-0.11
Global practice		0.12*	-0.09		0.01	0.14		0.15**	0.51		-0.03	0.52		0.11	0.10
mHR		0.20***	0.05		0.30***	0.28**		0.11	0.08		0.22***	0.23*		0.15**	0.12
sHR		0.31***	0.39		0.26***	0.32**		0.21**	0.29*		0.15**	0.24*		0.33***	0.27
Interactions															
mHR* Industry			0.05			-0.08			0.16			-0.17			0.05
sHR* Industry			0.09			0.08			-0.19			-0.00			0.17
mHR* Ownership			0.22			0.18			0.35			0.48			0.13
sHR* Ownership			-0.31			-0.21			-0.03			-0.01			0.02
mHR* Global practice			0.40			0.01			-0.22			-0.26			-0.02
sHR* Global practice			-0.16			-0.14			-0.17			-0.34			0.04
ΔR²		0.23	0.01		0.22	0.01		0.13	0.02		0.12	0.03		0.20	0.01
ΔF		14.87***	0.75		15.28***	0.26		7.47***	0.69		7.27***	1.34		11.99***	0.24
Adjusted R²	0.06	0.27	0.27	0.12	0.32	0.31	0.02	0.14	0.13	0.10	0.21	0.21	0.02	0.20	0.19
F	15.44***	15.72***	8.18***	32.35***	19.75***	9.82***	6.76**	7.51***	4.07***	28.86***	11.49***	6.46***	5.72**	11.17***	5.59***

Note: $N = 220$; Standardized coefficients (betas) are reported.
* $p < 0.05$
** $p < 0.01$
*** $p < 0.001$

Table 5. Regression Results for Firm Performance

Respective interaction term	Firm Performance						
	Model 1	Model 2	Model 3 mHR	Model 4 sHR	Model 5 Industry	Model 6 Ownership	Model 7 Global practice
Step 1: Control							
Firm size (ln)	0.11	0.08	0.08	0.08	0.08	0.04	0.08
Industry (IT = 1)	-0.13	-0.14*	-0.14*	-0.14*	0.20	-0.14*	-0.13
Ownership (non-local = 1)	0.08	0.08	0.09	0.09	0.08	-0.65*	0.09
Global practice	0.12	0.13	0.12	0.13	0.14*	0.13	0.45
mHR	0.03	-0.01	0.03	0.15	0.03	0.04	0.05
sHR	0.07	0.04	-0.06	-0.02	0.00	-0.02	-0.00
Step 2: HRBPs							
Employee development		-0.04	-0.70*	-0.21	-0.07	-0.09	-0.04
Career development		0.12	0.36	0.24	0.13	0.19	0.04
Performance-based compensation		-0.06	0.38	0.08	0.04	-0.23*	0.25*
Selective hiring		-0.00	-0.29	-0.05	0.01	-0.03	-0.07
Strategic HR planning		0.08	0.27	0.12	0.08	0.07	-0.02
Step 3: Interactions							
Employee development × respective interaction term			1.03*	0.27	0.09	0.17	-0.03
Career development × respective interaction term			-0.38	-0.21	0.00	-0.21	0.15
Performance-based compensation × respective interaction term			-0.70	-0.26	-0.48	0.67*	-1.11***
Selective hiring × respective interaction term			0.46	0.09	-0.03	0.17	0.31
Strategic HR planning × respective interaction term			-0.26	-0.04	0.06	0.01	0.29
ΔR^2		0.01	0.04	0.00	0.02	0.04	0.06
ΔF		0.56	2.10	0.17	0.79	0.77	2.75*
Adjusted R^2	0.06	0.05	0.07	0.03	0.04	0.06	0.08
R^2	0.08	0.09	0.14	0.10	0.11	0.13	0.15
F	3.13**	1.95*	2.03**	1.36	1.58	1.92*	2.25**

Note: $N = 220$; standardized coefficients (betas) are reported.
* $p < 0.05$
** $p < 0.01$
*** $p < 0.001$

five HRBPs were entered into the equation, it did not add much to the variance explained. All five practices were insignificant. This confirmed *Hypothesis 4a*.
Model 3 and Model 4 present the results of considering the interactions between HRBPs and the two HR orientations. The influence of HRBPs on firm performance remained insignificant even when firms adopted either strategic orientation or mimetic orientation. Hence, *Hypothesis 4b* was confirmed. When firms behave similarly, there is no effect on superior firm performance. The interactions between the extent of globalization and the five HRBPs were examined in Models 5 to 7. The interaction blocks were not significant when the HRBPs were considered together with industry and ownership. However, the global practice interaction block was significant. When individual HRBPs were examined, it was found that only performance-based compensation was significant. However, the sign was negative, implying that a less globalized firm employing the performance-based compensation practice had a better firm performance. Since most items were not significant, *Hypothesis 4c* was confirmed.

Discussion and Conclusion

In this study, we integrated globalization arguments with institutional theory and the resource-based view, and examined the extent of convergence of human resource best practices for a sample of firms of diverse industries and countries operating in Hong Kong. We found that both mimetic and strategic HR orientations of firms were related to their higher level of adoption of HRBPs. These results lend support to the convergence thesis, suggesting that globalization fosters a greater degree of mimetic and strategic HR orientations, which in turn leads to greater use of HRBPs. Moreover, in the ANOVA analyses, the adoption of HRBPs was not due to differences in ownership (country origins).

However, the convergence thesis remained plausible when we further examined the data. First, we found that the direct effects of the globalization measures on the adoption of HRBPs were not strong in our sample. The three indices of globalization had relatively small effects when it came to predicting HRBP adoption, except for intention to adopt global practices, which had some impact on employee development and performance-based compensation. Moreover, the interaction effects of these three globalization measures with mimetic and strategic HR orientations were not significant. Finally, we found that firm size, an organizational factor, remained a significant predictor of HRBP adoption. Against the convergence argument of globalization, Warner (2002) contends that globalization may have a divergent and uneven impact on employment practices, industrial relations, and HRM in the Asia-Pacific region. We concur with Warner's "soft convergence" argument. The firms in our study have not been unanimously adopting HRBPs at a time of increasing globalization. This is also consistent with Von Glinow et al.'s (2002) conclusion.

The effects of the adoption of HRBPs on performance were examined from a resource-based view. Conceptually, no performance differences would be expected. The empirical analysis confirmed this proposition. Hence, proposing the use of HRBPs to enhance firm performance is paradoxical. On the one hand, there is a global trend of firms converging towards adopting similar HRBPs for the sake of legitimacy and other reasons. On the other hand, adopting HRBPs would result in very little performance difference among firms, and it would be very misleading for managers to adopt best practices if their objective were to enhance firm performance. While the trend towards globalization may pose similar challenges to firms as they operate in a converging economy (Zivnuska/Ketchen/Snow 2001), if firms intend to obtain an edge over their rivals based on their human assets, they need to develop unique HR solutions to deal with these challenges.

The results of this study, however, should be interpreted with some limitations in mind. First, we employed three proxies to measure globalization. Although these proxies were carefully designed and received support from the literature, it is clear that there is a need for valid measures of a firm's degree of globalization. With more sophisticated measures, we can better examine the various effects of globalization on the adoption of HRBPs. Second, we collected our data through a self-reported survey on just one occasion. This may have created the problem of common method variance bias. Third, the cross-sectional nature of the data made it difficult to ascertain causality. If there is a temporal effect of globalization and firms' HR orientations, then this study would not have been able to detect it.

Despite these limitations, this study has shown that the convergence argument is still plausible for HRBP adoption. As firms face increasing competition due to globalization, the way they manage their human resources remains an important issue to be addressed as this could provide a source of competitive advantage to them. Nevertheless, merely following the crowd is not a wise strategy. More research in this area is called for.

References

Anakwe, U. P./Igbaria, M./Anandarajan, M., Management Practices Across Cultures: Role of Support in Technology Usage, *Journal of International Business Studies*, 31, 2000, pp. 653–666.
Arthur, J. B., Effects of Human Resources Systems on Manufacturing Performance and Turnover, *Academy of Management Journal*, 37, 1994, pp. 670–687.

Bae, J./Rowley, C. 2001, The Impact of Globalization on HRM: The Case of South Korea, *Journal of World Business*, 36, 4, 2001, pp. 402–428.
Barney, J., Firm Resources and Sustained Competitive Advantage, *Journal of Management*, 17, 1991, pp. 99–120.
Child, J./Tse, D. K., China's Transition and Its Implications for International Business, *Journal of International Business Studies*, 32, 2001, pp. 5–21.
Christmann, P./Taylor, G., Globalization and the Environment: Determinants of Firm Self-regulation in China, *Journal of International Business Studies*, 32, 2001, pp. 439–458.
De Cieri, H./Dowling, P. J., Strategic International Human Resource Management: An Asia-Pacific Perspective, *Management International Review*, Special Issue 1997, pp. 21–42.
Delaney, J. T./Huselid, M. A., The Impact of Human Resource Management Practices on Perceptions of Organizational Performance, *Academy of Management Journal*, 39, 1996, pp. 949–969.
Delery, J. E./Doty, H., Model of Theorizing in Strategic Human Resource Management: Tests of Universalistic, Contingency, and Configurational Performance Predictions, *Academy of Management Journal*, 39, 1996, pp. 802–835.
DiMaggio, P. J./Powell, W. W., The Iron Cage Revisited: Institutional Isomorphism and Collective Rationality in Organizational Fields, *American Sociological Review*, 48, 1983, pp. 147–160.
Dyer, L./Reeves, T., Human Resource Strategies and Firm Performance: What Do We Know and Where Do We Need to Go?, *International Journal of Human Resource Management*, 6, 1995, pp. 656–670.
Eden, L./Lenway, S., Introduction to the Symposium "Multinationals: The Janus Face of Globalization", *Journal of International Business Studies*, 32, 2001, pp. 383–400.
Ferner, A./Quintanilla, J., Multinationals, National Business Systems and HRM: The Enduring Influence of National Identity or a Process of "Anglo-Saxonization", *International Journal of Human Resource Management*, 9, 1998, pp. 710–731.
Fey, C. F./Bjorkman, I., The Effect of Human Resource Management Practices on MNC Subsidiary Performance in Russia, *Journal of International Business Studies*, 32, 2001, pp. 59–75.
Fields, D./Chan, A./Akhtar, S., Organizational Context and Human Resource Management Strategy: A Structural Equation Analysis of Hong Kong Firms, *International Journal of Human Resource Management*, 11, 2000, pp. 264–277.
Ghoshal, S., Global Strategy: An Organizing Framework, *Strategic Management Journal*, 8, 1987, pp. 425–440.
Gomez-Mejia, L.R./Balkin, D.B./Cardy, R., *Managing Human Resources*, New York: Prentice Hall International 1995.
Gooderham, P. N./Nordhaug, O./Ringdal, K., Institutional and Rational Determinants of Organizational Practices: Human Resource Management in European Firms, *Administrative Science Quarterly*, 44, 1999, pp. 507–531.
Guillen, M. F., Is Globalization Civilizing, Destructive or Feeble? A Critique of Five Key Debates in the Social Science Literature, *Annual Review of Sociology*, 27, 2001, pp. 235–260.
Hannon, J. M./Huang, I. C./Jaw, B. S., International Human Resource Strategy and Its Determinants: The Case of Subsidiaries in Taiwan, *Journal of International Business Studies*, 26, 1995, pp. 531–554.
Harris, L. C./Ogbonna, E., Strategic Human Resource Management, Market Orientation, and Organizational Performance, *Journal of Business Research*, 51, 2001, pp. 157–166.
Harukiyo, H./Hook, G., *Japanese Business Management: Restructuring for Low Growth and Globalization*, London: Routledge 1998.
Harvey, M. G./Buckley, M. R./Novicevic, M. M., Strategic Global Human Resource Management: A Necessity When Entering Emerging Markets, in Ferris, G. R. (ed.), *Research in Personnel and Human Resources Management*, vol. 19, New York: JAI Press 2000, pp. 175–242.
Huang, T., Are the Human Resource Practices of Effective Firms Distinctly Different from Those of Poorly Performing Ones? Evidence from Taiwanese Enterprises, *International Journal of Human Resource Management*, 11, 2000, pp. 436–451.
Huselid, M. A., The Impact of Human Resource Management Practices on Turnover, Productivity, and Corporate Financial Performance, *Academy of Management Journal*, 38, 1995, pp. 635–672.
Huselid, M. A./Jackson, S. E./Schuler, R. S., Technical and Strategic Human Resource Effectiveness as Determinants of Firm Performance, *Academy of Management Journal*, 40, 1997, pp. 171–188.

Jones, M. T., Globalization and Organizational Restructuring: A Strategic Perspective, *Thunderbird International Business Review*, 44, 2002, pp. 325-351.
Kerr, C./Dunlop, J. T./Harbison F. H./Myers, C., *Industrialism and Industrial Man*, Harmondsworth: Penguin 1973.
Koch, M. J./McGrath, R. G., Improving Labor Productivity: Human Resource Management Policies Do Matter, *Strategic Management Journal*, 17, 1996, pp. 335-354.
Lau, C. M./Ngo, H. Y., Organization Development and Firm Performance: A Comparison of Multinational and Local Firms, *Journal of International Business Studies*, 32, 2001, pp. 95-114.
Lee, J./Miller, D., People Matter: Commitment to Employees, Strategy and Performance in Korean Firms, *Strategic Management Journal*, 20, 1999, pp. 579-593.
MacDuffie, J. P., Human Resource Bundles and Manufacturing Performance: Organizational Logic and Flexible Production Systems in the World Auto Industry, *Industrial and Labor Relations Review*, 48, 1995, pp. 197-221.
Marchington, M./Grugulis, I., "Best Practice" Human Resource Management: Perfect Opportunity or Dangerous Illusion? *International Journal of Human Resource Management*, 11, 2000, pp. 1104-1124.
McGaughey, S. L./De Cieri, H., Reassessment of Convergence and Divergence Dynamics: Implications for International HRM, *International Journal of Human Resource Management*, 10, 1999, pp. 235-250.
Meyer, J. W./Boli, J./Thomas, G. M./Ramirez, F. O., World Society and the Nation-State, *American Journal of Sociology*, 103, 1997, pp. 144-181.
Ngo, H. Y./Turban, D./Lau, C. M./Lui, S., Human Resource Practices and Firm Performance of Multinational Corporations: Influences of Country Origin, *International Journal of Human Resource Management*, 9, 1998, pp. 632-652.
Ohmae, K., *The Borderless World*, New York: Harper Business 1990.
Pfeffer, J., *Competitive Advantage through People*, Boston, MA: Harvard Business School Press 1994.
Ritzer, G., *The McDonaldization of Society: An Investigation into the Changing Character of Contemporary Social Life*, Newbury Park, CA: Pine Forge Press 1993.
Rondinelli, D./Rosen, B./Drori, I., The Struggle for Strategic Alignment in Multinational Corporations: Managing Readjustment During Global Expansion, *European Management Journal*, 19, 2001, pp. 404-416.
Rosenzweig, P. M./Nohria, N., Influences on HRM Practices in MNCs, *Journal of International Business Studies*, 25, 1994, pp. 229-251.
Rowley, C./Bae, J., Globalization and Transformation of Human Resource Management in South Korea, *International Journal of Human Resource Management*, 13, 2002, pp. 522-549.
Rowley, C./Benson, J., Convergence and Divergence in Asian Human Resource Management, *California Management Review*, 44, 2002, pp. 90-109.
Scott, W. R., *Institutions and Organizations*, Thousand Oaks, CA: Sage Publications 1995.
Shaw, J. B./Kirkbride, P. S./Fisher, C. D./Tang, S., Human Resource Practices in Hong Kong and Singapore: The Impact of Political Forces and Imitation Processes, *Asia Pacific Journal of Human Resources*, 33, 1993, pp. 22-39.
Von Glinow, M. A./Drost, E. A./Teagarden, M. B., Converging on IHRM Best Practices: Lessons Learned from a Globally Distributed Consortium on Theory and Practice, *Human Resource Management*, 41, 2002, pp. 123-140.
Warner, M., Globalization, Labour Markets and Human Resources in Asia-Pacific Economies: An Overview, *International Journal of Human Resource Management*, 13, 2002, pp. 384-398.
Wright, P./McMahan, G. C., Theoretical Perspectives for Strategic Human Resource Management, *Journal of Management*, 18, 1992, pp. 295-320.
Wright, P./McMahan, G. C./McCormick, B./Sherman, W. S., Strategy, Core Competence, and HR Involvement as Determinants of HR Effectiveness and Refinery Performance, *Human Resource Management*, 37, 1998, pp. 17-29.
Yip, G. S., *Total Global Strategy: Managing for Worldwide Competitive Advantage*, Englewood Cliffs, NJ: Prentice Hall 1995.
Zivnuska, S./Ketchen, D./Snow, C. C., Implications of the Converging Economy for Human Resource Management, in Ferris, G.R. (ed.), *Research in Personnel and Human Resources Management*, vol. 20, Greenwich, CT: JAI Press 2001, pp. 371-405.

Management
International Review
© Gabler Verlag 2004

Elizabeth Maitland/Stephen Nicholas/William Purcell/
Tasman Smith

Regional Learning Networks: Evidence from Japanese MNEs in Thailand and Australia

Abstract

- Japanese firms have been depicted as 'learning organizations', with regional governments implementing incentives regions to attract Japanese multinational enterprises (MNEs).
- To test for regional learning networks, firm-specific surveys were undertaken of Japanese subsidiaries in Thai and Australian manufacturing and Japanese parent investment decisions in Southeast Asia, Australia, China and the EU.
- Japanese parents regionalized their investment decisions, treating Australia and Southeast Asia as different investment regions. Further, regional networks were created. For both Australia and Thailand, Japanese buyers established regional networks when parent B2B know-how was transferred to their Thai and Australian subsidiaries, and when Australian and Thai-based subsidiaries implemented B2B pre and post-contractual practices with indigenous suppliers.
- There was no evidence that experienced and large size Japanese MNEs learned from these regional subcontracting networks.

Key Results

- Our empirical evidence suggests that countries in the Southeast Asia region were involved in a location tournament or a zero-sum prisoner's dilemma game, where each country offers the same types of incentives.

Authors

Elizabeth Maitland, Senior Lecturer in International Business, School of International Business, University of New South Wales, Sydney, Australia.
Stephen Nicholas, Professor of International Business, School of Business, University of Sydney, Sydney, Australia.
William R. Purcell, Professor of International Business and Head, Newcastle Graduate School of Business, The University of Newcastle, Callaghan, NSW, Australia.
Tasman Smith, Professor of Marketing, The Thammasat Business School, Thammasat University, Bangkok, Thailand.

Introduction

Countries do not learn. Regions do not learn. Firms learn. When firms create national learning networks, then countries can be said to be "learning countries" in the sense that the country has a high concentration of learning firms. Similarly, regions can be said to be "learning regions" in the sense that the region has an agglomeration of cross-border learning firms. Building network capabilities and learning from partners have been identified as important components underpinning firm growth (Gulati et al. 2000, Nelson/Winter 1982, Kogut/Zander 1993, Khanna et al. 1998, Grant 1996b, Martin 1996, Martin/Salomon 1999). Networks across borders and the agglomeration of firms in a particular region create regional networks. Not all firms are learning organizations, nor are all regional agglomerations of firms learning regions. Japanese firms have been depicted as the model for 'organizational knowledge creation', with their ability to create new knowledge and disseminate it throughout the organization (Nonaka/Takeuchi 1995, Dyer/Nobeoka 2000). In particular, Japanese supplier-buyer, or B2B relationships, have been identified as archetypal learning networks, where both the core buyer and the tiered suppliers learn to improve existing products as well as develop new ones.

Japanese MNEs are also dominant investors in the Asian region. This paper focuses on two interrelated issues: the creation by Japanese MNEs of regional networks, and whether Japanese regional B2B buyer-supplier networks are regional learning networks. Evidence from Japanese firms' regional investment decisions allows us to identify regional investment networks. Using data from Japanese MNEs in two different regional networks, Southeast Asia and Australia, we analyze whether these regional networks are learning networks. While private firms create regional networks, government policy can influence the incidence and types of the regional networks. We develop insights into the role of host government incentive policy in developing regional networks.

Japanese Firms as Learning Organizations at Home

Japanese firms have been depicted as distinctively innovative and learning organizations (Nonaka/Takeuchi 1995). Japanese firms bring about continuous innovation in products and services through their B2B supplier-buyer competencies that ensures newly created knowledge is widely shared within the organization. Embedded in long-term relational contracts, Japanese B2B competencies developed in response to war-time government mandates, immediate post-war labor surpluses and the high growth and labor short economy of the 1960s (Nishiguchi/Brookfield 1997, Odaka et al. 1988). These long-term relational contracts for parts and components comprise a system of tiered suppliers stratified according to each supplier's range and level of technical expertise, attitudes to risk and relative bargaining power (Aoki 1988, Nishiguchi/Brookfield 1997, Nishiguchi 1994, Asanuma 1989, Roehl 1989). B2B practices involve the buyer transferring codified and tacit know-how, embodied in product specifications, pricing regimes, shipment scheduling and quality control mechanisms to suppliers. These practices not only allow learning, but also facilitate problem-solving and monitoring by attenuating information asymmetries between the partners. Suppliers learn to achieve reliability in quality and delivery and meet targeted percentage price reductions, over a specified time through rationalization or productivity improvement (Asanuma 1989). Buyers learn to commit to suppliers by assessing suppliers' performance and ranking suppliers into tiers. Buyer commitment and supplier reputation allow both parties to invest in relation-specific human capital (design engineers) and physical capital (machines). For both parties, these relation or network specific assets act as an additional incentive device to ensure contract compliance, attenuate opportunistic behavior and preserve the long-term supply relationship, given low second-best uses and high switching costs when specialized assets are present (Monteverde/Teece 1982, Odagiri 1992). Repeat contracting between buyer and supplier furthers learning and creates trust and cooperation, which also acts as an incentive for maintaining the subcontracting system over time (Aoki 1994, Sako 1992).

The internationalization of Japanese firms in the 1980s saw these Japanese B2B practices transplanted to non-Japanese cultural environments, raising the question of whether Japanese subcontract architecture could be successfully transplanted into non-Japanese environments (Beechler/Yang 1994, Koike 1988, Gordon 1985, Aoki 1994, Florida/Kenney 1991). The transferability of Japanese buyer-supplier practices overseas has been explored from a number of perspectives. First, non-Japanese firms imitate Japanese buyer-supplier organization, including just-in-time (JIT) and input quality control (Roehl 1989, McMillan 1990, Nishiguchi/Anderson 1995, Helper/Levine 1991, 1995, Sako et al. 1998, Cusumano/Takeishi 1991, Richardson 1993, Oliver/Wilkinson 1988, 1992). Second, Japanese B2B subcontracting might be transferred by Japanese buyers transplanting Japanese suppliers into host economies, or Japanese suppliers might "go it alone" investing overseas without their buyers (Lamming 1990, Kumon et al. 1994, Martin et al. 1995, Martin 1996, Florida/Kenney 1991, Kawabe/Kamiyama 1997, Cho 1997, Gittelman/Graham 1994). Finally, Japanese buyers might enter into subcontracting arrangements with local suppliers, transferring Japanese supplier-buyer know-how to indigenous firms. There is a paucity of research on this topic. There are no research studies on learning within Japanese regional networks involving Japanese subsidiary buyers and their indigenous suppliers.

The topic of regional learning networks involving MNEs and indigenous firms is a major topic for public policy makers. Learning by indigenous firms from regional learning networks promises to integrate host country firms into wider global networks, transfer know-how from foreign firms to the domestic economy and further the growth of countries that form part of host to regional learning networks. This paper analyzes these issues by assessing whether Japanese subsidiary buyers and indigenous suppliers in Southeast Asia and Australia create regional learning networks.

Regional Networks

Governments around the world and especially those in industrializing economies are engaged in fierce competition to attract foreign direct investment (FDI). The Southeast Asian countries of Singapore, Indonesia, Malaysia, Philippines and Thailand compete among themselves and with other regions, such as Australia, for foreign firms. MNEs are attracted to a country and region by policy and non-policy factors. Policy factors can be divided into incentive policies and non-incentive policies (Loree/Guisinger 1995). Incentive policy variables include tax and profit repatriation regulations, tariffs and subsidies. Non-policy incentives impact MNEs' investment decisions, but are not primarily implemented to attract foreign investment, such as government investment in infrastructure and setting exchange rates. Non-policy factors are location specific variables in MNEs' location decisions that government cannot influence, such as market size, raw material availability and cultural proximity.

Governments use incentive policies to create clusters of regional interdependent production within the wider global economy, providing certain states or regions with an early start or first mover advantage. State policies seek to create a path-dependent location process, laying down layer after layer of new firms upon inherited location formations (David 1984, Scott 1996). Of course, non-policy factors as well as incentive policy create regional industry agglomerations or clusters, where firms share net benefits from locating together, such as sharing of information, infrastructure, supply networks, labor markets and ancillary (legal and financial) services (David 1984, Scott 1996, Wheeler/Mody 1992). Clusters are 'sticky,' with countries or regions attracting further new investment quickly or shedding firms only reluctantly.

The battle for agglomeration economies might lock firms into sub-optimal regional clusters as much as optimal ones (Loree/Guisinger 1995). The eastern US 'rust belt' is an example of a 'sticky' sub-optimal cluster only slowly shedding firms while Silicon Valley and the M4 corridor in Britain might be modeled as optimal clusters quickly attracting firms. Hypothesis 1 tests for the existence of regional clusters. If Japanese MNEs perceive the Southeast Asian countries as a separate investment region from Australia, North America, Europe and China, then regional clusters exist.

Hypothesis 1 is that there are significant differences between the attractiveness of the Southeast Asia region and other regions, including Australia, creating regional investment networks.

Empirical Testing for Regional Japanese Networks

A list of Japanese MNEs that invested in Southeast Asia (Singapore Indonesia, Malaysia, Thailand, Philippines), Australia, China, North America and the EU was collected from *Who Owns Whom* (1997). A questionnaire survey was translated from English into Japanese, back translated, then independently reviewed and revised in Japanese before being sent to headquarters executives in Japan. Following Dillman (1978) a reminder letter was sent to all non-responding firms within four weeks of the first mail-out (Claycomb et al. 2000). The initial and follow-up mailing yielded responses from 134 firms from the total sample of 390 firms, or a return rate of 34 percent, with a balance between manufacturing (63 percent) and non-manufacturing (31 percent) Japanese MNEs. Kruskal-Wallis *post-hoc* pair-wise test of the differences in mean ranks was used to test for regional investment patterns (Bryman/Cramer 1997, Siegal/Castellan 1988).

Table 1 ranks the importance of each country as an investment location (using a scale between 1 for no importance to 5 for high importance). Reading across the table for Thailand, bolded numbers indicate significant differences be-

Table 1. Rank Importance of Countries as Japanese MNEs' Investment Locations[a, b]

	Mean	1	2	3	4	5	6	7	8	9
1 China	4.0	4.0	3.6	**3.3**	**3.3**	**3.1**	**3.0**	**2.8**	**2.8**	**2.2**
2 North America	3.6	4.0	3.6	3.3	3.3	3.1	**3.0**	**2.8**	**2.8**	**2.2**
3 Europe	3.3	**4.0**	3.6	3.3	3.3	3.1	3.0	2.8	**2.8**	**2.2**
4 Thailand	3.3	**4.0**	3.6	3.3	3.3	3.1	3.0	2.8	2.8	**2.2**
5 Indonesia	3.1	**4.0**	3.6	3.3	3.3	3.1	3.0	2.8	2.8	**2.2**
6 Singapore	3.0	**4.0**	**3.6**	3.3	3.3	3.1	3.0	2.8	2.8	**2.2**
7 Malaysia	2.8	**4.0**	**3.6**	3.3	3.3	3.1	3.0	2.8	2.8	**2.2**
8 Philippines	2.8	**4.0**	**3.6**	**3.3**	3.3	3.1	3.0	2.8	2.8	2.2
9 Australia	2.2	**4.0**	**3.6**	**3.3**	**3.3**	**3.1**	**3.0**	**2.8**	2.8	2.2

Notes:
[a] Cells with means in bold indicate a significant difference (Kruskal-Wallis Test, alpha = 0.05).
[b] Means are on a scale 1 (no importance) to 5 (high importance).

tween Thailand (3.3) and China (4.0) and Australia (2.2), while unbolded means indicate no differences (i.e., Singapore, Philippines Indonesia, Malaysia, North America and the EU). Australia was ranked significantly different from all other regions. While Southeast Asian countries and Australia were ranked significantly different from the other regions, the Southeast Asian countries were not ranked significantly different among themselves. Japanese MNEs treat Southeast Asia and Australia as different regional networks. Are these regional networks "learning" networks and is there significant difference in learning between Japanese buyers and indigenous suppliers in Southeast Asia and Australia?

Learning Networks: Agency Costs and Sunk Organizational Capital

Japanese domestic B2B practices created learning networks between buyer and supplier. These B2B competencies are difficult or impossible to assemble through the market, since they involve nonimitable and nonmobile assets (Barney 1986, Montgomery/Wernerfelt 1988, Peteraf 1993, Teece 1982, 1986, Teece et al. 1997). Foreign investment allows the internal transfer of firm specific competencies between parent and overseas subsidiary.

Hypothesis 2 is that Japanese MNEs transfer B2B and other competencies to their subsidiaries in Thailand and Australia.

According to Spender (1996, p. 48), learning routines, such as those embedded in the subcontracting relationship, involve processes for communicating the knowledge previously generated by others. Knowledge is usually classified into codified knowledge, which can be transferred through manuals or written rules, and tacit knowledge, which involves "knowing how" rather than "knowing about" (Polanyi 1962, 1966, Leroy/Ramanantsoa 1997, Huber 1991, Inkpen 1995, Kim 1993). Knowledge is "sticky," requiring B2B relationships to implement tailored mechanisms to transfer knowledge from those who create it to those who need to use it. Such transfers and use of knowledge within the B2B relationship represent learning, and when the transfer occurs between suppliers, buyers and parents in Japan, regional learning networks are formed.

The amount of inter-firm learning depends on the behavior of both the Japanese buyers and the indigenous suppliers. Japanese buyers optimize rents on their supplier-buyer practices only when indigenous suppliers cooperate in operating the Japanese B2B system. Opportunistic suppliers can appropriate the Japanese subsidiary's B2B know-how, while failing to implement B2B practices (Williamson 1985, Holstrom 1979, Carlos/Nicholas 1993). To attenuate supplier opportunism, and optimize the transfer of B2B practices, Japanese subsidiaries implement monitoring and control mechanisms as part of their pre- and post-contractual relationship with suppliers (Kale et al. 2000). Pre-contracting B2B marketing arrangements involve seeking quotes, providing specifications on the components before sourcing and contacting several suppliers. The post-contractual B2B practices involve establishing trust and cooperation, transferring designs, drawings, technical know-how, and tools and machinery, as well as advising suppliers on quality, delivery scheduling and management practice.

The potential for opportunism and the costs of monitoring will be positively correlated with the Japanese buyer's dependence on indigenous suppliers. As an alternative to contracting with local suppliers, subsidiaries can vertically integrate by undertaking input production in-house, use Japanese transplants or rely on imports from their parents.

Hypothesis 3 is that the level of B2B practices transferred to indigenous suppliers will vary between regions depending on the subsidiaries' reliance on inputs sourced in-house, through imports and from transplants.

Learning in B2B relationships benefits from history. Japanese subsidiaries and their indigenous suppliers' administrative history creates an organizational infrastructure comprising processes, routines and ways of doing things (Bartlett/Ghoshal 1989, Nelson/Winter 1982, Winter 1987). These formal and informal channels, routines, procedures, norms and cultures allow buyer and supplier to coordinate their supply activities. The firm-specific channels and codes for dealing with information represent 'sunk' organizational capital made by both parties (David 1994, Kogut/Zander 1993, Nelson/Winter 1982, Teece et al. 1997). Such organizational capital includes the way the suppliers and buyers interact, sharing common codes of communication and common understandings. Sharing codes of communication and common understandings allow joint inputs into problem solving and, as a result, learning. Learning is encouraged when the firm's organizational design allows frequent interactions between individuals and within groups (Kogut 1983, Kogut/Zander 1993, Itami/Roehl 1987, Huber 1991). These codified and tacit routines are capabilities that may be thought of as a genetic code, uniquely defining how the two firms perform their joint activities.

Learning is not easy. The stickiness of much tacit, ambiguous, difficult to communicate and idiosyncratic B2B knowledge acts as a barrier to transferring knowledge from originator (buyer) to user (supplier) and to new contracting parties (Grant 1996a, Kogut/Zander 1993, Polanyi 1962, 1966, Leroy/Ramanantsoa 1997, Huber 1991, Inkpen 1995, Kim 1993). Operationalized in inter-firm patterns and routines of doing things, Japanese subcontract relationships typically allow learning through continuous improvement, transfer of plans and machinery, JIT and labor training (Nelson 1991, Nishiguchi 1994, Asanuma 1989). Learning is encouraged when B2B architecture allows frequent inter-firm interactions between individuals and groups, allowing new information to be generated and experiments to be run (Dosi et al. 1992). Weak inter-firm B2B practices will be strengthened through the experience of frequent interaction between buyer and supplier (Dyer/Nobeoka 2000, Kogut 2000). The more experienced a buyer firm is in dealing with indigenous suppliers, the greater is the learning. Learning can be measured by the higher incidence of B2B practices between experienced buyers and suppliers compared to less experienced buyers and suppliers.

Hypothesis 4 is that Japanese subsidiaries with years of B2B subcontracting experience with indigenous suppliers will display a significantly greater incidence of B2B practices than recent arrivals.

Similarly, large firms with a greater capacity to make investments in 'sunk' organizational infrastructure will experience greater learning than will small firms. Large firms are faster learners, since their investment in firm-specific infrastructure, including channels and routines for dealing with information flows and knowledge transfer, promote learning (David 1994). Such learning can also be measured by the higher incidence of B2B practices in large buyers.

Hypothesis 5 is that the large Japanese buyers will display a higher incidence of B2B practices than small Japanese buyers.

Testing for Regional Learning Networks

To assess learning by Japanese subsidiaries in Southeast Asia and Australia, we undertook three identical surveys of Japanese MNEs in Australian manufacturing in 1993 and 1997, and Thai manufacturing in 1999. The Australian samples are aggregated into a single sample. The Australian samples were primarily drawn from the 1992 and 1996 *Directories of Japanese Business Activity in Australia.* The Thai sample was drawn from the *1999 List of Members, Japanese Chamber of Commerce, Bangkok.* A survey instrument was designed in English, translated into Japanese and then independently back-translated. The same Japanese language questionnaire was used in all three surveys. The questionnaires were mailed to the CEOs of each Australian subsidiary, together with a letter of endorsement from the Japanese Chamber of Commerce and Industry. A follow-up letter was mailed approximately three weeks after the initial mail-out, enclosing another survey questionnaire (Claycomb et al. 2000). Follow-up telephone calls were subsequently made to all non-responding firms. Mail surveys are difficult to conduct in Thailand. Fifty-six Japanese subsidiary managers agreed to be interviewed. A copy of the survey was sent by mail, then a face-to-face interview was held to complete the survey.

The population and sample characteristics are given in Table 2. As can be seen from Table 2, the Australian sample firms, with a 30–38 percent response rate, were widely distributed across the manufacturing sector. The 1993 Austra-

Table 2. Sample Characteristics for Manufacturing Firms and Standard Manufacturing Classifications

Industry Sector	Survey Mailing List Estimate		Respondents			
	Firms	Employees	Firms	Employees	Response Rate (percent)	Employee Ratios (percent)
1993/94 Australian Manufacturing	53	26 200	20	10 187	38	39
1997 Australian Manufacturing	84	31 345	25	17 144	30	55
Aggregate Australian Manufacturing	137	57 682	45	27 331	33	47
1999 Thai Manufacturing	130	58 143	56	28 222	43	49

ASIC Classification	1993 Australian Sample	1997 Australian Sample	Aggregate Australian	1999 Thai Sample
2000-Food	3	6	9	5
2000-Textile and Furniture	1	3	4	9
3000-Paints, Plastics and Rubber	3	1	4	6
3000-Machinery	4	1	5	5
3000-Electrical	4	5	9	17
3000-Auto Parts & Components	5	4	9	10
3000-Instruments	–	5	5	–
3000-Cosmetics & Household	–	–	–	4
TOTAL	20	25	45	56

Note: Australia-Japan Economic Institute A Directory of Japanese Business Activity in Australia 1992 and 1996, Sydney; 1999 List of Members, Japanese Chamber of Commerce, Bangkok

lian manufacturing sample was broadly representative of the size distribution of the population, but the 1997 sample included more large firms, with our respondents accounting for 30 percent of the population and 55 percent of total Japanese manufacturing employment. To overcome any bias toward large firms, the learning results were analyzed for firm size. The response rate for Thai subsidiaries was 43 percent, and the firms were broadly representative of the size distribution of the population.

Learning outcomes were measured by significant changes in the means of the codified and tacit knowledge transfers. T-tests were used to measure the difference in proportions; Kruskal-Wallis one-way analysis of variance by ranks was used to determine whether the means from different samples were from the same population; and the Mann-Whitney U test was employed as a non-parametric version of an independent sample t test (Bryman/Cramer 1997, Siegal/Castellan 1988).

Table 3. Mean Score of the Competencies of Japanese MNEs

	Australia 1993 Mean (SE)	Australia 1997 Mean (SE)	Australia Aggregate Mean (SE)	Thailand 1999 Mean (SE)
COMPETENCIES				
Product quality	3.7 (0.17)	3.8 (0.0)	3.8 (0.0)	3.9 (0.0)
Product price	3.2 (0.23)	3.7 (0.0)	3.5 (0.10)	3.7 (0.0)
Work organization	3.1 (0.22)	3.0 (0.0)	3.0 (0.10)	3.1 (0.0)
Management expertise	3.1 (0.21)	3.0 (0.0)	3.0 (0.10)	3.1 (0.0)
After sale service	3.4 (0.20)	3.3 (0.18)	3.3 (0.13)	3.1 (0.10)
Advertising & marketing	3.0 (0.25)	3.1 (0.13)	3.0 (0.13)	2.8 (0.10)
In-house quality control	**3.7 (0.18)**[a]	**3.3 (0.16)**[a]	**3.5 (0.12)**[b]	**3.7 (0.0)**[b]
SUBCONTRACT PRACTICES				
Keeping delivery dates	3.3 (0.19)	3.3 (0.16)	**3.3 (0.12)**[a]	**3.7 (0.0)**[a]
Quality of inputs	3.3 (0.23)	3.3 (0.16)	3.3 (0.13)	3.4 (0.)
TOTAL	3.3	3.3	3.3	3.4

Note: 1 – no; 2 – low; 3 – medium; 4 – high. [a] Mann-Whitney U test significant at 0.05.
[b] Mann-Whitney U test significant at 0.10.

Table 3 confirms *Hypothesis 1*, that Japanese parents transferred tacit and codified know-how, including B2B competencies, to their Australian and Thai subsidiaries. Competencies related to quality (product quality and in-house quality control) were ranked highest by managers of both Australian and Thai subsidiaries, although all the basic Japanese competencies in Table 3 were rated in the medium-high range. Mann-Whitney tests show that Thai subsidiaries scored in-house quality control and delivery dates significantly higher than did the Australian subsidiaries. The significantly lower score for Australian subsidiaries was due to firms with less than 12 years operating experience in Australia in the 1997 sample.

Tables 4 and 5 show that both Australian and Thai subsidiaries implemented B2B subcontracting practices. However, there were significant differences in the

Table 4. Pre-contractual Sourcing by Japanese Buyers in Australia and Thailand

	Australian Aggregate Mean (SE)	Thai Mean (SE)
Seek quotations	3.9 (0.0)	3.7 (0.0)
Establish long term relationships	3.5 (0.11)	3.3 (0.11)
Provide details of input to potential suppliers, then seek quotations	3.4 (0.13)	3.7 (0.0)
Always contact two or more firms	**3.2 (0.13)**[a]	**3.5 (0.10)**[a]
Average Score	3.5	3.6

Note: based on scale 1–4, with 1 = no, 2 = low, 3 = medium, 4 = high. [a] Mann-Whitney U test significant at 0.05. [b] Mann-Whitney U test significant at 0.10.

Table 5. Post-contractual Relationship by Japanese Buyers in Australia and Thailand

	Aggregate Australian Mean (SE)	Thai Mean (SE)
Establish long-term relationship	3.4 (0.13)	3.1(0.12)
Visit the supplier regularly	3.2 (0.14)	3.1 (0.09)
Transfer designs and drawings	2.7 (0.17)	2.6 (0.15)
Transfer other technical know-how	2.7 (0.16)	2.5 (0.14)
Transfer tools and machinery	2.2 (0.19)	2.3 (0.12)
Advise on specifications/procurement	3.0 (0.17)	3.2 (0.10)
Advise on quality control	3.0 (0.18)	3.1 (0.11)
Advise on delivery times	3.0 (0.18)	3.1 (0.09)
Advise on management	2.3 (0.18)	2.1 (0.11)
Train operatives	2.1 (0.17)	2.2 (0.12)
Average Score	2.7	2.7

Note: Based on scale 1-4, with 1 = never, 2 = rarely, 3 = sometimes, 4 = usually.
[a] Mann-Whitney U test significant at 0.05. [b] Mann-Whitney U test significant at 0.10.

reliance on indigenous subcontractors by Japanese subsidiaries in Australia compared to Thailand. Japanese MNEs in Thailand sourced eight percent of their parts and components in-house compared to 22 percent in Australia. Thai subsidiaries imported 48 percent of their components and relied on Japanese firms in Thailand for another 19 percent of their parts. Thai suppliers only accounted for 28 percent of Thai subsidiary inputs, with 16 percent using long-term and 12 percent using short-term contracts. In contrast, Australian subsidiaries only imported 22 percent of their inputs, and less than one percent of components were procured from transplanted Japanese firms. Australian suppliers accounted for 57 percent of the inputs purchased by Japanese subsidiaries, with 35 percent involving contracts of more than three years duration. These data suggest that the operation of the regional subcontract system in Australia and Thailand might display significant differences.

In spite of the different reliance on indigenous suppliers in Australia and Thailand, Table 4 shows that Japanese pre-contractual sourcing practices were ranked overall 3.5 by Australian and 3.6 by Thai subsidiaries. The only significant difference in pre-contractual subcontracting behavior was that Thai subsidiaries ranked contacting two or more firms for quotes significantly higher than Australian subsidiaries.

Similarly, Japanese buyers in Australia and Thailand ranked post-contractual sourcing arrangements with the same mean score of 2.7 (rarely-sometimes) in Table 5. Although Japanese subsidiaries in Australia depended heavily on indigenous suppliers, while Japanese buyers in Thailand relied more on imports and Japanese transplants, there were no significant differences in the overall transfer of B2B practices. *Hypothesis 3* is not confirmed. The greater reliance on indigenous suppliers in Australia did not lead to a higher incidence of B2B pre- and post-contractual practices.

Table 6. Post-contractual B2B Practices by Experience and Size by Japanese Buyers in Australia

	Experienced	Inexperienced	Large	Small
Visit the supplier regularly	3.4	2.9	**3.6**	**2.9**
Establish long-term relationship with supplier	**3.5**	**3.2**	3.4	3.3
Advise on material specifications/procurement	2.8	3.1	**3.3**	**2.6**
Help with quality control and testing	2.9	3.0	**3.3**	**2.6**
Help in delivery times	2.4	2.9	**3.1**	**2.2**
Transfer designs and drawings	2.4	2.9	2.9	2.5
Transfer technical know-how	2.6	2.8	2.8	2.6
Transfer tools and machinery	2.0	2.3	2.3	2.1
Advise on management	2.6	1.9	2.5	1.9
Train operatives	2.0	2.3	2.4	1.9

(Mann-Whitney test found significant at 0.05 level are bold)

The existence of regional learning networks was measured by the higher incidence of B2B practice in experienced versus inexperienced firms. Experienced buyers were those with more than 12 years experience in Australia and in Thailand, while recent arrivals were those with less than 12 years experience. Table 6 shows that experienced Australian subsidiaries did not implement pre- or post-contractual sourcing arrangements more intensely than recent arrivals, except that experienced buyers establish long-term relations with suppliers significantly more frequently than recent arrivals. Table 7 reveals no significant differences in post-contractual practices between experienced and inexperienced Thai suppliers. To provide a further test of learning by experienced firms, the Australian and Thai samples were divided into three experience groups, those operating for more than 20 years, those operating 8–20 years and those with less than 8 years

Table 7. Post-contractual B2B Practices by Experience and Size by Japanese Buyers in Thailand

	Experienced	Inexperienced	Large	Small
Visit the supplier regularly	3.0	3.2	3.3	3.0
Establish long-term relationship with supplier	3.3	2.9	3.3	2.9
Advise on material specifications/procurement	3.3	3.1	3.3	3.1
Help with quality control and testing	3.0	3.2	3.3	3.0
Help in delivery times	3.0	3.1	3.1	3.0
Transfer designs and drawings	2.8	2.4	2.6	2.5
Transfer technical know-how	2.4	2.6	2.7	2.4
Transfer tools and machinery	2.2	2.5	**2.6**	**2.1**
Advise on production methods	2.7	2.6	**2.9**	**2.4**
Advise on management	2.2	2.0	2.2	2.1
Train operatives	2.2	2.2	2.1	2.2
Coop staff	2.1	1.7	1.9	1.9

(Mann-Whitney test found significant at 0.05 level are bold)

experience. Mann-Whitney and difference in proportion tests were run on the two subsamples, with the firms with 8–20 years experience deleted. The results revealed no significant differences for the Thai firms between experienced and more recent arrivals. For the Australian firms with more than 20 years experience, the only significant differences were that they visited suppliers and established a long-term relationship more frequently than recent arrivals. Hypothesis 4 is not supported, with no evidence that experience promoted regional learning networks for Australian or Thai subsidiaries.

The theory also suggested that large firms learn faster since they have invested more in sunk organizational capital than small firms. Size and experience were not significantly correlated in the Thai or Australian samples. In Table 7, large Thai buyers advised on production and transferred tools significantly more frequently than small Thai subsidiaries, but other post-contractual practices were not significantly different. Large Japanese subsidiaries in Australia ranked establishing a long-term relationship and advising on quality and delivery times significantly higher than did small subsidiaries (See Table 6). Hypothesis 5 received little verification, with only limited support that size was an important factor in learning by large Japanese buyers in Australia.

Conclusion

Our data show that Japanese parents regionalized their investment decisions, treating Australia and Southeast Asia as different investment regions. Further, regional networks were created. For both Australia and Thailand, Japanese buyers established regional networks when parent B2B know-how was transferred to their Thai and Australian subsidiaries, and when Australian and Thai-based subsidiaries implemented B2B pre and post-contractual practices with indigenous suppliers. Increased intensity in the use of B2B practices, especially transferring know-how, advising suppliers and training supplier staff, was used to measure regional network learning. We found no evidence that experienced and large size Japanese MNEs learned from these regional subcontracting networks.

It might be argued that it would be an error to see the replication of Japanese domestic subcontracting practice as the benchmark for successful subcontracting relationships in Australia or Thailand. The subcontracting system in Japan is the outcome of a path dependent process that Japanese firms may not recreate at home if given the choice (Odaka et al. 1988, Nishiguchi/Brookfield 1997). In Australia and Thailand buyers were given the choice to build subcontracting practices from scratch, by selectively transferring key elements of Japanese practice to their overseas operations. If Japanese buyers were satisfied with their suppliers, then the absence of improvements in the initial transfer of B2B subcontracting practices should not be interpreted as a failure to learn. But, Japanese buyers were not satisfied with their Australian or Thai suppliers' B2B performance, scoring average performance low-medium (2.7). Satisfaction with crucial supplier practices, especially availability and reliability of delivery, were rated particularly poorly. For Japanese buyers, there was scope for learning in the buyer-supplier B2B relationship.

We have poor information on learning by indigenous suppliers. Japanese buyers rated the co-operation of their Australian and Thai suppliers as medium-high. Buyer-supplier alliances can be analyzed as learning races, where the object of the B2B architecture is to promote joint learning (Khanna et al. 1998). Indigenous firms adopted Japanese B2B practices, with Japanese subsidiaries rating the co-operation of their Australian (3.3) and Thai suppliers (3.2) higher in executing Japanese subcontracting practices than they scored themselves (2.7 in Table 5). Experienced Japanese subsidiaries ranked their suppliers' post-contractual co-operation higher than did recent Japanese arrivals. These findings suggest that indigenous suppliers performed well in the "learning race." Without increased incidence of B2B practices by Japanese subsidiaries, indigenous suppliers were constrained in their ability to learn.

These results have important implications for government policy. There is considerable debate on the role of incentives policy in attracting investment and whether countries in a region compete against each other for foreign investment through incentive policies. The survey evidence reveals that investment incentives are not the most important factor in the location choice. Aharoni's (1966) interviews with executives showed that incentives did not bring about the decision to locate overseas, a result confirmed by other studies (Lim 1983, Mody/ Srinivasan 1998, Wheeler/Mody 1992, Hughes/Dorrance 1984, Chen 1998). While not provoking the overseas investment decision, incentives were assigned a secondary role of influencing the precise location of investment (Taylor 1993). In a survey of World Bank projects, Guisinger (1985) challenged much of this research, finding that two out of three investments only went ahead because of investment incentives. To assess incentive effectiveness, Guisinger (1992) called for a country's incentives to be measured against other factors, such as other countries' incentive policies.

Relative incentive effectiveness links incentive policies directly to predatory bidding wars. States promote investment incentives as devices for attracting MNEs to their country within a region. Aware of location tournaments, MNEs play countries off against one another in order to attain the best incentive package (Loree/Guisinger 1995, Scott 1996, Weigand 1983, Wheeler/Mody 1992). In competitive bidding wars, all countries in a region increase their incentives simultaneously, but no country increases its relative investment share, a classic zero-sum prisoner's dilemma game (Loree/Guisinger 1995). If all states reduced their incentives, MNEs would still invest, but each state would provide a lower level of incentive payment.

Our empirical evidence supports the case that countries in the Southeast Asia region were involved in a location tournament. Using Kruskal-Wallis and Kruskal Wallis pair-wise tests, Japanese parents did not perceive any significant differences between the Southeast Asian countries across the six incentive policies, comprising import tariffs and barriers, import tax exemptions, tax reductions, free trade zones and government subsidies. This suggests that Asian countries were involved in a zero-sum prisoner's dilemma game, where each country offers the same types of incentives. If all countries reduced their incentives, there could well be no change in the overall distribution of Japanese investment. Each country would save on the level of incentives, with Japanese MNEs receiving a lower level of incentive payments. The presence of a zero-sum prisoner's dilemma game within the Southeast Asian region alerts policy makers to the fact that successively increasing incentives does not guarantee an increase in a country's share of Japanese investment. Rather, strengthening regional co-operation in investment regimes promises to attenuate bidding wars between neighboring Southeast Asian states.

Secondly, the presence of Japanese investment in the region is not sufficient to ensure that local firms and foreign subsidiaries are part of a regional learning network. Policy makers face a challenge to implement "fine tuned" incentives, industry policies and environments for high performing local firms to encourage regional networks to be transformed into regional learning networks.

References

Aharoni, Y., *The Foreign Investment Decision Process*, Boston: Division of Research, Graduate School of Business Administration, Harvard University 1966.
Aoki, M., *Information, Incentives and Bargaining in the Japanese Economy*, Cambridge: Cambridge University Press 1988.
Aoki, M., The Japanese Firm as a System of Attributes: A Survey and Research Agenda, in Aoki, M./Dore, R. (eds.), *The Japanese Firm: The Sources of Competitive Strength*, Oxford: Oxford University Press 1994, pp. 11–40.
Asanuma, B., Manufacturer-Supplier Relationships in Japan and the Concept of Relation-Specific Skill, *Journal of Japanese and International Economics*, 3, 1989, pp. 1–30.
Barney, J. B., Strategic Factor Markets: Expectations, Luck, and Business Strategy, *Management Science*, 32, 1986, pp. 1231–1241.
Bartlett, C. A./Ghoshal, S., *Managing Across Borders: The Transnational Solution*, Boston: Harvard Business School Press 1989.
Beechler, S./Yang, J. Z., The Transfer of Japanese-Style Management to American Subsidiaries: Contingencies, Constraints, and Competencies, *Journal of International Business Studies*, 25, 3, 1994, pp. 467–491.
Bryman, A./Cramer, D., *Quantitative Data Analysis with SPSS for Windows: A Guide for Social Scientists*, New York: Routledge 1997.

Carlos, A./Nicholas, S., Managing the Manager: An Application of the Agent Principal Model to the Hudson's Bay Company, *Oxford Economic Papers*, 45, 1993, pp. 243-256.
Chen, J. H., The Effects of International Competition of Fiscal Incentives on Foreign Direct Investment, *Economia Internazionale*, 51, 1998, pp. 497-516.
Cho, D., Electrical Component Factories, in Itagaki, H. (ed.), *The Japanese Production System: Hybrid Factories in East Asia*, London: Macmillan 1997, pp. 231-262.
Claycomb, C./Porter, S./Martin, C., Riding the Wave: Response Rates and the Effect of Time Intervals Between Successive Mail Survey Follow-Up Efforts, *Journal of Business*, 48, 2000, pp. 157-162.
Cusumano, M. A./Takeishi, A., Supplier Relations and Management: A Survey of Japanese, Japanese-Transplant, and US Auto Plants, *Strategic Management Journal*, 12, 1991, pp. 563-588.
David, P., *High Technology Centre and the Economics of Locational Tournaments* (mimeo), Stanford: Stanford University 1984.
Dillman, D.A., *Mail and Telephone Surveys: The Total Design Method*, New York: John Wiley and Sons 1978.
Directory of Japanese Business Activity in Australia, 1992, Sydney: Australia-Japan Economic Institute 1992.
Directory of Japanese Business Activity in Australia, Sydney: Australia-Japan Economic Institute 1996.
Dosi, G./Teece, D. J./Winter, S., Towards a Theory of Corporate Coherence: Preliminary Remarks, in Dosi, G./Giannetti, R./Toninelli, P. A. (eds.), *Technology and Enterprise in a Historical Perspective*, Oxford: Clarendon Press 1992, pp. 185-211.
Dyer, J. H./Nobeoka, K., Creating and Managing a High Performance Knowledge-Sharing Network: The Toyota Case, *Strategic Management Journal*, 21, 2000, pp. 345-367.
Florida, R./Kenney, M., Transplanted Organizations: The Transfer of Japanese Industrial Organization to the US, *American Sociological Review*, 56, 1991, pp. 381-398.
Gittelman, M./Graham, E., The Performance and Determinants of Japanese Affiliates in the European Community, in Mason, M./Encarnation, D. (eds.), *Does Ownership Matter? Japanese Multinationals in Europe*, Oxford: Oxford University Press 1994, pp. 127-158.
Gordon, A., *The Evolution of Labour Relations in Japan: Heavy Industry, 1853-1955*, Cambridge MA: Harvard University Press 1985.
Grant, R. M., Prospering in Dynamically-Competitive Environments: Organizational Capability as Knowledge Integration, *Organizational Science*, 7, 1996a, pp. 375-387.
Grant, R. M., Toward a Knowledge-Based Theory of the Firm, *Strategic Management Journal*, 17, 1996b, pp. 203-215.
Guisinger, S., *Investment Incentives and Performance Requirements*, New York: Praeger 1985.
Guisinger, S., Rhetoric and Reality in International Business: A Note on the Effectiveness of Incentives, *Transnational Corporations*, 1, 2, 1992, pp. 111-123.
Gulati, R./Nohria, N./Zaheer, A., Strategic Networks, *Strategic Management Journal*, 21, 2000, pp. 203-215.
Helper, S./Levine, D., Long-term Supplier Relations and Product Market Structure: An Exit-Voice Approach, *CCC Working Paper* 1991.
Helper, S./Levine, D., Supplier Relations in Japan and the United States: Are They Converging?, *Sloan Management Review*, 36, 1995, pp. 77-84.
Holstrom, B., Moral Hazard and Observability, *The Bell Journal of Economics*, 10, 1979, pp. 74-91.
Huber, G. P., Organizational Learning: The Contributing Processes and a Review of the Literature, *Organizational Science*, 2, 1991, pp. 88-117.
Hughes, H./Dorrance, G., Economic Policies and Direct Foreign Investment with Particular Reference to the Developing Countries of East Asia, Paper prepared for Commonwealth Secretariat, January 1984.
Inkpen, A., *The Management of International Joint Ventures: An Organizational Learning Perspective*, New York: Routledge 1995.
Itami, M./Roehl, T. W., *Mobilizing Invisible Assets*, Cambridge, MA: Harvard University Press 1987.
Kale, P./Singh, H./ Perlmutter, H., Learning and Protection of Proprietary Assets in Strategic Alliances: Building Relational Capital, *Strategic Management Journal*, 21, 2000, pp. 217-237.

Kawabe, N./Kamiyama, K., The Auto Parts Industry, in Itagaki, H. (ed.), *The Japanese Production System: Hybrid Factories in East Asia*, London: Macmillan 1997, pp. 170-205.
Khanna, T./Gulati, R./Nohria, N., The Dynamics of Learning Alliances: Competition, Cooperation and Relative Scope, *Strategic Management Journal*, 19, 1998, pp. 193-210.
Kim, D. H., The Link Between Individual and Organizational Learning, *Sloan Management Review*, 35, 1, 1993, pp. 37-50.
Kogut, B., Foreign Direct Investment as a Sequential Process, in Kindleberger, C. P./Audretsch, D.B. (eds.), *The Multinational Corporation in the 1980s*, Cambridge, MA: M.I.T. Press 1983, pp. 38-56.
Kogut, B., The Network as Knowledge: Generative Rules and the Emergence of Structure, *Strategic Management Journal*, 21, 2000, pp. 405-425.
Kogut, B./Zander, U., Knowledge of the Firm and the Evolutionary Theory of the Multinational Corporation, *Journal of International Business Studies*, 24, 1993, pp. 625-46.
Koike, K., *Understanding Industrial Relations in Modern Japan*, Basingstoke: Macmillan 1988.
Kumon, H./Kamiyama, K./Itagaki, H./Kawamura, T., Industrial Analysis by Industry Types, in Abo, T. (ed.), *Hybrid Factory: The Japanese Production System in the United States*, New York: Oxford University Press 1994, pp. 123-180.
Lamming, R., Strategic Options for Automobile Suppliers in the Global Market, *International Journal of Technology Management*, 5, 1990, pp. 649-684.
Leroy, F./Ramanantsoa, B., The Cognitive and Behaviour Dimensions of Organizational Learning in a Merger: An Empirical Study, *Journal of Management Studies*, 34, 1997, pp. 871-894.
Lim, D., Fiscal Incentives and Direct Foreign Investment in Less Developed Countries, *The Journal of Development Studies*, 18, 1983, pp. 207-212.
List of Members, Japanese Chamber of Commerce, Bangkok 1999.
Loree, D. W./Guisinger, S. E., Policy and Non-Policy Determinants of U.S. Equity Foreign Direct Investment, *Journal of International Business Studies*, 2nd Quarter, 1995, pp. 281-299.
Martin, X., *Supplier Capabilities and Buyer Foreign Direct Investment As Determinants of Supplier Foreign Direct Investment: A Longitudinal Analysis*, Paper prepared for conference on Longitudinal Studies of Foreign Market Entry, University of Chicago at Urbana-Champaign, April 1996, pp. 18-20.
Martin, X./Mitchell, W./Swaminathan, A., Recreating and Extending Japanese Automobile Buyer-Supplier Links in North America, *Strategic Management Journal*, 16, 1995, pp. 589-619.
Martin, X./Salomon, R., *Knowledge Transfer Capacity: Implications for the Theory of the Multinational Corporation* (mimeo), 1999.
McMillan, J., Managing Suppliers: Incentive Systems in Japanese and US Industry, *California Management Review*, 32, 1990, pp. 38-55.
Mody, A./Srinivasan, K., Japanese and U.S. Forms as Foreign Investors: Do They March to the Same Tune?, *Canadian Journal of Economics*, 31, 4, 1998, pp. 778-799.
Monteverde, K./Teece, D., Supplier Switching Costs and Vertical Integration in the Automobile Industry, *Bell Journal of Economics*, 13, 1982, pp. 206-213.
Montgomery, C./Wernerfelt, B., Diversification, Ricardian rents, and Tobin's q, *Rand Journal of Economics*, 19, 1988, pp. 623-633.
Nelson, R./Winter, S., *An Evolutionary Theory of Economic Change*, Cambridge, MA: Harvard University Press 1982.
Nelson, R. R., Why do Firms Differ, and How Does it Matter?, *Strategic Management Journal*, 12, 1991, pp. 61-74.
Nishiguchi, T., *Strategic Industrial Sourcing: The Japanese Advantage*, New York, Oxford: Oxford University Press 1994.
Nishiguchi, T./Anderson, E., Supplier and Buyer Networks, in Bowman, E./Kogut, B. (eds.), *Redesigning the Firm*, New York: Oxford University Press 1995, pp. 65-84.
Nishiguchi, T./Brookfield, J., The Evolution of Japanese Subcontracting, *Sloan Management Review* Fall, 1997, pp 89-101.
Nonaka, I./Takeuchi, H., *The Knowledge-Creating Company: How Japanese Companies Create the Dynamics of Innovation*, New York: Oxford University Press 1995.
Odagiri, H., *Growth Through Competition, Competition Through Growth: Strategic Management and the Economy in Japan*, Oxford: Clarendon Press 1992.

Odaka, K./Ono, K./Adachi, F., *The Automobile Industry in Japan: A Study of Ancillary Firm Development*, Tokyo: Kinokuniya Company and Oxford University Press 1988, pp. 43-67.

Oliver, N./Wilkinson, B., *The Japanization of British Industry*, London: Basil Blackwell 1988.

Oliver, N./Wilkinson, B., *The Japanization of British Industry: New Developments in the 1990s*, Oxford: Blackwell 1992.

Peteraf, M. A., The Cornerstones of Competitive Advantage: A Resource-Based View, *Strategic Management Journal*, 14, 1993, pp. 179-191.

Polanyi, M., *Personal Knowledge: Towards a Post-critical Philosophy*, Chicago: University Press 1962.

Polanyi, M., *The Tacit Dimension*, New York: Anchor Day 1966.

Richardson, J., Parallel Sourcing and Supplier Performance in the Japanese Automobile Industry, *Strategic Management Journal*, 14, 1993, pp. 339-350.

Roehl, T., A Comparison of US-Japanese Firms' Parts-Supply Systems: What Besides Nationality Matters?, in Hayashi, K. (ed.), *The US – Japanese Economic Relationship: Can It be Improved?*, New York: New York University Press 1989, pp. 127-154.

Sako, M., *Prices, Quality and Trust: Inter-Firm Relations in Britain and Japan*, Cambridge: Cambridge University Press 1992.

Sako, M./Lamming, R./Helper, S. R., Supplier Relations in the Multinational Automotive Industry, in Mudambi, R./Ricketts, M. (eds.), *The Organisation of the Firm: International Business Perspectives*, London: Routledge 1998, pp. 178-194.

Scott, A. J., Regional Motors of the Global Economy, *Futures*, 28, 1996, pp. 391-411.

Siegal, S./Castellan, J., *Nonparametric Statistics for the Behavioural Sciences*, New York: McGraw-Hill 1988.

Spender, J. C., Making Knowledge the Basis of a Dynamic Theory of the Firm, *Strategic Management Journal*, 17, 1996, pp. 45-62.

Taylor, J., An Analysis of the Factors Determining the Geographical Distribution of Japanese Manufacturing in the UK, 1984-91, *Urban Studies*, 30, 7, 1993, pp. 1209-1224.

Teece, D. J., A Behavioural Analysis of OPEC: An Economic and Political Synthesis, *Journal of Business Administration*, 13, 1982, 127-160.

Teece, D. J., Transaction Cost Economics and the Multinational Enterprise, *Journal of Economics Behaviour and Organization*, 7, 1986, pp. 21-45.

Teece, D. J./Pisano, G./Shuen, A., Dynamic Capabilities and Strategic Management, *Strategic Management Journal*, 18, 1997, pp. 509-533.

Weigand, R., It Pays to Know Your Way Through the Government Maze of Give-Backs, Grants, Tax Holidays and Subsidies, *Harvard Business Review*, 61, 1983, pp. 146-152.

Wheeler, D./Mody, A., International Investment Location Decisions: The Case of U.S. Firms, *The Journal of International Economics*, 33, 1992, pp. 57-76.

Who Owns Whom? Volume 1 Australasia & the Far East, Bucks: Dun & Bradstreet Ltd 1997.

Williamson, O., *The Economic Institutions of Capitalism: Firms, Markets, Relational Contracting*, New York: Free Press 1985.

Winter, S. G., Knowledge and Competence as Strategic Assets, in Teece. D. (ed.), *The Competitive Challenge*, Cambridge, MA: Ballinger 1987, pp. 159-184.

Mannsoo Shin

Convergence and Divergence of Work Values among Chinese, Indonesian, and Korean Employees[1]

Abstract

- This study analyzes the cross-national comparison of work values among employees in China, Indonesia, and Korea.

- First, this research compares various levels of organizational commitment of workers in the three countries, and tries to explain why there are differences or similarities in commitment level.

- Second, this paper seeks to identify the key variables affecting the level of commitment. It also analyzes to what extent various relationships between predictors and commitment are consistent across the three Asian countries. This issue is related to identifying specific measures or conditions where commitment can be developed.

- This paper also discusses the influence of cultural work values on level of commitment. Using Hofstede's work value items, this paper tries to identify and document which work values are converging, and which values are diverging among the three countries.

Key Results

- Results of the initial regression analysis indicated that there was an explicit relationship between employees' organizational commitment and several predictors such as formalization, centralization, skill variety, and task autonomy. A subsequent inclusion of Hofstede's 20 cultural work value items in the multiple regression analyses revealed evidence for both convergence and divergence trends. These results provide some basis for both standardized and differentiated international human resource management practices among the three countries.

Author

Mannsoo Shin, Professor of International Business, Korea University Business School, Seoul, Korea.

Introduction

This study analyzes the relationship between organizational commitment and individual work values of Chinese, Indonesian and Korean workers. Given the rapid globalization trend in Asia by multinational corporations (MNCs), much research is needed that focuses on cross-cultural values in Asian countries. This research could provide important insights to international human resource managers in designing better management strategies. Asian countries such as China, Indonesia, and Korea will likely continue to be important global manufacturing sites for MNCs in the years ahead. In fact, a majority of the worldwide manufacturing labor force is already located in Asia. Yet in the international human resource management literature, until now there has been a lack of research that studies job related values of Asian workers. Within the existing literature, one of the central debates is over the extent to which an MNC's overall human resource management system should be standardized, and over the extent to which local management practices should be adopted in managing organizational units in different countries (England 1975, Kelley et al. 1981, Hofstede 1984, Adler 1986, Ralston et al. 1992, Triandis 1995). The answer to this question may depend on to what extent work values and attitudes of the workers in different countries are similar or dissimilar, and to what extent those diverse configurations of value systems actually affect managerial attitudes and behaviors such as organizational commitment. Given the importance of the outcome of that debate, this paper aims to study the issue using survey data from ten manufacturing organizations in China, Indonesia and Korea.

First, this research seeks to compare various levels of organizational commitment of workers in those three countries. In addition, it tries to explain why there are differences or similarities in commitment level. Although each of the three countries is located in Asia, each individual country may be unique in some of its sociocultural as well as economic characteristics. Second, this paper seeks to identify the key variables affecting the level of commitment. Third, it also analyzes to what extent various relationships between predictors and commitment are consistent across the three Asian countries, and to what extent these relationships are consistent with existing commitment literature. This issue is related to identifying specific measures or conditions where commitment can be developed. To answer those questions, this paper first examines various variables determining organizational commitment of workers including nationality, demographic, organizational, and task variables that have been widely investigated in the literature. The second stage of analysis focuses on the influence of cultural work values on commitment. Using Hofstede's (1994) 20 work value items, this paper tries to identify and document which work values are converging, and which values are diverging among the three countries. This will provide some basis for discussion on standardization versus localization issues of international human resource management. These findings will also identify which specific measures would be appropriate to motivate local labor forces. For example, which would Chinese workers prefer: a participative management style or a directed management style? How important is it to be promoted to higher jobs or to have a good relationship with a direct supervisor for Asian workers? Would a competition based pay structure work? Results on cross-cultural analysis will provide clues to these intriguing questions.

Literature Review

The Concept of Organizational Commitment

Commitment has been identified as an important variable in understanding the work behavior of employees in organizations. In their early work, Porter at al. (1974) explained that organizational commitment consists of an individual's (1) belief in and acceptance of organizational goals and values (Identification), (2) willingness to exert effort toward organizational goal accomplishment (Involvement), and (3) strong desire to maintain organizational membership (Loyalty). Their 15 item research instrument has been popularly used, although there have been debates on the discriminant validity among the three subcomponents (Morrow 1983, Reichers 1985). It has also been argued that Porter's definition of commitment basically covers only an individual's psychological attachment to the organization. In fact, people can also be committed to the company mainly because of the social and economic investment made (side bets) in the form of pensions or seniority. This 'side bets' approach views commitment as an outcome of the perceived costs of leaving rather than as a favorable feeling toward the company. In addition, the individual can choose to remain in an organization simply because of a lack of alternative job opportunities. This may be particularly common in times of recession when there is high unemployment.

Incorporating the above side bets view, Allen and Meyer's (1990) definition of commitment consists of three parts: (1) affective, (2) continuance (or calculative), and (3) normative aspects of organizational commitment. They argue that the affective component of organizational commitment refers to the employee's emotional attachment to, identification with, and involvement in the organization. The continuance commitment items in their measure can actually consist of two parts: costs or sacrifices that the employee associates with leaving the organization, and lack of job alternatives. The normative component in turn refers to the employee's feeling of obligation to remain with the organization.

Commitment Research on Asian Countries

A review of the literature reveals that there is a lack of research on organizational commitment in foreign countries. Among a few cross-cultural research studies on organizational commitment, one popularly held determinant of organizational commitment is the employee's nationality (Luthans et al.1985, Agarwal/ Ramaswami 1993, Randall 1993, Sommer et al. 1996). Most of the few commitment studies on Asian countries published in English journals tend to concentrate on Japan, Korea, Singapore, and Hong Kong (Marsh/Mannari 1977, Luthans et al. 1985, Lincoln/Kalleberg 1985, Near 1989, Putti et al. 1989, Sommer et al. 1996). Most studies used the commitment concept from Porter's Organizational Commitment Questionnaire (OCQ 1974) or used the Cook and Wall instrument (1980) that focuses on the affective aspect of commitment. Reliabilities for OCQ range from 0.76 to 0.94, which is an acceptable range (Randall 1993). The levels of commitment of Asian employees reported in the literature were 3.21 (Luthans et al. 1985) and 3.13 (Lincoln/Kalleberg 1985) for Japan, and 3.29 (Luthans et al. 1985) and 3.42 (Sommer et. al. 1996) for Korea, on a 1 to 5 likert scale.

Although Japanese and Korean workers were found to have lower commitment levels than their US counterparts [3.34 in Lincoln and Kalleberg's (1985) study or 3.61 in Luthans et al.'s (1985) study], Japanese and Korean workers are generally perceived by westerners both to be highly committed to their work and their company, and to have a strong work ethic. This high level of commitment was also believed to be one of the key success factors for rapid economic development. In contrast, Southeast Asian and Chinese workers are portrayed as being relatively less loyal to their company, and as having an unpredictable motivation level. Sometimes they are described as being constant job hoppers and as not being sufficiently capable (Lasserre/Schutte 1995). The quality of Chinese workers is generally perceived as unsatisfactory, although the labor shortage became problematic in burgeoning coastal areas (Chen/Jin 1991).

Antecedents to commitment that were previously studied among Asian employees also include organizational structure, job characteristics, and demographics, as in the studies for western workers. Marsh and Mannari (1977) argued that the variables related to commitment were universal rather than culture-specific for Japanese and US workers. Luthans et al. (1985) concluded that two demographic variables, age and tenure, were consistently determining variables for commitment for Japanese, Korean, and US samples. Near (1989), however, argued that although social interaction, fairness, and job content were universally affecting commitment for Japanese and US workers, freedom on the job (for Americans), and age (for Japanese) were found to be culture specific. Therefore, more research is needed to determine which variables associated with commitment are universally valid or otherwise culture-specific (Redding et al. 1994).

Research Questions

To accomplish the goals of this study, the following research questions were formulated. First, what is the relationship between predictors including nationality and the organizational commitment composites and factors? Second, to what extent are organizational and task variables universal in explaining organizational commitment? If found to be universal, the implication would be that western management techniques could be effective management tools even in the Asian context. Third, what are the differences and similarities in employees' responses for work value items and for the organizational commitment among Chinese, Indonesian, and Korean workers? How would those work value variables influence a universally significant role across the three countries or a unique role to a particular country in predicting commitment? The results lead to a discussion on whether cultural adaptation or standardization of the management system is appropriate in terms of international human resource management.

Samples and Measure

Samples and Demographics

China and Indonesia have been among the most important host countries to MNCs investing in Asia. Their great market potential, relatively cheap labor cost, and well endowed natural resources have been reasons for MNCs to set up large-scale manufacturing operations in this region. In both China and Indonesia, there are about 6,000 manufacturing operations by Korean companies in various industrial sectors ranging from garments and textiles to electronics and, recently, automobiles. One of the major concerns in managing a manufacturing subsidiary is over how to deal effectively with the local labor force. Less committed workers would show low morale and high absenteeism and turnover, which together lead to low factory productivity. In contrast, highly committed workers would work harder, would be willing to take on more responsibility, and would be willing to participate voluntarily in company events, together leading to higher productivity.

All respondents are blue-collar workers coming from 10 manufacturing organizations: four in China, four in Indonesia, and two in Korea. The Chinese and Indonesian firms are subsidiaries of the Korean firms. All the manufacturing sites represent major investments by large Korean-based multinational firms in the electronics, textiles, and food industries. The manufacturing sites averaged

$100 million in annual sales, and the sites had an average of 846 employees. The actual sample was composed of 459 Indonesians, 126 Chinese, and 221 Korean employees of those 10 companies. The average ages of Indonesian, Chinese, and Korean samples were 26.5, 23.7, and 25.0, respectively, which suggests that the sample tends to represent the relatively young manufacturing labor force. The average tenure for Indonesian and Korean workers was four years and five months, whereas the average tenure for Chinese workers was only two years and five months.

Research Instruments

Questions were asked concerning the organizational commitment variables, other organizational variables, and task variables. The respondents were also asked to provide demographic information such as sex, age, tenure with organization, and years of education. The instruments used for this study were Allen and Meyer's (1990) Organizational Commitment Instrument, Pugh et al.'s (1968) Organizational Structure Measure, and Hackman and Oldham's (1974) Job Diagnostic Survey Measure. Allen and Meyer's measure was selected for this study because it is one of the most widely used measures and has achieved acceptable levels of validity and reliability (Hackett et al. 1994, Dunham et al. 1994).

All the commitment scores were measured on a 1 to 7 likert scale. Organizational structure variables focused on formalization and centralization, and the variables were measured with five items and two items, respectively (Pugh et al. 1968). Each item was measured using a 1 (very inaccurate) to 5 (very accurate) likert scale. Five job characteristic variables were based on Hackman and Oldham's (1974) Job Diagnostic Survey. They are skill variety, task identity, task significance, autonomy, and feedback from the supervisor. Demographic variables included in the survey were gender, age, years of education, and tenure with the current employer. To further examine the national differences in commitment level, Hofstede's (1994) cultural measure was used in the subsequent multiple regression analysis. The instrument consists of twenty items that cover the individual work value system. The survey consists of three parts. The first eight questions ask the respondent to evaluate the importance of each factor in thinking of an ideal job rather than the current job. The second part asks employees the importance of various attributes in their private life. The remaining six questions measure the level of agreement for various managerial issues including competition, organizational structure, and rule observance. All the questions were evaluated using a 1 (of utmost importance, or strongly agree) to 5 (of little importance or strongly disagree) likert scale.

Translation of the English version of the questionnaire into Chinese, Indonesian and Korean was conducted by professional translators to ensure cross cultural consistency and equivalence in connotations of the questionnaire items. The translated local versions were later checked using a back-translation method by other professional persons who were fluent in both English and the local languages, followed by a back-translation of the instruments. Finally, the back translation versions were compared with the original English instrument.

Findings

Internal Reliability and Factor Structure of Organizational Commitment

The internal consistency of the scale was tested using the Cronbach alpha coefficient. The Cronbach alphas obtained for the Allen and Meyer's 24 items using the entire sample were 0.74. For each construct, relatively low but acceptable internal consistency levels were found for the affective (0.63) and continuance (0.70) factors. But the Cronbach alpha value for the normative component was too low (0.26) to conduct further meaningful analysis. The alpha value for the normative component was not changed much even if one or two items were eliminated. From the results of a varimax rotated factor analysis, two factors of commitment clearly emerged. The first factor was labeled affective commitment, and the second factor, continuance commitment. Items for which factor scores were at least 0.4 were selected in the analysis. Factor loadings for all the items except items 4, 9, 12 have at least 0.4. Thus the affective commitment factor contains seven items out of the original eight items, and the continuance commitment factor contains six items. Internal consistency for formalization was also acceptable (0.67). The reliabilities for the five dimensions of Hofstede's instrument were also checked. Alpha levels for five dimensions ranged from 0.20 to 0.62, which generally indicates poor internal consistencies: 0.51 for individualism, 0.33 for power distance, 0.23 for masculinity, 0.20 for uncertainty avoidance, and 0.62 for long-term orientation. The alpha levels did not change much even if one or two items were excluded. Also the alpha levels did not improve even at the national level analysis. Therefore, the five-dimensional level analysis Hofstede originally proposed may not be meaningful for the sample. Given the situation, an alternative method for analysis would be individual item level analysis. The item level analysis would not allow one to directly compare the results with the existing literature, which is based on Hofstede's traditional four (or five, if long-term orientation was included) dichotomy cultural model. However, Hofstede's twenty items still represent a broad spectrum of work related values, and thus those items may still be relevant to Asian workers, although the reliabilities for the five dimensions are low.

Table 1. A Comparison of Organizational Commitment by Nationality

Item	Indonesia (N = 459)		China (N = 126)		Korea (N = 221)		F value, sig
	Mean	Std	Mean	Std	Mean	Std	
Affective Commitment (AC)							
• AC1: spend the rest of my career	5.08[b]	0.79	5.18	0.89	4.12	0.76	113.5, 0.0001
• AC2: enjoy discussing my company outside	4.36[a, b]	1.60	4.73[a]	1.59	3.99	1.43	9.5, 0.0001
• AC3: feel that company's problems are my own	4.91[b]	1.53	4.64[a]	1.61	3.79	1.52	38.3, 0.0001
• AC5R: do not feel like 'part of the family'	5.58[b]	1.15	5.65[a]	1.26	4.26	1.27	98.7, 0.0001
• AC6R: do not feel 'emotionally attached'	5.62[a, b]	1.39	5.98[a]	1.39	4.09	1.46	107.0, 0.0001
• AC7: company has a great deal of meaning	4.34[a, b]	1.81	5.35[a]	1.58	3.81	1.28	34.1, 0.0001
• AC8R: do not feel a strong sense of belonging	5.71[a, b]	1.12	4.73	1.68	4.42	1.37	83.3, 0.0001
	5.13[b]	1.61	5.29[a]	1.44	4.37	1.42	22.3, 0.0001
Continuance Commitment (CC)							
• CC2: hard to leave company even if I wanted to	4.63[a, b]	0.89	3.15[c]	0.89	4.27	0.84	128.4, 0.0001
• CC3: too much disrupted if I decided to leave	4.87[a]	1.55	3.13[c]	1.92	4.75	1.55	58.6, 0.0001
• CC5: staying is matter of necessity	3.70[a, b]	1.76	3.08[c]	1.80	4.33	1.64	21.5, 0.0001
• CC6: have too few options to consider leaving	5.63[a, b]	1.11	2.58[c]	1.80	4.36	1.52	267.5, 0.0001
• CC7: one consequence of leaving is the scarcity of alternatives	4.46[a, b]	1.55	3.85	1.96	3.70	1.36	19.9, 0.0001
• CC8: leaving requires personal sacrifice	4.47[a]	1.62	3.43[c]	1.47	4.23	1.36	21.8, 0.0001
	4.71[a, b]	1.57	3.06[c]	1.75	4.23	1.34	56.3, 0.0001
Overall Organizational Commitment (OC)	4.85[a, b]	0.68	4.20	0.52	4.20	0.67	84.9, 0.0001
Age	26.5[a, b]	6.3	23.7	6.2	25.0	5.6	11.4, 0.0001
Years of Education	7.3[a, b]	2.7	11.7	2.3	12.2	0.8	429.8, 0.0001
Tenure (month)	52.5[a]	60.7	28.7[c]	54.4	52.5	48.6	9.3, 0.0001

[a] Tukey HSD Test, sig dif (p < 0.05) between Indonesian and Chinese workers
[b] Tukey HSD Test, sig dif (p < 0.05) between Indonesian and Korean workers
[c] Tukey HSD Test, sig dif (p < 0.05) between Chinese and Korean workers

A Comparison of Commitment Among Three Nations

The affective commitment (AC) and continuance commitment (CC) levels were determined by computing the mean of all the items included in each factor. Overall commitment scores were the means of both AC and CC. Table 1 summarizes the detailed analysis of the organizational commitment of workers in each country. Quite surprisingly, Chinese workers show the highest level of affective commitment (5.18), followed by Indonesian (5.08) and Korean workers (4.12). For all the seven items except AC7, Chinese and Indonesian workers' responses are statistically higher than those of Korean workers.

These results indicate that both Chinese and Indonesian workers are more emotionally attached to their organization, and that they believe that their company's problems are their own. This finding may differ from the prior perception of managers who stated that workers in the head office are likely to be more loyal than the local labor force in China and Indonesia. Generally, workers at the head office would seem more likely to identify with company goals and objectives because the socialization process takes place more frequently and quickly. This study shows, however, that both Chinese and Indonesian workers are emotionally attached to their company, that they prefer a paternalistic work environment, and that various morale boosting programs such as in-house sports events and social get-togethers may be effective tools for motivating these workers to get involved in their work.

Even in the continuance commitment aspect, Indonesian workers show a higher level of commitment than Korean workers. They feel that they do not have comparable job alternatives. If they decide to quit their job, they may have to endure serious hardship. Indonesian workers say that they would like to maintain their current employment in part out of necessity, and as a result, Indonesian workers may be more sensitive to higher wages and better fringe benefits. Extrinsic awards, also, could be more effective tools for motivating Indonesian workers than for motivating their Chinese or Korean counterparts.

Another interesting finding is the relatively low level of continuance commitment among the Chinese workers. This result implies that they may not be worried much even if they lose their current job. Perhaps this finding may be related to the socio-political characteristics of China. In a socialist country like China, people are not usually worried about losing jobs because they believe that the government is supposed to provide jobs until the age of retirement. Another possible explanation may be the labor market conditions in Tienjin where three of the Chinese manufacturing subsidiaries in the sample are located. Since many foreign companies are rushing into these areas, local workers may be able to easily switch jobs should they so desire.

National Comparison of the Relationship Between Commitment and Determinants

Table 2 shows the intercorrelation matrix among independent variables for the sample Asian workers. Probably because of the wide range of job-related value items covered and the large number of the sample (n = 806), a large proportion of the 190 correlations shown were statistically significant. However, the correlations among Hofstede's 20 items are not generally strong. Also it is quite evident that they are rather small in magnitude. The average for 190 correlations is 0.12. The highest correlation observed is 0.47 between V10 (thrift) and V11 (persistence), both of which are related to the long-term orientation dimension. The lowest is –0.10 between V2 (physical working conditions) and V19 (rule orientation). Also, V6 (consulted by direct supervisor) and V7 (advancement for higher job levels) show a high level of association (0.40). In addition, there are modest correlations found between V3 (good relations with direct superior) and V4 (job security), V5 (work with people who cooperate well) and V6 (consulted by direct supervisor). Despite several modest correlations, all twenty items were first simultaneously included in the multiple regression analysis, and the VIF (variance inflation factors) were checked for possible multicolinearity. Most VIF values were between 1 and 2. However, there was a multicolinearity effect detected between age and tenure for both Chinese and Korean samples. Since age and tenure are supposed to be correlated, it is not a major concern for further analysis.

A series of multiple regression analyses were conducted to identify key variables determining the organizational commitment of workers. Four demographic variables including sex, age, education, and tenure were included in the analysis. Two organizational variables (formalization and centralization) and five task-related variables were also included.

When excluding work value variables, R^2 for AC for Indonesia, China and Korea were 0.21, 0.37, and 0.29, respectively. However, R^2 for CC (0.10, 0.19, and 0.12) were substantially lower than in AC. Table 3 also shows that there are other significant relationships between organizational commitment and antecedents. Formalization has a strong positive relationship, and centralization also has a moderate relationship with commitment. This result shows a good contrast to many research findings in western countries where both formalization and centralization are normally negatively associated with commitment.

Cross-cultural Comparison of Work Values

Table 3 reports the results of multiple regression that was performed within each country and across the entire sample to explain the relationship between work-

Table 2. Intercorrelation among Variables

Variable	Mean	SD																														
HOFS1	3.80	0.94	1.00																													
HOFS2	4.13	0.82	0.34	1.00																												
HOFS3	3.93	0.85	0.21	0.33	1.00																											
HOFS4	4.27	0.82	0.20	0.26	0.34	1.00																										
HOFS5	4.20	0.82	0.22	0.34	0.35	0.30	1.00																									
HOFS6	3.54	0.98	0.30	0.35	0.36	0.34	0.16	1.00																								
HOFS7	3.85	0.94	0.26	0.30	0.30	0.22	0.24	0.32	1.00																							
HOFS8	3.73	0.96	0.04	0.17	0.30	0.22	0.22	0.24	0.40	1.00																						
HOFS9	4.17	0.78	0.16	0.17	0.30	0.30	0.26	0.20	0.30	0.34	1.00																						
HOFS10	3.81	0.80	0.21	0.21	0.23	0.21	0.24	0.29	0.20	0.27	0.30	1.00																					
HOFS11	4.03	0.81	0.19	0.26	0.22	0.13	0.28	0.35	0.28	0.24	0.23	0.29	1.00																				
HOFS12	3.27	0.95	0.13	0.17	0.13	0.13	0.19	0.20	0.13	0.11	0.26	0.24	0.47	1.00																			
HOFS13	3.07	0.92	0.11	0.02	0.02	0.01	0.07	0.10	0.03	-0.00	0.02	0.12	0.33	0.29	1.00																		
HOFS14	3.23	0.99	0.11	0.09	0.01	0.05	0.03	0.07	0.08	-0.00	0.04	-0.01	0.00	0.04	0.03	1.00																	
HOFS15	3.03	1.00	0.05	-0.02	0.10	0.05	0.05	0.09	0.02	0.10	0.07	0.07	0.00	0.00	0.01	0.28	1.00															
HOFS16	2.47	1.11	0.04	-0.10	-0.03	-0.06	-0.09	-0.01	-0.0	-0.00	-0.04	-0.00	-0.01	0.12	0.09	-0.05	-0.00	1.00															
HOFS17	3.41	1.12	0.05	0.02	0.08	0.03	0.09	0.08	0.12	0.18	0.13	0.01	0.07	0.02	0.06	-0.02	0.06	-0.03	0.11	1.00													
HOFS18	2.75	1.09	0.07	0.01	0.04	0.04	0.03	0.11	0.07	0.05	0.01	0.06	0.07	0.02	0.05	0.06	0.03	0.06	0.17	0.06	1.00												
HOFS19	3.18	1.07	0.17	0.15	0.04	0.08	0.13	0.14	0.09	0.01	0.04	0.13	0.09	0.22	0.08	0.04	-0.01	0.05	0.05	0.08	0.12	1.00											
HOFS20	3.28	1.07	0.06	0.03	0.09	0.01	0.05	0.13	0.05	0.18	0.06	0.05	0.07	0.05	0.03	0.03	0.00	0.01	0.05	0.08	0.07	0.17	1.00										
SEX	0.44	0.50	-0.14	-0.04	-0.01	-0.12	-0.08	-0.08	-0.06	0.02	-0.01	-0.03	0.02	-0.07	-0.02	0.04	-0.09	0.01	-0.11	0.03	-0.12	-0.04	1.00									
AGE	25.6	6.17	0.10	-0.03	-0.03	0.01	0.56	0.08	-0.00	-0.01	-0.02	0.01	0.03	0.08	0.04	-0.05	0.16	0.10	0.00	0.14	0.04	-0.44	1.00									
EDU	9.30	3.29	-0.03	-0.15	0.13	-0.08	0.01	0.10	0.05	0.30	0.08	-0.03	0.10	-0.05	0.02	-0.08	0.19	0.13	0.22	0.16	-0.10	0.17	0.10	0.14	1.00							
TENU	48.7	57.2	0.10	0.01	-0.04	-0.01	0.03	-0.02	-0.04	-0.06	0.06	0.05	0.09	0.06	0.05	-0.02	0.10	0.07	0.02	0.03	0.10	0.01	-0.30	0.84	0.07	1.00						
FORM	5.1	0.90	0.14	0.22	0.08	0.12	0.08	0.09	0.08	-0.03	0.06	0.11	0.05	0.09	-0.14	-0.02	0.04	-0.07	-0.09	-0.05	0.15	0.02	-0.08	0.02	-0.29	0.05	1.00					
CENT	4.77	1.17	0.09	0.02	0.13	0.08	0.10	0.19	0.13	0.05	0.05	0.04	0.13	0.07	0.03	0.05	0.07	0.03	0.11	0.05	0.11	0.05	-0.11	0.18	0.04	0.14	0.17	1.00				
JOB1	5.25	1.37	-0.04	-0.01	0.05	0.12	0.02	0.06	0.02	0.03	0.11	0.09	0.02	0.08	-0.08	-0.08	0.15	-0.04	0.01	-0.08	-0.04	-0.00	-0.21	0.11	-0.12	0.05	0.22	0.09	1.00			
JOB2	5.32	1.33	-0.01	0.05	0.05	0.13	0.13	0.02	0.04	0.04	0.00	0.06	0.09	0.02	0.06	-0.03	0.02	0.03	0.05	-0.01	-0.05	-0.12	0.00	-0.01	-0.17	0.04	-0.31	0.03	0.28	1.00		
JOB3	5.10	1.46	0.07	0.02	0.06	0.13	0.13	0.08	0.06	0.05	0.08	0.05	0.04	0.14	-0.03	-0.03	0.06	-0.02	-0.03	-0.06	0.03	0.01	-0.19	0.10	-0.15	0.06	0.22	0.06	0.08	0.38	0.45	1.00	
JOB4	4.52	1.68	0.08	0.01	0.02	0.16	-0.03	0.06	0.06	0.03	0.07	0.14	0.02	0.04	-0.09	-0.12	0.03	0.01	-0.04	-0.01	-0.04	-0.14	0.08	0.03	-0.17	0.04	-0.31	0.10	0.02	0.28	0.25	0.28	1.00
JOB5	5.06	1.41	0.08	0.03	0.02	0.16	0.02	-0.02	0.08	-0.00	0.07	0.09	0.01	0.11	-0.11	-0.09	0.05	0.00	-0.00	-0.13	0.02	0.02	-0.18	0.03	-0.23	-0.02	0.28	-0.02	0.39	0.47	0.36	0.38	1.00

Table 3. Overall Multiple Regression

Explanatory Variables		Indonesia		China		Korea		Total	
		AC	CC	AC	CC	AC	CC	AC	CC
Cultural System (Hofstede Work Value Items)	H1: time for personal/family life								0.10
	H2: physical working conditions		0.14		0.27	0.21	0.20	0.15	0.12
	H3: relationship with direct superior	0.12		0.15				0.08	
	H4: security of employment								
	H5: work with people cooperating well								
	H6: direct superior's consultation							−0.09	
	H7: advancement to higher level jobs	−0.10	−0.17		−0.13			−0.06	−0.09
	H8: variety and adventure in the job								
	H9: personal steadiness and stability		0.16						
	H10: thrift					−0.13			
	H11: persistence (perseverance)								
	H12: respect for tradition	−0.10	−0.16	−0.18	−0.15		0.21	−0.13	0.09
	H13: feeling nervous frequency at work	−0.09			−0.20			−0.05	
	H14: afraid in expressing disagreement			0.29		0.27	0.12	0.08	
	H15: most people can be trusted		0.08		−0.15		0.15	−0.05	
	H16: answering ability to subordinates	0.07					0.10	0.06	
	H17: agreement to two boss structure					−0.08		−0.05	
	H18: competion does more harm than good				0.28				
	H19: company rule should not be broken	0.17	0.13		0.14	0.11		0.08	0.19
	H20: failure in life is their own fault								
Personal Variables	Sex (dummy variable)	0.15							
	Age		−0.05				0.13	0.01	−0.06
	Years of Education	0.00						−0.03	
	Tenure (Number of Years Working)								
Org. Variables	Formalization	0.24	0.17	0.25	0.18	0.09	0.23	0.16	0.18
	Centralization		0.09	−0.12					0.11
Task Variables	Skill Variety	0.14				0.08	0.08	0.12	
	Identity				−0.19	0.11		0.08	−0.04
	Significance			0.13				0.05	
	Autonomy					0.09			
	Feedback		0.05	0.20				0.10	
F value		0.07	6.7	8.6	4.6	13.3	0.08	23.4	20.4
R² (with all the explanatory variables)		11.3	0.17	0.46	0.38	0.46	8.1	0.43	0.24
R² (without cultural variables)		0.28	0.10	0.37	0.19	0.29	0.29	0.35	0.17
		0.21					0.12		

Numbers in the cells represent significant regression coefficients at least $p < 0.1$ level. But all the missing cells mean insignificant coefficients.

ers' value systems and commitment. In this analysis Hofstede's 20 work items and existing variables were treated as the predictor variables and the commitment levels as the dependent variables. The results summarized in Table 3 show that overall, cultural value items were generally good predictors of commitment. The multiple regression analysis including Hofstede's work value items as independent variables showed a substantial improvement in the explanatory power. For example, R^2 values for affective commitment for Indonesia, China, and Korea changed from 0.21, 0.37, and 0.29 to 0.28, 0.46, and 0.46, respectively.

Table 4. A Grouping of Hofstede's 20 Work Value Items

Universal Values	Strong	G1(sig., consistent in all 3 countries, and positive β) <u>V3</u> (relationship with direct superior) G2(sig., consistent in 2 countries, and positive β) <u>V2</u> (I*, K*: physical working conditions) **V15** (C*, K: most people can be trusted) **V19** (I, C: company rules should not be broken) **V20** (C, K: one's failure is one's own fault) G3(sig., consistent in 2 countries, and negative β) <u>V7</u> (I, C: promotion to higher level jobs) **V13** (I, C: feeling nervous at work)
	Weak	G4 (sig., in a total sample only, and positive β) <u>V1</u> (time for personal life) **V4** (job security) G5(sig., in a total sample only, and negative β) <u>V6</u> (direct superior's consultation) **V8** (variety and adventure in job)
Particular Values	Strong	G6 (sig., not consistent in β sign) <u>V12</u> (C−, K+: respect for tradition) **V14** (I−, K+: afraid in expressing disagreement to superiors) **V16** (I+, C−: can be a good manager without having answering abilities)
	Weak	G7(sig., in one country only, and positive β) <u>V9</u> (I: personal steadiness and stability) **V17** (I: avoiding dual reporting) G8(sig., in one country only, and negative β) <u>V10</u> (K: thrift) **V18** (K: competition does more harm than good)
Indeterminate Values		G9 (not sig.) <u>V5</u> (work with people who cooperate well) **V11** (perseverance)

* C: China, I: Indonesia, K: Korea.
Five levels of consistency in beta coefficient sign among the three countries are: highly consistent (if same signs are shown for the three countries), moderately consistent (two countries only), one country only, total sample only (relationship was not significant at the country level, but significant at the aggregate level), and not consistent (coefficient signs are in the opposite directions).
The relationship between a particular work value and commitment can be either significant or not significant. Significant variables can be classified into one of the ten possible groups because there are five levels of consistency, and two sign directions (either + or −). Therefore, the maximum number of groups for classification would be eleven. But the actual results show only nine groups.

On the other hand, some differences were found among the three countries. As in Table 4, the relationship with work value items and commitment can be multiple. The 20 items can be classified into several categories depending on the following three factors: 1) whether each item is statistically significant, 2) level of consistency in beta coefficient signs across the three countries[2], and 3) sign of coefficient. Based on that classification scheme, Hofstede's work value items were grouped as Universal Values, Particular Values, and Indeterminate Values[3].

Discussion

National Differences in Organizational Commitment Level

It is interesting to see that even though all three countries are located in Asia, they show substantially different commitment structures. Indonesian workers are high on both affective (5.08) and continuance (4.63) commitment, and Chinese show a high affective (5.18) but very low continuance (3.15) commitment. In contrast, Korean samples are in the middle range on both (4.12, and 4.27). One interesting puzzle, then, is why current commitment levels for Chinese and Indonesian workers are relatively high, whereas ones for Korean workers are rather low.

First of all, in the Korean sample, the survey participants were not middle-aged white-collar managers but, instead, rather young blue-collar workers with a relatively short job tenure. There is a common tendency for the commitment level to be lower for workers who are at the bottom of the organizational hierarchy.

Casual observers might point to higher Korean productivity per worker in positing that Korean workers would have higher commitment than their Chinese and Indonesian counterparts. However, besides commitment, there are many other factors influencing productivity such as equipment, technical capability, work intensity, and so forth.

Also, one may argue that the Chinese and Indonesian workers do not form a representative sample of workers in each country. On average, the surveyed Indonesian and Chinese workers are better paid and work under better physical conditions than do workers in local firms. All eight sample subsidiaries except one in Indonesia built new plants when they started their operations. The plants have been in operation for an average of just 5.3 years. Given the new factory environment and their own short tenure, Indonesian and Chinese workers might be satisfied with their current jobs and their place of employment.

Another possible explanation for the high commitment level of Chinese and Indonesian workers would be the strict hiring practice adopted by Korean subsidiaries in the sample. Many personnel managers stress the importance of their selective recruitment system. For example, one expatriate executive of a sample subsidiary said:

> Currently there are a dozen Korean technicians sent from the head office to assist local technical staff. But keeping expatriates is very expensive, and we must localize production function as soon as possible. To do this, we need many good skilled technicians in our factory. That is why we are very selective in hiring new workers. We do not normally hire workers who had work experience with our competitors or who had quit jobs many times. A couple of years ago, a few of our workers moved to a newly established Japanese plant in nearby area because they were offered higher pay. But in a couple of months, a couple of workers asked whether they could come back to our factory because I think they had much greater job pressure [there] than here. However, we politely declined their request. I am sure that they know our policy.

Another interesting question regarding Chinese workers is why they have such a low continuance commitment in contrast to their fairly high affective commitment. There may be a few possible explanations for this phenomenon. Perhaps workers in China are less concerned about the loss of jobs because China is a socialist country, where a job is more or less guaranteed by the state. In other words, they know that they would have alternative work opportunities available in case of leaving the current employer. The second explanation would be the characteristics of the labor market in Tienjin where three sample firms are located. Tienjin, as the fourth largest city in China, has been able to attract many foreign manufacturing companies. There are reportedly more than 4,300 foreign firms operating in this area. This presence of numerous foreign subsidiaries may provide ample job opportunities for Chinese workers. Another possible reason for low continuance commitment may be due to the sample bias of the Chinese workers who tend to be younger (mean age is 23.7 years) with significantly shorter tenure (mean tenure, 28.7 months) than their Indonesian (26.5 years, 52.5 months) or Korean (25.0 years, 52.5 months) counterparts. Reichers (1985) argues that commitment may evolve over time. At the early career stage, organizational commitment tends to exist in the form of psychological attachment. But as time passes, emotional attachment may decrease in importance and continuance commitment will emerge because of some structural factors, such as increased pension, seniority and pay increase. Also, as discussed above, the continuance commitment items are not measured accurately with only cost-related items. Inclusion of benefit-related items in the continuance commitment would be recommended in future studies.

If indeed there are substantial differences in commitment among the three Asian countries, a differentiated management approach may be appropriate. First,

Chinese workers can be relatively easily motivated by emotion-related morale boosting programs such as frequent get-togethers, celebration parties for achieving quotas, superiors' attendance at employees' family occasions such as weddings and funerals, company sporting events, encouragement of unity between managers and workers, and so forth. Essentially, Chinese workers would appreciate collegial treatment in a family-like atmosphere. However, incentive systems such as a bonus increase may not prove to be effective, given the low level of continuance (or calculative) commitment (CC5) for Chinese. In the case of Indonesian workers, both holistic and pragmatic approaches in motivating workers would work effectively.

Determinants of Organizational Commitment

The current finding that a more formalized job process would be related to the higher commitment of Asian employees is quite consistent with Sommer et. al.'s (1996) result for Korean employees, and also with Lincoln and Kalleberg's (1985) study on Japan. It appears quite evident that to develop commitment, subsidiaries' management systems in China and Indonesia need to be more streamlined with clear written rules and procedures. Formal job descriptions and manuals need to be developed and actively utilized for day-to-day operations.

Lincoln and Kalleberg's (1985) research indicates that formalization is negatively associated with commitment for US samples, because of increased stress and burden to individuals associated with formalization. The difference in the findings on formalization may be due to cultural factors: Asians in general have a higher uncertainty avoidance tendency than do westerners. However, it may be premature to jump to the conclusion that western workers prefer a less formalized job structure, whereas Asian workers want formalized job roles due to a different cultural orientation.

An alternative argument would be that there are, in fact, many non-cultural institutional differences existing between an Asian organization and a typical western organization. Asian management styles are not systematically developed yet. The difference in formalization may simply reflect the fact that western organizations have sufficient formalization, whereas the Asian subsidiary operations still have a long way to go to reach a comparable formalization level with western firms. To make this argument more convincing, further research that includes comparable western subsidiaries in the sample is required.

There is also a related issue of localization to be considered when Korean overseas subsidiaries choose their level of formalization. Currently, many Korean companies are pressured to localize their subsidiaries' operations mainly through replacing expatriate managers with local staff. However, simply replacing local personnel to reduce operating costs without developing a certain formalized management system may turn up more uncertainties, and thus lead to lower commitment of workers. This may eventually result in low productivity in the long run. To develop a more formalized operation both at home and abroad, Asian multinationals may have to adopt more formal management techniques perhaps from US, Japanese or European firms.

This study shows that a more centralized organizational structure appears to have mixed relationships with higher commitment. At least one thing made clear from the findings is that more research needs to be done to confirm that the delegation of decision-making authority to lower levels in the organization would help to improve commitment for Asian blue-collar workers.

Five job-related variables appear to have a strong positive correlation with commitment across the three countries, and this result is quite consistent with previous studies. Again, as in the case of formalization, various job related programs used in advanced countries might also be transferred to an Asian setting to improve the commitment of workers.

Convergence-Divergence of Work Values

Universally Related Work Values

Universal work values consistently found in sample countries suggest the standardized management approach will be appropriate in international human resource management practices. Specifically, 'having a good relationship with direct superior' (V3) showed a strong and positive association with commitment for all the countries. This means that developing a good working relationship is the most universal attribute in explaining the commitment of Asian workers among the 20 work values. Asian workers feel psychologically secure when they have comfortable relations with their supervisors. This finding is also consistent with the relatively high scores of sample countries in Hofstede's power distance index. For example, in the power distance dimension, Indonesia and Korea were located in the fourth (78) and the third quartile (60), whereas the US is located in the second quartile (40). Perhaps in the case of western workers, other work values may be more closely related to commitment such as time for personal or family life (V1), advancement for higher level jobs (V7), and an element of adventure in the job (V8).

One may argue, however, that the reason for the importance of 'having a good relationship with direct superior' may be due to sample characteristics rather than cultural characteristics. Since Indonesian and Chinese workers are employed by foreign companies, they may have more difficulty in getting acquainted with foreign expatriate managers or local supervisors than workers in local firms due to the existence of a foreign organizational culture in the company. However the findings show that Korean workers also view 'having a good relationship with direct superior' as one of the key determining values of commitment. In fact, the beta coefficient for the Korean sample (0.21) is higher than that of the Indonesian sample (0.12) or the Chinese sample (0.15).

Commitment of Indonesian and Chinese workers is also found to have a consistent and strong relationship with rule orientation (V19). They tend to think that company rules should not be broken even if the employee thinks keeping rules is not in the best interests of the company. In case of China, this may be due to a strong socialist norm that official rules are stubbornly observed. Chinese tend to think that any deviation to group regulations should be brought to disciplinary measures. Strong association of the rule-observing tendency with commitment of Indonesian workers is perhaps related to the long tradition of European colonial influence.

However, the results show that for Korean workers the rule observance variable does not have a significant relationship with commitment. This is an interesting result, given the fact that Korean culture is perceived to be a rather high context culture where there are many implicit rules and peculiarities to follow in conducting business. However, in reality, this inflexible structure of rules in Korea is greatly alleviated by rather flexible processes of rule implementation.

There is a popular Korean expression, *Buk-Gamjung*, which can be literally translated as subjective feeling or expectation of people on how the laws and regulations should be actually applied to each particular case. Koreans tend to believe that whether the rules should be harshly or generously applied depends on many contextual factors such as motivations, rank, age, and position of the person in question. This peculiar concept of *Buk-Gamjung* is quite prevalent in every aspect of daily life in Korea. Another explanation for the insignificant relationship between the rule observance tendency and commitment would be related to the characteristic of Korean management style that stresses verbal communication rather than formalized, written communication for fast decision making. Since rule observation is one of the strong determinants of commitment for Indonesian and Chinese workers, the Korean management style should be adapted to the local environment. Perhaps successful local operations may require developing a clear set of rules and regulations.

'Having a good physical working condition' (V2) is found to have a significant relationship with commitment for both Indonesians and Koreans. This indicates that a cleaner and more comfortable factory environment could be a good way to further develop commitment in Indonesian and Korean workers.

'Frequency of feeling nervous at work' (V13) is negatively correlated with commitment, and this relationship is significant for both Indonesian and Chinese workers. Therefore, reducing tension in the workplace would be an effective way to promote commitment. This could be achieved in two ways. The first approach would be to improve the physical working environment. For example, minor changes such as repainting the factory interior wall with bright colors, decorating the wall for special occasions, making a lounge area for rest in the factory, and allowing light music in the workplace may be some ways to alleviate tension. However, the more basic approach to reduce tension would be redesign of the existing workflow to better accommodate local conditions. Even such a small change as adjusting the height of the machine may reduce the work tension of line workers.

Quite surprisingly, the relationship between 'advancement to higher level jobs' (V7) and commitment was significantly negative. This may be the opposite of what is expected in a typical western organization. Perhaps Indonesian and Chinese workers do not value the opportunities for promotion to higher positions at the present time. Considering that they are rather young blue-collar workers in developing countries, major motivations for working might be more tangible things than long-term career opportunities. If the survey were conducted for white-collar employees, the results might have been different. In relation to this finding, one of the expatriate managers interviewed said:

> Many Indonesian workers are just happy for being low-level workers for a long time. Sometimes we would like to identify capable workers and train them to promote to supervisory positions. If promoted, they could earn as much as twice a regular worker makes. However, some local supervisors do not want to take managerial responsibilities. They do not want to be pressured. I guess that they are worried about possible conflicts with other local workers or with expatriate managers of the company.

At the present stage, motivating Indonesian and Chinese workers with promising career opportunities may not be an effective strategy due to their different value orientation. Foreign companies operating in this region need to take care not to overemphasize the opportunities for fast promotion to higher jobs when they recruit blue-collar workers.

'Stability in the private life' (V9) and 'avoiding dual boss structure in the company' (V17) were found to be significant for Indonesian workers. They do not want an abrupt change in their lives and maybe they are happy with what they are now. Indonesian workers do not generally want any conflicts or uncertainties that may arise due to a dual reporting structure in the organization.

'Employment security' (V4) was found to be positively correlated with the affective commitment, and 'time for personal and family life' (V1) was also found to be positively correlated with continuance commitment at the aggregate level. However, 'adventure in a job' (V8) and 'being consulted by direct supervisor' (V6) were negatively correlated. Negative correlation between commitment and 'being consulted by direct supervisor' (V6) again confirms the general tendency of high power distance for Asian workers. This suggests that the participative management style, which is quite popular in many advanced countries, may not be appropriate for Asian factory workers at this stage.

Particularly Related Work Values

'Afraid in expressing disagreement to superiors' (V14), 'respect for tradition' (V12), and 'can be a good manager without having precise answers on the subordinates' job related questions' (V16) have different (either positive or negative) relationships with commitment depending on the country. Perhaps these values are the areas where MNCs need to adapt their management systems differently to each nation. For example, in Indonesia and Korea, a typical manager's role may be perceived to be much broader than just problem solving or decision making. In other words, workers may expect a manager to be also an effective social leader in the work group. However, these inconsistent variables need to be further investigated to confirm international differences.

Measures of Organizational Commitment and Work Values

Several conclusions can be drawn from the results above regarding commitment measure. First, the concept of organizational commitment developed and tested mostly in western countries can be applied to China, Indonesia, and Korea. A varimax rotated factor solution using Allen and Meyer's instrument indicates that the affective and continuance components are measurable.

The internal consistencies, however, both for affective and continuance construct items need to be improved. Also, one item (AC4R) for the affective commitment and three items (CC1R, CC4R, CC6) for the continuance commitment were eliminated after reviewing factor loading scores. Of those four eliminated, three items were reverse coded. This indicates that more effort is required to improve the current instrument, particularly on reverse coded items. In improving the current continuous commitment measure to Asian workers, two other points need to be noted. The current eight items of continuance commitment basically measure the degree of intention to stay in a job based on two evaluations: perceived costs with leaving the company (CC2, CC3, CC4R, CC5, and CC8) and lack of other job alternatives (CC1R, CC6, and CC7). Leaving costs measured in the above items are either personal difficulties expected or accumulated assets in the company (e.g., pension or seniority) to be lost with leaving. However, the items do not really measure one's benefits anticipated with staying in the company. Anticipated benefits may be in the form of technical training to be learned, ongoing experience with advanced management systems, or the possibility of rapidly accumulating some savings. In fact, these are often quite common motivators for working for a company in such developing countries as China and Indonesia. Perhaps the current continuance commitment items could not capture such benefit related motivations, and that might be the reason why Chinese workers show very low continuance commitment scores. Therefore, inclusion of benefit related items in the measure may capture a more accurate continuance commitment level.

Another elaboration on items related to lack of alternatives could be made in the Asian context. The current items (CC1R, CC6, and CC7) measure the availability of alternative jobs assuming that individuals could move to available positions easily if they so desired. Because of some cultural characteristics in the Asian context, however, this may not be true even if jobs are available in the labor market. First, there is a strong possibility that individuals are still binding themselves not to move due to their psychological obligation to remain with the current employer. Unfortunately, the current study could not measure the normative commitment construct, and thus could not investigate this aspect further. Second, if indeed there were a tendency for newly established foreign companies not to hire workers who had histories of job hopping, as seemed to be the case in some Korean subsidiaries in this study, then that may also explain why workers do not switch jobs even if alternative employment is available. Therefore, inclusion of items measuring the degree of cultural or institutional peculiarities existing in the labor market would help one better understand why workers continue to stay at their current organization.

Also, one of the alternative means of redefining the organizational commitment concept comes from the multiple commitments view (Reichers 1985, Randall 1990). Reichers (1985) argued that the organization in the organizational commitment concept should not be viewed as monolithic, that the commitment of individuals is not based on undifferentiated attachment to the organization. It should be viewed rather as a collection of multiple commitments to various groups that comprise the organization. Given the collectivist culture of Asian countries, it would be interesting to study how organizational commitment is different from commitment to small work groups, supervisors, top management or labor unions.

One other issue regarding the validity of the commitment measure in collectivist cultures relates to the current questionnaire format focusing on individual response. In an individualistic culture, this questionnaire format is of course quite appropriate because individuals tend to have clear personal ideas and attitudes on management issues, and also because individuals are expected to reveal their views candidly. This, however, may not be the case in a collectivist culture. It could be argued that workers in a collectivist culture have clearer views of what their work groups share in terms of common beliefs. Also, they may be more likely to respond to survey questions by giving the collectivist view of their work group. Perhaps in future studies a few items could be added in regards to the commitment within a small work group. These items would enable the researcher to look into small group commitment, which may be a more important concept than individual commitment in a collectivist cultural context.

Based on his monumental empirical research, Hofstede (1991) identified five distinctive cultural dimensions that are power distance, individualism (or collectivism), uncertainty avoidance, masculinity (or femininity), and long-term orientation (or Confucian dynamism). However, applying Hofstede's five cultural constructs in the current sample appears to be problematic. Reliabilities ranged from 0.20 (uncertainty avoidance) to 0.51 (individualism). The greatest strength of his model is that it provides a simple tool of comparing the dynamic structure of various cultures. However, critics of the model argue that the sample employees in IBM who participated in Hofstede's study were not representative samples of each country, and that the research results may be biased. This is particularly so in most developing countries. Out of 53 countries studied, about two thirds were developing countries. Employees in IBM subsidiaries in most developing countries then tended to be far more qualified than average local employees and to be highly western influenced. One example showing clear evidence of a biased result would be the masculinity orientation of the Korean sample. According to Hofstede's index, Korean samples are 41st out of 53 countries, which suggests that they should have a highly feminine cultural orientation. On the contrary, Korean employees tend to have a highly male oriented culture, and Korean companies usually put a heavy emphasis on tangible output such as productivity and growth. Another criticism of the Hofstede model relates to possible cultural change since the study was initially conducted more than a couple of decades ago. Many social, economic, ideological, economic, and technological changes have taken place since then. All these environmental changes may influence the cultural orientation of workers to varying degrees. Therefore, one should be cautious in interpreting Hofstede's model today, particularly in developing countries.

As in the data analysis section above, an alternative approach to using Hofstede's cultural model would be item level analysis rather than dimensional analysis. Much existing cross cultural research using Hofstede's five culture dimensions in interpreting the results assumes that culture is stable and common among many subgroups in a nation. Besides, Hofstede's cultural dimension map does not allow either subgroup or individual level analysis which many organizational behavior researchers are interested in. However, with item level analysis using Hofstede's framework researchers could capture more specific psychographics of sample workers, and still make some references to Hofstede's five dimensions.

Conclusion

To investigate further the meaning of national differences, Hofstede's cultural work values were used in the analysis replacing the nationality variables. There was a strong relationship found between cultural work value systems and organizational commitment. The nature of this relationship, however, varied by country, and for the commitment factors. Several points need to be noted.

Having a good relationship to a direct superior was found to be a universally determining variable of commitment. This implies that Asian workers are highly relation-oriented. Asian workers generally value the intimate interpersonal relationship to superiors. Asian countries have been experiencing rapid industrialization. Yet it is believed that many of the traditional core values and beliefs remain intact. Traditionally Chinese and Korean cultures have been heavily influenced by Confucian ideologies that emphasize the importance of obligation toward family members: parents, husband and wife, and siblings. Also Indonesian subordinates tend to have a very passive role toward their superiors. MNCs should make efforts to develop measures to improve the subordinate-supervisor relationship. However, frequency of feeling nervous at work is negatively correlated with commitment, for both Indonesian and Chinese workers. Therefore, various tension reducing measures need to be developed to promote commitment.

There are some areas found where different human resource management approaches are required depending on the country. In general, workers in each country tend to have different attitudes on communication patterns with supervisors, attitudes on innovation and new change, and qualifications on effective supervisors. Perhaps those issues require further studies to develop appropriate international human resource management strategies.

This study has some limitations. Further studies are required to test whether the findings based on surveys in these eight Korean subsidiaries and two head offices are generalizable. It would be ideal to extend the study to include comparable local companies in the same industry and in the same geographic area. Since the current sample of workers is young (with an average of 3.5 years of tenure), perhaps older workers with longer job tenure should be included in future studies. The relationship, also, between organizational commitment and outcome variables such as productivity or worker satisfaction should be investigated.

Acknowlegement

1 Funding for this research was provided by SK Research Grant.

References

Adler, N. J., Cross-Cultural Management Research: The Ostrich and the Trend, *Academy of Management Review*, 8, 1986, pp. 226-232.
Agarwal, S./Ramaswami, S. N., Affective Organizational Commitment of Salespeople: An Expanded Model, *Journal of Personal Selling and Sales Management*, 13, 1993, pp. 49-70.
Allen, N. J./Meyer, J. P., The Measurement and Antecedents of Affective, Continuance and Normative Commitment to the Organization, *Journal of Occupational Psychology*, 63, 1990, pp. 1-18.
Chen, P./Jin, P., Managing Human Resources in China, in Putti, J. M. (ed.), *Management: Asian Context*, Singapore: McGraw-Hill 1991.
Cook, J./Wall, T. D., New Work Attitude Measures of Trust, Organizational Commitment and Personal Need Non-fulfilment, *Journal of Occupational Psychology*, 36, 1980, pp. 1140-1157.
Dunham, R. B./Grube, J. A./Castaneda, M. B., Organizational Commitment: The Utility of Integrative Definition, *Journal of Applied Psychology*, 79, 1994, pp. 370-380.
England, G. W., *The Manager and His Values*, Cambridge, MA: Ballinger 1975.
Hackett, R. D./Bycio, P./Hausdorf, P. A., Further Assessments of Meyer and Allen's (1991) Three-Component Model of Organizational Commitment, *Journal of Applied Psychology*, 79, 1, 1994, pp. 15-23.
Hackman, J. R./Oldham, G. R., The Job Diagnostic Survey: An Instrument for the Diagnosis of Jobs and the Evaluation of Job Redesign Projects, *JSAS Catalog of Selected Documents in Psychology*, 4, 1974, pp. 148.
Hofstede, G., Cultural Dimensions in Management and Planning, *Asian Pacific Journal of Management*, 1, 2, 1984, pp. 81-89.
Hofstede, G., *Cultures and Organizations: Software of the Mind*, London: McGraw-Hill 1991.
Hofstede, G., *Value Survey Module 1994 Manual*, The Netherlands: Institute for Research on Intercultural Cooperation, University of Limburg 1994.
Kelley, L./Worthley, R., The Role of Culture in Comparative Management: A Cross-Cultural Perspective, *Academy of Management Journal*, 24, 1981, pp. 164-173.
Lasserre, P./Schutte, H., *Strategies for Asia Pacific*, London: MacMillan Business 1995.
Lincoln, J. R./Kalleberg, A. L., Work Organization and Workforce Commitment: A Study of Plants and Employees in the US and Japan, *American Sociological Review*, 27, 1, 1985, pp. 738-760.
Luthans, F./McCaul, H. S./Dodd, N. G., Organizational Commitment: A Comparison of American, Japanese, and Korean Employees, *Academy of Management Journal*, 28, 1985, pp. 213-219.
Marsh, R. M./Mannari, H., Organizational Commitment and Turnover: A Predictive Study, *Administrative Science Quarterly*, 22, 1977, pp. 57-75.
Morrow, P. C., Concept Redundancy in Organizational Research: The Case of Work Commitment, *Academy of Management Review*, 8, 1983, pp. 486-500.
Near, J. P., Organizational Commitment among Japanese and US Workers, *Organizational Studies*, 10, 1989, pp. 281-300.
Porter, L. W./Steers, R./Mowday, R. T./Boullan, P. V., Unit Performance, Situational Factors, and Employee Attitudes in Spacially Separated Work Units, *Organizational Behavior and Human Performance*, 15, 1974, pp. 87-98.
Pugh, D. S./Hickson, D. J./Hining, C. R./Turner, C., Dimensions of Organizational Structure, *Administrative Science Quarterly*, 13, 1968, pp. 65-105.
Putti, J. M./Aryee, S./Liang, T. K., Work Values and Organizational Commitment: A Study in the Asian Context, *Human Relations*, 42, 1989, pp. 57-288.
Ralston, D. A./Gustafson, D. J./Elsass, P. M./Cheung, F./Terpstra, R. H., Eastern Values: A Comparison of Managers in the United States, Hong Kong, and the People's Republic of China, *Journal of Applied Psychology*, 77, 5, 1992, pp. 664-671.
Randall, D. M., The Consequences of Organizational Commitment: Methodological Investigation, *Journal of Organizational Behavior*, 11, 1990, pp. 361-378.
Randall, D. M., Cross Cultural Research on Organizational Commitment: A Review and Application of Hofstede's Value Survey Module, *Journal of Business Research*, 26, 1993, pp. 91-110.

Redding, S. G./Norman, A./Schlander, A., The Nature of Individual Attachment to the Organization: A Review of East Asian Variations, in Triandis, H. C./Dunnette, M. D./Hough, L. M. (eds), *Handbook of Industrial & Organizational Psychology*, second edition, 4, Palo Alto, G: Consulting Psychologists Press 1994, pp. 647-688.
Reichers, A. E., A Review and Reconceptualization of Organizational Commitment, *Academy of Management Review*, 10, 1985, pp. 465-476.
Sommer, S. M./Bae, S./Luthans, F., Organizational Commitment across Culture: The Impact of Antecedents on Korean Employees, *Human Relations*, 49, 1996, pp. 977-993.
Triandis, H. C., *Individualism and Collectivism*, Boulder, Colorado: Westview Press 1995.

mir *Edition*

Carsten Röh

IuK-Technik und internationale Unternehmensführung

Kommunikation – Koordination – Konfiguration

2004, XVII, 326 pages, pb., € 59,90 (approx. US $ 59,90)
ISBN 3-409-12552-3

Information technology and particularly the internet is at the centre of the current technology debate. It offers a large potential for business applications, especially in an international context.

This work focuses on and analyses new aspects of IT looking at its impacts on communication, coordination and configuration aspects of international management.

Target groups are students and teachers of business administration, especially in the fields of organisation and international management, scientists of international management and managers.

Betriebswirtschaftlicher Verlag Dr. Th. Gabler GmbH, Abraham-Lincoln-Str. 46, 65189 Wiesbaden

Management
International Review
© Gabler Verlag 2004

William T. Stanbury/Ilan B. Vertinsky

Economics, Demography and Cultural Implications of Globalization: The Canadian Paradox[1]

Abstract

- In this paper we explore the effects of globalization on Canada's economy and on the political and cultural identities of Canadians.

- We begin the paper with a description of the economic, technological and social forces which lead to global integration (or "globalization") and the removal or reduction of barriers erected by borders. We examine the extent to which these forces have influenced the economy of Canada in the last two decades and its interactions with the rest of the world. In particular, we investigate whether "globalization" is manifested by changes in the locus of control and/or extension of the geographical horizons of Canadian economic agents. We conclude that, while the foreign trade component in Canada's GDP has increased significantly, much of the integration process has been regional, not global.

- The degree of regional integration is especially pronounced in the sector of cultural products where US exports overwhelm Canadian consumption. This is a source of concern for Canadian politicians who fear that Canada is losing its distinct cultural identity. The response to this perceived threat was a complex regime of regulations and subsidies aimed at protecting domestic production of cultural goods and services. These measures, however, had a very limited impact. While production has shifted to an extent from the US to Canada and the gap in exports/imports of cultural products has declined, the contents of the products continue to reflect the tastes of the bigger US market.

Key Results

- The paper points out that despite of the overwhelming flow of American cultural products Canada remained distinct in the dimensions of culture that matter most. Paradoxically the major factor that helped create and preserve the distinct character of Canadian culture was the "globalization" of its population through immigration. New immigration rules in 1962 and 1967 combined with a policy of multiculturalism announced in 1971 helped to create a distinct dynamic identity for Canada which has resisted the forces of globalization and Americanization.

Authors

William T. Stanbury, Professor Emeritus and former UPS Professor of Regulation and Competition Policy, Faculty of Commerce and Business Administration, The University of British Columbia, Vancouver, BC, Canada.

Ilan B. Vertinsky, Director, Vinod Sood Professor and Senior Fellow at the Centre for International Business Studies, The University of British Columbia, Vancouver, BC, Canada.

William T. Stanbury/Ilan B. Vertinsky

Introduction

"Globalization" can be said to involve several intertwined processes: the intensification of international trade and the movement of capital across borders; denser and more extensive communication networks; and an increasing flow of people (both temporarily and permanently) across borders (Friedman, 1998). The economic dimensions of globalization reflected in the integration of markets and the extension of the geographic horizons of economic agents imply increases in the influence of markets and competition as the primary means of allocating scarce resources. Hence efficiency becomes a prime driver in shaping society. One result is often a reduction in the role and size of governments and relatively less emphasis on distributional equity. Increases in the density and extent of communication networks results in the export and import of cultural products. No doubt, this is largely a matter of business. Yet it also "foretells the contact and interpretation of national cultures at an intensity scarcely conceivable in older, slower epochs" (Jamieson 1998, p. 58). The diffusion of mass media and import of cultural products, largely from the US, is far greater than "anything known in earlier forms of colonization" (Jamieson 1998, p. 56). Add to this the dominance of the English language as the lingua franca in the economic world and "globalization" becomes equated with "Americanization." For a country like Canada with a small population neighboring the US giant, the combination of economic integration and the expectation of even greater inflow of cultural products from the US may appear as threats, not only to national sovereignty, but also to a distinct "national identity."

In this paper, we argue that Canadian governments over the past two decades have accepted (some times reluctantly) the inevitability of North American regional integration as a means of adjusting to the forces of *economic* globalization. In doing so, however, they have attempted to contain (or even reduce) the importance of US-made cultural products sold in Canada by implementing a variety of measures to protect and promote comparable domestic products. These policies have focused on the artifacts of *popular* culture, and they are an extension of policies that had been put in place over the four previous decades or so as new technologies facilitated the inflow of US cultural products. Yet, while these policies have had a modest impact, Canada has a "national culture" that is quite distinctive from that of the US (and other countries) when one looks at the deeper, less ephemeral attributes. Changes in immigration policy made in 1962 and 1967, which encouraged the flow of immigrants from a variety of non-European countries, combined with a policy encouraging cultural diversity or multiculturalism (announced by Prime Minister Trudeau in 1971), have created aspects of a distinctive "Canadian identity." For Canadian nationalists, the crucial point is to be distinct from the United States. This identity is based in part on values that are less responsive to the pressures for standardization and efficiency-seeking, and is reflected in a society that promotes diversity of ethnicity-based cultures and where distributional concerns continue to be of great importance.

The paper begins with an analysis of the effects of economic global integration on Canada. We show that Canada's dependence on international trade has increased significantly in the past two decades more than other countries. Yet much of the integration process has been *regional* (North American), not global. This process of regional integration, however, is not complete. Indeed, in spite of the Free Trade Agreement (FTA) of 1989, and the North American Free Trade Agreement (NAFTA) of 1994, the Canada-US border continues to matter. This is in part because of protectionist interests in both countries, but perhaps more importantly because of the momentum of trade patterns and customs. Adjusting for distance and market size, Canadians trade with *other Canadians* more intensively than they do with foreigners (see Helliwell 1996). The dominance of the United States, however, in the trade of "cultural" goods and services is unchallenged.

Next we provide a brief analysis of trends in the export and imports of cultural goods and services. We note in the following section that Canada, like most other nations, has not been able to prevent US cultural products from dominating the sale of a number of artifacts of popular culture – despite considerable efforts to do so.

The US has successfully used trade policy to challenge Canada's protectionist policies in the case of "split-run" magazines. The GATT and WTO have reduced the ability of Canada to discriminate against imports from foreign countries. The result has been that Canada recognizes that it will have to modify its large stock of policies aimed at protecting and promoting Canada's popular culture products as it did with respect to magazines.

Finally, we note that Canada's multiculturalism policies were developed beginning in 1971 as a response to domestic political circumstances. They were a means to placate sensitivities of non-English and non-French immigrant populations largely in Western Canada at a time when the French fact was becoming more important at the national level. In 1962 and 1967 changes in immigration policy soon changed the ethnic composition of the immigrants to Canada and, in time, greatly increased ethnic diversity. These policies have changed the nature of Canada. It is now a society that encourages diversity and resists "American melting-pot policies," and also the pressures for efficiency-seeking standardization. This section also analyzes how this ethnic and cultural mosaic has helped Canada to preserve its distinctive political and social culture, where regional and ethnic interests thrive, and the Westminster model of government remains at the centre of a distinctive set of political institutions and patterns of behavior.

Economic Aspects of Globalization in Canada

The path of the world to economic integration has been molded by changes in the technological, economic, and social demographic environments and domestic and international political processes (see Friedman 1998). At a fundamental level, market integration can be viewed as a consequence of private and public economic agents responding to opportunities and threats that emerge from these changes. Thus, for example, the shrinkage of "distance" brought about by rapid technological changes in diverse areas ranging from transportation to communications to information technology has fostered integration through the globalization of business activity. Benefits of economies of scale associated with modern mass production technologies in some industries provide further strong incentives for international division of labor and globalization of markets, while the advancement of flexible manufacturing technology and enhanced communication systems in other sectors fosters economic integration through foreign direct investment (FDI). Increases in the international flow of people, information, and ideas contributed further to the globalization of markets. Since the late 1940s, the process of market integration has accelerated as several rounds of GATT and WTO negotiations have led to a significant reduction in tariffs, other trade barriers, and constraints on foreign direct investment. In addition to global integration and regional market integration, agreements have resulted in trade creation (not only trade diversion)[2] and further increases in international investment flows. During this period the world saw increases in trade and foreign direct investment far exceeding the growth of world production.

Canada's economic reliance on international trade and foreign direct investment has grown, reflecting these trends of market integration. Indeed, Canada's exports as a percentage of GDP increased from 25.6% in 1989 to 45.3% in 2000 (Canada 2001). This increase in the integration of its economy to markets outside its borders is larger relative to other trading countries, such as Japan, Germany, and the US. In Japan, the share of exports as a percentage of GDP increased insignificantly from 10.7% to 10.8% during the same period. In Germany the share remained constant at 29.6%. In the US, the share increased from 9.3% of GDP in 1989 to 10.8% in 2000. Canada's ratio of inward FDI to GDP increased from 18.7% in 1989 to 25.1% in 1999. Of the G7 nations, only the UK has a higher ratio of foreign direct investment to GDP (27.4% in 1999) than Canada. The share for the G7 total was 10.8% (with the Japanese ratio pulling the average down with a miniscule ratio of 0.9%).

But has Canada truly experienced economic globalization? Canada's trade and investment flows have always reflected the dominance of its economic relationship with its neighbor. This relationship, however, strengthened with the implementation of the Free Trade Agreement with the US in 1989. Between

1980–1989, there was no great change in the composition and relative share of Canada – US trade in the Canadian GDP. Exports to the US rose from 15% of GDP in 1989 to 28% in 1998 and 32% in 2001. The share of Canadian merchandise exports going to the US as a percentage of all merchandise exports increased from 71% to 84% between 1989 and 1998 and to 85% in 2001. Japan, the second largest trade partner behind the US, took only 4% of Canadian exports. Paralleling the growth of international trade over the decade (1989–1999) has been a *fall* of inter-provincial trade in Canada from 27% of GDP to less than 19% (Harris 2001). In terms of FDI the story is similar. The US accounted in 2000 for about 64% of total inward FDI in Canada (though the share of Canada's FDI in North American FDI fell from 26% in 1986 to about 13% in 1998) (Harris, 2001, Industry Canada 2001).

The FTA offered Multinational corporations (MNCs) located in the US access to the advantages of central locations in a larger market. US location also reduced the political risks associated with possible changes to the FTA. Integration also reduced the need for US firms to invest within the region since they could serve it from domestic locations. Overall, however, market integration increased the attractiveness of investment in the region and this increase compensated, to a degree, for the decline in intra-regional flows. Thus in the decade ending in 2000, Canadian inward FDI increased by 72% and outward FDI increased by 136%, while inward US FDI increased by 213% and outward FDI by 189%. The rest of the world experienced an increase in inward FDI of 209% while the outward FDI increased by 238%.

The integration of markets also highlighted also an increase in regional specialization and the emergence of sectoral geographical clusters. Freer movement of goods and services allowed concentration of investment in geographical centers which enjoyed the benefit of agglomeration (e.g., Silicon Valley in the US).

While the economic importance of the border between the US and Canada has been reduced, the "borderless" region has not emerged yet. McCallum (1995), studying trade flows among Canadian provinces and US states, concluded that the trade generating powers of the Canadian federation are more than an order of magnitude larger than those of the European Union. Helliwell (1996), considering the effects of the FTA and NAFTA, suggests that international trade flows (adjusting for distance and market size) remain much less dense than national trading ties even after all tariffs are removed. When one considers the political-economic consequences of market integration, the vision of a future borderless region and world are becoming more distant. The US (especially near domestic election times) is not always playing the role of a generous hegemon pursuing global market integration irrespective of immediate benefits. Despite official rhetoric that emphasizes a free market ideology, it is pursuing selective liberalization, protecting some sectoral interests (see Krugman 2002). Its recent disputes with Canada (e.g., the softwood lumber dispute) highlight the importance of the border. The vision of broader continental integration is threatened by what the smaller economies in the continent view (or fear) as an integrated Western Hemisphere with the US as its economic hub.

What have been the consequences of market integration for Canada? An important argument for policy-led market integration is the impact that free trade has on productivity. After more than a decade the picture that emerges with respect to productivity is not clear. Several forces were at play, leading to an increase in the productivity growth gap between Canada and the US. The lower value of the Canadian dollar relative to the US dollar reduced the incentive to improve productivity. The emergence of regional clusters in the US, especially those related to computers and then information technologies was not matched in Canada. The reduction in tariffs did not foster rationalization which could have resulted in increased productivity growth (Head/Ries 1999). However, there is evidence that the FTA increased the exit of low productivity firms in Canada.

Six years after the FTA, manufacturing output per plant in Canada increased by 34% while the number of plants declined by 21%. Fewer plants operating at a larger scale appear to imply rationalization of the industry. The findings of Head and Ries (1999) show, however, that Canadian tariff decreases appear to have reduced the scale and number of Canadian manufacturing plants. US tariff reduction had the opposite effect on scale and no effect on entry. The effects of tariff reduction were, however, more pronounced in larger firms. The 34% increase in output per plant was explained as a consequence of (a) a shift in output towards high scale industries (12%), (b) an impact of US tariff reduction 9.4% less 8.5% contraction due to Canadian tariff reduction, and (c) an exchange rate depreciation accounting for 10%. Baggs, Head, and Ries (2002) showed in another study that trade liberalization led to a decrease in the probability of survival of low productivity firms. The consequences of the productivity gap are reflected in part in the differential economic growth in Canada and the US. The two countries' growth rate was quite similar from 1975 to 1985 (indeed, percentage-wise GDP grew faster in Canada). From 1989 to 1999 the GDP in the US grew significantly faster while in Canada growth stagnated. The extraordinarily good performance of the US economy validated in the eyes of many Canadians (and some policy makers) the US economic governance paradigm. Harris (2001, p. 5) suggests that:

> The United States during the 1990's, with low inflation and low unemployment, has had a two-fold effect on Canada. First it has quashed a lot of doubt by many-market proponents about the performance and merits of US style market capitalism. Historically, there has always been a lot of antipathy by Canadian policy makers toward the US model of economic development, and while this has certainly not disappeared it has been considerably muted by the development in the 1990's. Second, the

fact that the United States has done so well relative to Canada has raised the export dependency of Canada on the United States and increased the potential benefits of catching-up with the US.

The increased dependency, which in the past stimulated policy incentives aimed at diversifying Canada's exports, seemed to have the opposite effect of seeking ways to deepen the regional integration process and make it more secure (though with each trade dispute there is often much talk of diversification). As a small economy,[3] Canada is seeking to increase its market access security by promoting multi-lateralism through the WTO and APEC. These two processes of global market integration, however, are slow and are not viewed as credible substitutes to deepening the economic integration with the US. The economic performance of the US has raised another concern about Canada's future – the threat of a "brain drain." NAFTA made temporary migration of skilled workers less difficult. In the past few years there was an increase of migration from Canada to the US (about 3,000 to 4,000 visas were granted). The number of temporary migrants was not significant though it attracted attention to the depreciation of the Canadian dollar, Canadian tax levels, and the decline in the relative standard of living of Canada.

While the pressures to seek even deeper regional economic integration have intensified, policy makers in Canada were alarmed by the trends in one sector where US dominance is unchallenged: trade in cultural products. We now turn to that matter.

International Trade in Cultural Products: The US as Powerhouse

According to a UNESCO report (2000) trade in cultural products represented 2.8% of all world imports in 1998. There has been an increase from US $4.7 billion ($12 per capita) in 1980 to $213.7 billion (or $44.7 per capita) in 1998. Cultural goods as defined by UNESCO include "printed matter and literature, visual arts, cinema and photography, radio, televisions, games and sporting goods." Canada is a major consumer of cultural goods. Once the exports of hardware are excluded, the global dominance of the US in exports of cultural goods (movies, TV programs, recordings, computer games, computer software and magazines, books, and other publications) is unchallenged.

In 1996, international sales of software and entertainment products ($60.2 billion) exceeded those of any other industry. Indeed, from 1991 to 1996 the US exports of intellectual property rose 94% (Farhi/Rosenfeld 1998). The surge in US exports of cultural products can be attributed to: (a) rising incomes and corresponding increases in sales of related hardware (e.g. TV sets); (b) fewer barriers in borders due to trade agreements; (c) the spread of the English language; (d) a focus on entertainment values, and (e) the concentration of aggressive US based multinationals in the entertainment business.

The focus on pop culture goods that appeal to global sensibilities, e.g., freedom, speed, individuality, sex, violence, and opportunity for common people, is regarded with suspicion by foreign politicians who see "American values" dominating domestic popular culture. According to France's former minister of Culture, Jack Lang, "American culture is pure entertainment. It is without restraint, without shame. [it] finds the soul of the child in the adult." (quoted in Farhi/ Rosenfeld 1998). Waxman (1998) echoes the sentiment, arguing that US popular culture exerts a powerful influence across the globe, shaping attitudes, trends, and styles. Movies and TV shows "reflect ideas and values and offer powerful images of US society." In 1997, US film distributors earned $ 5.85 billion at foreign box offices. Now, foreign markets generate more revenue for Hollywood than does the domestic one.[4] A large US market ensures a focus on US tastes in movies, TV, and other entertainment products. It offers economies of scale advantages to US producers of films (although Hollywood is increasingly shaping its films to better fit foreign markets). Similar economies of scale advantages can be seen in other cultural products. For example, US magazines produced for large US markets can be exported globally and compete with domestic publications, which do not enjoy the same cost advantages for editorial content (virtually zero for US exported magazines). *Reader's Digest*, for example, is produced in 19 languages with 48 foreign editions and sold 28 million copies internationally (14.7 million in the US) and *Cosmopolitan*, with 36 foreign editions, sold 4.5 million copies internationally versus 2.7 million in the US. Aronson (2001) observes that the foreign editors of US magazines rely very heavily on the editorial content of the US parent, (e.g. for *Glamour* in Latin American the US content is between 80–90% of the total editorial content). While some of the foreign editions are joint ventures, many involve licensing deals: the US parent ensures that it maintains the image and character of the US brand, thus the magazine becomes a dissemination of American culture. The declining cost of direct satellite broadcasting, the ability to instantly transfer with little cost digital information to consumers everywhere (e.g. permitting downloading of music through the Internet) is further eroding the role of borders as defense lines of culture. Canada, with a long border (almost 8,900 km) and a common language with the US, is more susceptible to US influence than other more distant nations.

Examination of the trade patterns between Canada and the US in cultural products confirms the tight economic links between Canada and the US In 1990, Canadian exports to the US of cultural products in Canadian dollars (current May 2002 prices) amounted to $ 747 million while exports from the US to Canada were $2.803 billion (a ratio of 3.8 in favor of the US). By 2000, Canada's exports rose by more than 300% from 1990, reaching in Cdn $3.060 billion. US exports to Canada rose 96% reaching $5.497 billion (a ratio of 1.8 in favor of the US). While the gap between exports and imports closed to a certain extent, the threat felt in Canada has not diminished. While Canada has increased its efforts to *export* its cultural products, policy makers do not see the contradiction in attacking US "cultural imperialism" effected through the export of popular cultural products by the US, and doing exactly the same thing – albeit less successfully. Canadian popular culture is said to foster cultural diversity and gives foreign consumers more choice; American pop culture "swamps indigenous cultures" and results in "homogenization." Indeed, economic integration allowed Canadian producers of cultural products to export to the US meeting the demands of a US market, responding largely to US tastes and values. In 2000, of the total imports of cultural products, the United States' market share was 86%. The share of Canadian exports of total US imports of cultural products was 16%. If the magnitude of trade in cultural products was indeed a reflection of integration and loss of cultural identity, the number should have been of great concern to Canadian politicians. The response of politicians to what appeared to be a cultural threat was a set of policies which have not stemmed the tide. These are described and analyzed in the next section. We shall later argue however, that trade numbers and balances are about business seeking protection from foreign competitors not cultural imperialism and that these numbers represent the market of popular culture not the deeper dimensions of Canadian cultural distinctiveness. Canadians, as the rest of the world, have preferences for entertaining popular culture promoted by giant multinationals. Consuming these cultural products for the last eight decades does not seem to have changed the core values of the Canadian society, however.

Globalization and Cultural Industries in Canada

Definitions, Policy Objectives, and Context

There are many definitions of "culture." At its broadest, a culture is a total pattern of human behavior and its products embodied in speech, action, artifacts. It is "the collective mental programming of the people in an environment" (Hofstede 1980, p. 42). It depends on learning – knowledge, values, beliefs are passed on from generation to generation. Culture is embodied in language, religion, political and legal systems, economic behavior and in social customs. It is also embodied in the artifacts of both "high" and "popular" cultural activities.

Culture is used by the organizers of society – politicians, religious leaders, academics and families – to impose and ensure order (Rothkop 1997). Along the same lines, Fukuyama (1998) argues that "a culture really consists of deeper moral norms that affect how people link together."

A much narrower and more superficial concept of culture[5] is being used when culture is taken to be the outputs of cultural industries: radio, television, motion pictures, video, sound recordings, publishing (books, magazines, newspapers), museums, art galleries, and the performing arts (ballet, theatre, concerts). It is often assumed or implied that such activities embody a nation's culture. In Canada, it is often claimed that the activities/products of cultural industries play an important role in creating/shaping "national identity." We propose to avoid the debate about the meaning or meanings of culture by focusing on government policies aimed at cultural industries and/or certain products of such industries. Cultural industries – often described as those heavily dependent upon copyright – currently account for 7.4% of Canada's GDP (compared to 5% in the US). Furthermore, these industries grew far more rapidly (6.6% p.a.) than the rest of the economy (3.3%) between 1992 and 2000 (Industry Canada 2001).

The most important contextual factor explaining Canada's efforts to protect and to promote domestic cultural industries/products has been the extent to which Canadians consume foreign (read US) popular cultural products. Various estimates provided in *Figure 1* indicate that about 45% of the books sold in Canada are produced by foreign companies; 35% of total magazine *circulation* in Canada is of foreign magazines; some 95% of feature films shown in Canadian theatres are foreign; 67% of English-Canadian TV viewing consists of foreign programs (almost all from the US) – for Francophones the comparable figure is under 25%; about 65% of the popular music broadcast on radio is of foreign origin; over 80% of retail sales of sound recordings in Canada are of foreign origin; but foreign newspapers have only a tiny share of the Canadian market (under 2%).

Policies to Protect and Promote Canada's Cultural Industries

The Minister of Canadian Heritage (the Hon. Sheila Copps) has summarized the goals of Canada's cultural policies as follows: "Ensure access to Canadian voices and spaces; Promote the creation of quality Canadian content; Reflect Canada's diversity; Present and protect Canada's heritage; Contribute to Canada's economic prosperity; [and] Foster dynamic international outreach." (Copps 1998, p. 2). Ms. Copps (1998, p. 2) continued, "To achieve these objectives, we pursue freedom of choice for consumers, freedom of expression by creators and partnerships at home and abroad." She also argued that, "Throughout this century, every Canadian government has taken the view and acted upon the view that the marketplace

Figure 1. Estimates of the Importance of Foreign Cultural Products in Canada

1. Books
- 45% of book sales in Canada are foreign (Cultural Industries Sectoral Advisory Group on International Trade 1999).

2. Feature Films
- 85% of revenue from film distribution in Canada goes to foreign companies (Cultural Industries Sectoral Advisory Group on International Trade 1999).
- 95% of screen time in Canada consists of foreign movies (Cultural Industries Sectoral Advisory Group on International Trade 1999).

3. Magazines
- 81% of English-language consumer magazines on Canadian newsstands are foreign.
- 63% of magazines' circulation revenue goes to foreign publishers (Cultural Industries Sectoral Advisory Group on International Trade 1999).
- Over 80% of newsstand space in Canada and 89% of newsstand sales go to foreign magazines (Department of Canadian Heritage 1998).
- Canada imports $818 worth of US periodicals, accounting for about 80% of all US exports of magazines (Department of Canadian Heritage 1998).

4. Television Broadcasting
- 60% of the English-language television programs in Canada are foreign (Copps 1998, p. 4).
- Under 25% of the TV viewing hours of Francophones in 2000 was of foreign programs compared to 67% by English-language viewers (Colville/Wylie 2001, p. 3).
- Viewing of TV programs with the highest level of Canadian content increased by 23% overall and by 50% in prime-time for English-language stations between 1997 and 2000 (Bertrand 2000, p. 3).

5. Radio Broadcasting
- 65% of popular musical selections played on Canadian radio stations comes from abroad (Stanbury 1998).

6. Sound Recordings
- 79% of the retail sales of tapes, CDs, concerts, merchandise, and sheet music in Canada accrue to foreign companies (Cultural Industries Sectoral Advisory Group on International Trade 1999).

7. Newspapers
- Foreign newspapers account for less than 2% of the number of daily or weekly papers sold in Canada. (Authors' estimate).

alone cannot guarantee Canadian content." It is useful to note that in most instances federal policies to protect Canadian cultural products alter the set of cultural products available to Canadians so as to give greater prominence to domestic ones at the expense of more strongly preferred foreign ones (Stanbury 1998).

The federal government has made use of almost every possible governing instrument to implement its policies designed to protect and promote a wide range of cultural industries/products. These include various types of regulation (most notably Canadian content requirements and foreign ownership rules), taxation (including "tax expenditures"), public enterprise (the best example being the Canadian Broadcasting Corporation[6]), loans, and loan guarantees (including "soft" loans), public expenditures (including direct cash subsidies and departmental operating programs), partnerships with the private sector, and suasion.

Figure 2. Governing Instruments Used to Implement Canada's Cultural Policies by Industry in 2002

Governing Instruments	Radio	TV	BDUs	Feature Film Prodn.	Magazine Publishing	Newspapers	Film Distrib.	Book Pub./Distrib.	Sound Recordings	New media/Internet	Art Galleries, Museums	Symph. Orchest; Ballet	Theatre Prodn.
1) Regulations													
• Cdn. content requirements	✓	✓	✓		✓								
• Foreign ownership rules	✓	✓	✓		✓	✓	✓	✓					
• Entry controls	✓	✓	✓										
2) Taxation													
• Preferential tax rates					✓								
• Special tax for Cdn Content			✓										
• Tax credits				✓									
3) Public enterprise	✓	✓		✓							✓	✓	
4) Loans/ guarantees				✓			✓	✓	✓	✓	✓		
5) Public expenditures													
• Subsidies/grants		✓		✓✓	✓	✓	✓	✓✓	✓✓	✓	✓	✓	✓
• Operating programs	✓			✓	✓			✓		✓	✓		
6) Partnerships with the private sector		✓	✓	✓	✓								
7) Suasion			✓			✓			✓				

Source: Author's analysis of scores of cultural policies in Canada.

Figure 3. Origins of Protectionist Policies in Cultural Industries in Canada

Cultural Industry/ Product	Commercial Introduction in Canada [in US]	Penetration Rate[a] a) 50% b) 75%	First Major Protectionist Measure	Second Major Protectionist Measure
• Book Publishing	Pre 1867	a) not applicable b) not applicable	1957: Canada Council provides grants to authors	1972: federal subsidies for "culturally valuable" books by Canadian publishers
• Magazine Publishing	Pre 1867	a) not applicable b) not applicable	Late 1800s: subsidized postal rates for Canadian periodicals (foreign ones excluded)	1965: tax and tariff laws changed to block split-run editions of foreign magazines
• Motion Pictures	c1910 [c 1900]	a) not applicable b) not applicable	1939: creation of National Film Board, a Crown corporation to produce films	1967: creation of Canadian Film Development Corp. which paid subsidies
• Radio Broadcasting	1920 [1920]	a) 1936 b) 1939	1923: licences limited to "British subjects"	1932: created a national broadcaster and regulator (CRBC)
• Television Broadcasting (over-the-air)	1952 [1946]	a) 1956 b) 1959	1952: created a national TV network owned by federal government (CBC-TV)	1961: Canadian content requirements set at 45%
• Cable TV (terrestrial)	1952 [c1950]	a) 1978 b) c1990	1968: Cable TV brought under the new *Broadcast Act* (so foreign ownership limited to 20%)	1980s: foreign specialty channels limited to twice the number of Canadian ones
• Communications Satellites (geosynchronous orbit)	1972 [1963]	a) 1972 b) 1979	1969: mixed enterprise given a monopoly in carrying telephone and broadcast signals	1983: ban on Canadian households receiving TV signals from foreign (i.e., US) satellites
• Specialty TV Channels (including pay TV, pay-per-view, and VOD)[b]	1982 (n = 4) [1970s]	a) 1982 b) c1990 (n = 19)	1982: Canadian content requirements (gradually increased over time)	1995: maximum ratio of foreign to Canadian channels reduced to 1 to 1 (from 2 to 1)
• DBS/DTH Satellite Broadcasting	1997 [1994]	a) not yet b) not yet	1997: Extensive Canadian content requirements from launch date	1998: 5% tax on all BDUs to finance Canadian content
• Internet	Early 1980s[c] [late 1970s]	a) 2000 b) expected in 2004	1999: CRTC decision *not* to regulate the Net (to be revisited in 5 years)	2001: legislation introduced to control retransmission of TV signals over the Net

[a] The year in which the penetration rate was 50%, then 75% of Canadian households.
[b] The first pay-TV channels began operation in February 1983. The first pay-per-view channels began in 1990; the first video on demand channels began in 1997.
[c] In the early 1980s, access to the Net was confined largely to universities and national defence. It wasn't until about 1990 that households began to gain access to the Net as more homes acquired a personal computer.

Source: Authors' analysis of the history of government policy interventions in various cultural industries.

As indicated in *Figure 2*, it is common for the federal government to use two or more governing instruments for the same cultural industry. "Canadian content" (CanCon) requirements are a peculiar Canadian institution whose title is quite misleading. These requirements (e.g., the regulation that requires that 60% of the total hours broadcast by TV stations consist of "Canadian" programs) have nothing at all to do with the substantive or thematic content of the cultural products in question. Rather, a "Canadian" TV program (or feature film or musical selection) is one which obtains a certain number of points based on the *citizenship* (i.e., being a Canadian or a Canadian Landed Immigrant) of particular persons associated with the production of the program notably actors in major roles, director, producer, and post-production technicians.[7]

Concerns about the political, economic, and cultural sovereignty of Canada have been an important theme in Canadian history since Canada became a nation in 1867. This is directly attributable to Canada's relationship to its huge, populous, and powerful neighbor to the south. We need also add the fact that the US is the originator or earliest adopter of most new communications technologies and signals carried on the wireless ones (e.g., radio and satellite TV) can be received by much of Canada's population.

It is clear from the information summarized in *Figure 3* that federal government policies aimed at protecting a variety of cultural industries or products originated long before the current wave of globalization in the 1980s. Of the 10 cultural industries/products (ranging from book publishing to the Internet), protectionist policies in seven began before the 1980s, and of these one began in the 1920s and two in the 1950s.

It is also clear from *Figure 3* that a great deal of cultural protectionism in Canada is associated with the introduction of new communications technologies into Canada, and a number of these involved wireless transmission of cultural products such as radio, television (over-the-air), geostationary communications satellites, and Direct-to-Home (DTH) satellite broadcasting.

Our detailed review of the evolution of protectionist policies in over a dozen cultural industries indicates that some have resulted in much more extensive and restrictive policies than others. We infer that the more extensive restrictive policies are the result of nationalists' perception of a higher *threat* to Canada's cultural or national identity, never defined, from US popular cultural products. It appears that the magnitude of the perceived threat depends heavily on the nature of the technology involved. In most cases, more extensive protectionist measures are associated with wireless methods of communication.

The Split-Run Magazines Case

On several occasions, Canada's efforts to protect its cultural industries have resulted in conflicts with the US (but no other country), but in only one case did the US government pursue the matter under a multi-lateral international trade agreement. That case dealt with split-run editions of US magazines printed and distributed in Canada.

The use of a new technology – transmission of editorial content from the US to Canada via satellite – precipitated the conflict in April 1993 when *Sports Illustrated* (SI) owned by US media giant Time Warner began publishing a split-run edition in Canada with most of the editorial content sent from the US by means of a satellite. Most of the advertising revenue came from Canadian businesses targeting Canadian customers. Canadian magazine publishers immediately and very loudly cried foul because satellite transmission obviated the provisions of Tariff Code 9958 established in 1965 designed to ban the import of split-runs and foreign magazines with more than 5% of their ads directed at Canadians[8].

The federal government quickly created the O'Leary Task Force on the Canadian Magazine Industry. In its report in March 1994, it recommended an excise tax on the printers or distributors of split-run magazines equal to 80% of the value of the ads in the magazines. On December 22, 1994 the Minister of Canadian Heritage said that the federal government would implement this recommendation and on November 3, 1995, the House of Commons passed Bill C-103 to do this. Royal Assent soon followed so that the hole in the dike was plugged 33 months after it was opened. At that time, SI had some 145,000 subscribers in Canada and had cancelled two of 12 editions during the past year due to insufficient interest by Canadian advertisers.

On March 11, 1996, the US filed its case against Canada's various protectionist magazine policies with the WTO arguing that they were inconsistent with Article III of GATT. It was the first case brought against Canada under the WTO since the latter began operations on January 1, 1995.

The decision of the WTO's Dispute Settlement Body on March 14, 1997 strongly supported the US position. Both countries quickly appealed. On June 30, the WTO Appellate Body issued its report – from which there was no appeal (WTO Panel 1997): Canada's 80% excise tax on split-runs was condemned as were its postal rate subsidies and other measures. There followed more lamentations by Canadian nationalists and demands for other WTO-proof forms of assistance to protect Canadian magazines.

On July 27, 1997 Canada said that it would implement the changes required by the WTO and meet the WTO's deadline of October 30, 1998. On October 8, 1998, Bill C-55, the "Foreign Publishers Advertising Services Act," was introduced. While it dismantled the offending provisions, it created new protectionist measures, most notably fines up to $250,000 on split run magazines that solicited ads from Canadian businesses. However, the Canadian editions of *Time* and *Reader's Digest* were exempted.

In April, 1999, Canadian and US officials held many meetings to negotiate changes to Bill C-55. Talks continued in May, but collapsed on May 19, and resumed shortly thereafter in secret. On May 26, 1999 Canada and the US reached an agreement in principle on the magazines issue (see Department of Canadian Heritage 1999). On July 1, 1999 an amended Bill C-55 came into effect. Its key provisions were as follows: a) A foreign publisher cannot sell more than 18% of its advertising aimed at Canada (the level had been 15% since January 1, 2001, and it went up to 18% on July 1, 2002); b) A foreign publisher who makes an investment in periodical publishing which has been approved under the *Investment Canada Act* will have unrestricted access to the Canadian advertising market; c) A foreign publisher who lawfully supplied advertising services directed at the Canadian market by means of a periodical during the year before the day on which the *Act* was introduced in the House of Commons (October 8, 1998), will be able to continue to supply advertising services directed at the Canadian market by means of that periodical. This means that *Time* and *Reader's Digest* are exempted.

The magazine case formally ended on June 1, 2000 when amendments to the *Income Tax Act* came into effect. The new section 19.01 permits full deductibility of expenses for advertisements published in issues of periodicals that contain at least 80% original editorial content (this is the code phrase for "Canadian content"), and 50% deductibility for advertising expenses in other periodicals regardless of ownership of the periodical. The new Section 19 applies to advertisements in issues of periodicals published after May 2000. It does not affect the criterion for claiming a deduction for advertising in newspapers.

After all this *sturm und drang*, what was the net result? A comprehensive set of measures to protect Canada's magazine industry have been replaced by another set of measures that meet the WTO requirements and those of the US government. These measures are slightly less protectionist, and larger direct cash subsidies have been substituted for the impugned measures. Thus about 440 magazines each received subsidies from about $12,000 to over $1.5 million (Department of Canadian Heritage 2002a). Finally, a new form of Canadian content requirement has been established for magazines based only on the citizenship of the author, photographer, or illustrator.

Lobbying on the International Stage for Special Treatment for Cultural Industries in Trade Agreements

Canada has long argued that culture, even cultural products, should not be subject to international agreements liberalizing and governing trade. Thus the effort to negotiate the so-called "cultural industries exemption" in the FTA (effective January 1, 1989) and carried over into the NAFTA (effective January 1, 1994). In practice, the exemption has been only of value in reassuring anxious nationalists because the US can take retaliatory action on other industries.

More recently, largely through the efforts of the federal Minister of Canadian Heritage Sheila Copps, Canada has been the leader in organizing nations and NGOs to help oppose the "cultural imperialism" of the US. France has been active in this matter as well. Late in June 1998, Heritage Minister Copps had two days of meetings with the culture ministers of 20 countries in Ottawa. The objective was to form a permanent network to try to limit the effects of trade liberalization agreements on the ability of nations to promote and protect cultural industries (see Copps 1998). The *bête noir* is the US, which was not invited to the meeting. That meeting helped to create the International Network for Cultural Diversity in 2000 in Santorini, Greece. It consists of 160 organizations from over 30 countries. Canada's efforts have hardly been viewed with favor by the US Canada has taken the lead in developing an international instrument intended to limit the effects of trade agreements on cultural industries (Department of Canadian Heritage 2002b).

Defense of Culture or Rent-Seeking?

Canada has long been a recipient of extensive inflows of US popular culture. Yet, when one stands back, what is remarkable is how *little* apparent effect the large inflow of US pop culture has had on the bigger and more important things that characterize Canada's national culture in the broad sense such as the following:

a. Attitudes toward government (the state is larger in Canada than the US and continues to expand).
b. The design of Canadian governments (Westminster model, and a highly decentralized form of federalism).
c. The use of higher taxes to create a "more caring/compassionate society" (emphasis on distributive equity rather than efficiency).
d. Extensive efforts to limit the role that open competition plays in many areas of Canadian life.
e. The encouragement of cultural diversity.

There is no evidence that the "soul of the nation" is in any way affected, for example, by whether or not the direct and indirect subsidies to sound recording enterprises owned by Canadians or the number of Canadian citizens who make pop recordings sold in Canada or abroad are increased or decreased. Supply will be affected, and possibly consumption, but the relationship between the latter and Canadian cultural identity is unknown. The policies described as cultural protection can be easily explained as the product of rent-seeking by those who work or invest in industries which produce the cultural products.[9] Indeed the contents of many cultural products produced in Canada are affected to a large degree by the preferences of the larger market in the US. Thus, place of production may not matter.

Immigration and Multiculturalism: The Globalization of Canada's Population

We have suggested in the beginning of this paper that economic integration, whether regional or global, tends to promote efficiency and standardization as basic values which shape society. Given the huge flows of cultural products and information, given a common border and proximity of most of Canada's population to the border, and given a common language, one must wonder why the expected cultural convergence between the US and Canada has not taken place?

Paradoxically it is "globalization" of Canada's population brought about by changes in immigration policy in 1962 and 1967 and a policy of multiculturalism first enunciated in 1971 that appear to be making Canada a distinct society which is resisting some of the forces created by economic globalization.

Immigration: Changing the Face of Canada

In a broad sense, Canada is a nation of immigrants. Aside from the descendants of the native Indians who inhabited the country prior to the arrival of the French and English in the early 1600s, almost all of the growth of Canada's population can be attributed to immigrants and their progeny.

Between 1871 and 1996, Canada's total population grew from 3.69 million to 29.67 million (Statistics Canada, 2003b). Net natural increase accounted for 74.7% of the total increase. Immigration amounted to 13.94 million – but emigration was 7.56 million. Thus *net* immigration accounted for 25.3% or one-quarter of the increase in Canada's population between 1871 and 1996 (Statistics Canada 2003b).

In 1962 and in 1967 Canada made important changes in its immigration policies that have – quite literally – changed the face of the nation.[10] Between 1955 and 1969, Canada received 2.15 million immigrants compared to the population of 20.0 million in mid-1966: 76% came from Europe, 6% from Asia 12% came from the US or West Indies, and 6% came from other countries (*Table 1*). Between 1970 and 1984, Canada received 2.01 million immigrants compared to the population of 24.8 million in mid-1981: 37% came from Europe, 30% from Asia and 10% from the US or West Indies and 23% from other countries. Between 1985 and 2001, Canada received 3.36 million[11] immigrants compared to the population of 30.01 million in mid-2001 of which 57% were from Asia, 20% from Europe, 8% from the US or West Indies, and 15% from other countries (*Table 1*). In summary terms, over the past three decades Europe lost its dominance in the supply of immigrants to Canada and Asia has become the primary source of immigrants. In 2000/01, 62% of Canada's 252,000 immigrants came from Asia.

Globalization: The Canadian Paradox

Table 1. Country of Origin of Immigrants to Canada, 1955 to 2001

Country of Origin	1955 to 1969	%[a]	1970 to 1984	%[a]	1985 to 2001	%[a]	(000s) 1996/97 to 2000/01	%[a]
Europe	1,643,183	76%	743,261	37%	685,449	20%	200.9	19%
Asia	133,855	6%	598,416	30%	1,903,126	57%	648.4	62%
US and West Indies	256,999	12%	209,539	10%	276,968	8%	63.9	6%
Other North and Central America	0	0%	9,383	0%	96,014	3%	15.4	1%
South America	0	0%	15,772	1%	130,296	4%	29.9	3%
Other Countries	120,734	6%	237,830	12%	269,839	8%	90.9	9%
Total Number of Immigrants	2,154,771	100%	2,011,876	100%	3,361,692	100%	1049.3	100%

[a] Total may not add to 100% due to rounding.
Sources: Statistics Canada (2002a).

Another way to examine the origins of Canada's immigrants is to consider this factor at the time of a particular census. This is done for 1996 in Table 2.[12] Of Canada's total population of 29.67 million in June 1996, 4.97 million (or 16.8%) were *first generation* immigrants. Of these, 1.06 million (or 21.2%) had arrived in Canada prior to 1961. An almost equal number (1.04 million) had arrived in the previous five years; while 1.09 million had arrived in the period 1981–90 (see Table 2).

Table 2. Origins of First Generation Immigrants in the 1996 Census by Period of Arrival (in 000s)

Place of Birth	Total	Before 1961	1961–1970	1971–1980	1981–1990	1991–1996
United States	245	45	50	74	46	29
Central/South America, Caribbean & Bermuda	553	15	63	164	179	137
Europe	2,331	953	544	357	281	198
Africa & West Central Asia & Middle East	440	10	41	89	142	158
Asia (E, SE, Southern)	1,352	28	82	297	435	511
Oceania & Others	49	4	9	15	10	10
Total	4,972	1,055	789	996	1,092	1,039
Total Population		18,238	21,568	24,820	28,031	29,672
Reference Year		1961	1971	1981	1991	1996

Source: Statistics Canada (2003a).

The change in the origin of immigrants can be seen by comparing the pre-1961 arrivals to the 1991–96 arrivals – both of which were counted in the 1996 Census. Of the pre-1961 immigrants 90.3% came from Europe. Of those arriving in 1991–96, 19.1% came from Europe while 49.2% came from East, South East, and Southern Asia, and 15.2% came from Africa, West Central Asia and the Middle East.

Although Canada did not officially create a category for refugees in its immigration policy until 1978, it regularly took in refugees, usually created by the actions of totalitarian governments or by war. In 1956–57, Canada took in 37,500 Hungarians; in 1968–69 it received 11,000 Czechoslovakians; in 1972 it took in 6,200 Ugandan Asians; it took in over 6,000 Chileans in 1973; between 1975 and 1978, Canada took in 9,000 refugees from Vietnam; in 1979 and early 1980 Canada received another 34,000 Vietnamese refugees. In 1986, Canada was awarded the Nansen Medal by the UN High Commissioner for Refugees. It was the first time a *nation* had received the award.

Immigrants have always tended to settle in parts of the country where there are significant numbers of persons who share their ethno-cultural heritage and language. Thus, there are large numbers of Canadians of Chinese and South Asian origins in British Columbia and Ontario, whereas persons of Caribbean descent tend to be concentrated in Ontario. Because Quebec attracts many French-speaking immigrants, it has the highest percentage of Canadians of Vietnamese, Haitian, and Lebanese origins. (Heritage Canada 2000, Part 1). While Toronto accounts for 8% of Canada's total population, it is home to 41% of Canadians for whom Chinese is their mother tongue, 42% of those whose mother tongue is Italian, and 35% of those whose mother tongue is Punjabi. Only 53.8% of Toronto's population claim English as their mother tongue (Galloway 2002).

As part of the wider process devolution of federal powers to the provinces, and to appease separatists in Quebec, the federal government has since 1991 allowed the Province of Quebec to have complete control over the number and source immigrants coming to Quebec. And Quebec gets to increase its share of the national quota to compensate for the "leakage" of newcomers who quickly move out of the province. It is the only province with this authority. Three factors appear to have motivated Quebec's demands: a) its share of Canada's population was shrinking slightly[13], b) Quebec's highly restrictive language law had discouraged immigrants from settling in Quebec – unless they already spoke French and c) Quebec's desire to acquire greater authority in almost every policy field, particularly those associated with a *national* government.

The 2001 Census revealed that the mother tongue of 17.8% of the population was *neither* official language: English (59.4%); French (25.9%). Fourteen languages, spoken by at least 100,000 persons, accounted for 72.5% of persons whose mother tongue was neither English nor French. The largest was Chinese, accounting for 2.9% of the total population in mid-2001 (Statistics Canada 2002b).

In 2000, Heritage Canada predicted that by 2006 visible minorities will represent between 14.7% and 20% of the population. Toronto, the largest city in Canada's largest province, will be the world's most multicultural city, ahead of New York and London. Vancouver, with the fastest growing and most diverse immigrant population in Canada, will be among the world's most integrated cities.

Multiculturalism in Canada

With ascendance of the French fact in Canada beginning in the 1960s (Thomson 1984), the federal government, led by Pierre Trudeau, emphasized that the federal government had to provide services in both official languages and to provide opportunities for both of Canada's "founding peoples", the French and the English. This was reflected in the *Official Languages Act* of 1969. While there is no question that the French and English accounted for the vast majority of the earliest settlers in the 1600s and for the next two hundred years, following Confederation many more national streams contributed to the river of immigrants who came to Canada. These other groups also wanted to be recognized in both the official rhetoric and in terms of Ottawa's largesse.

Political pressure, primarily from Western Canada, prompted the Trudeau Government in 1971 to announce support for "multiculturalism." This was done at the time when Quebec's rising power among the 10 provinces and Francophone power within the federal government was giving real force to official bilingualism and biculturalism. The Royal Commission on Bilingualism and Biculturalism reported in 1965 (interim report) and 1969 (final report). Multiculturalism was a cause John Diefenbaker had long supported. As prime minister and leader of the opposition Progressive Conservative Party, Diefenbaker wanted to get rid of the terminology of "hyphenated Canadians," i.e., Polish-Canadians, French-Canadians, Ukrainian-Canadians. But what started as a few millions in grants to keep alive certain foreign languages in Canada and to fund some of the folkways of the old world grew in both financial terms and in import. In particular, the vast increase in none European immigrants over the next 30 years helped to redefine multiculturalism in Canada. It led to the tremendous emphasis on the virtues of diversity.

Multiculturalism has strongly reinforced the idea and practice of Canada as a "mosaic" in contradistinction to the US model of a "melting pot."[14] The rapidly increasing ethnic diversity of the population is seen as a source of unity and an important part of the "Canadian identity" (Copps 1998, 1999).

In 1982, the Charter of Rights and Freedoms in the new constitution specified in section 27 that the Charter is to "be interpreted in a manner consistent with the preservation and enhancement of the multicultural heritage of Canadians."

The Department of Canadian Heritage administers Canada's multiculturalism policy said to be the first adopted by any nation. It argues that "Canadian multiculturalism is fundamental to our belief that all citizens are equal. Multiculturalism ensures that all citizens can keep their identities, can take pride in their ancestry, and have a sense of belonging. Acceptance gives Canadians a feeling of security and self-confidence, making them more open to, and accepting of, diverse cultures. The Canadian experience has shown that multiculturalism encourages racial and ethnic harmony and cross-cultural understanding, and discourages ghettoization, hatred, discrimination, and violence" (Department of Canadian Heritage 2003).

Section 3 of the *Canadian Multiculturalism Act* (enacted in mid-1988) declares the policy of the federal government in 10 paragraphs. Among the policy objectives are the following:

- Recognize and promote the understanding that multiculturalism reflects the cultural and racial diversity of Canadian society and acknowledges the freedom of all members of Canadian society to preserve, enhance, and share their cultural heritage;
- Recognize and promote the understanding that multiculturalism is a fundamental characteristic of the Canadian heritage and identity and that it provides an invaluable resource in the shaping of Canada's future;
- Promote the full and equitable participation of individuals and communities of all origins in the continuing evolution and shaping of all aspects of Canadian society and assist them in the elimination of any barrier to that participation;
- Preserve and enhance the use of languages other than English and French, while strengthening the status and use of the official languages of Canada.

According to the Department of Canadian Heritage, multiculturalism contributes to citizenship acquisition, participation and quality of life, and a strong sense of pride in what Canada stands for internationally. It is based on diversity within a common citizenship and fosters a sense of belonging and attachment to the country and to one another. Thus it promotes social cohesion (Heritage Canada 2000, Part 1). But as Canada's ethnic diversity increases, driven largely by immigration policy, yet greater efforts must be made by the federal government to counteract the centrifugal tendencies.

The Department of Canadian Heritage states that polls conducted by Ipsos Reid show that an increasing proportion of Canadians in 1999 more than 83% agree that the multicultural make-up is one of the best things about Canada. This compares with 78% in October 1998, 80% in June 1996 and 77% in February of 1993. And the most ethno-culturally diverse demographic group in Canada, youth, are the most enthusiastic. A 1999 survey showed that 96%

agree with the statement it is good that Canada has people of different racial backgrounds. Heritage Canada (2000) states that, "There is evidence of a stronger connection between multiculturalism and Canadians sense of identity. When Canadians were asked in 1999 about what contributes to their sense of identity and makes them different from Americans, multiculturalism came in second after the health care system."[15]

Conclusions

The emergence of a Canadian identity defined in terms of co-existence of different groups, the tensions that such differences create and the patterns of reconciliation that are involved have deep implications in terms of the values that must sustain the society. These values highlight the importance of equitable distribution rather than efficiency of allocation. They see a strong role for government in ensuring the supply of public goods and the maintenance of a security net. They provide the counter balance to market forces that drive convergence. The complex social and economic ties of immigrant communities with their homelands, and the interaction among groups and regions in Canada have helped to create a distinct identity for Canada, and one that continues to evolve. Thus the paradox: economic globalization and the forces of modernization that it fosters posed a serious threat to Canada's distinct social, political and cultural identities, but globalization and the increased international immigration it brought about, have formed a strong basis for Canada as a distinct society, despite a long and open border with the US and a common language.

The protection of culture by government can be seen either as an ineffective means to stop an inevitable process of convergence brought about by globalization in some (and not necessarily important) aspects of culture or perhaps more plausibly can be seen as means for protection of Canadian cultural industries. Indeed, in many cases, irrespective of where and by whom cultural products are produced they are produced to meet the demands and preferences of a global market in which the US plays a dominant role.

Endnotes

1 An earlier version of this paper was presented at the Conference "Cultures of Economy – Economic Cultures", sponsored by the Bavarian American Academy held in Munich, Germany, June 20–22, 2002. Funding from SSHRC Canada is gratefully acknowledged.

2 Trade diversion refers to situations in which imports from free trade agreement member countries increase, displacing imports from non-member countries.
3 Canada's population in 2002 was 31 million versus 287 million for the U.S. Canada's GDP per capita is 20% *below* that of the US (Little 2002).
4 Note that non-box office revenues are an increasing part of the revenues flowing to the makers of motion pictures, i.e., video rights, TV rights, merchandise tie-ins, etc. See www.factbook.net/wbglobal_rev.htm.
5 The UNESCO (2000) definition of culture includes cultural heritage, printed matter and literature, music, the performing and visual arts, cinema and photography, radio and television, and socio-cultural activities.
6 The CBC is Canada's largest cultural institution. In 2001, the CBC owned had 97 broadcasting stations, 1,164 rebroadcasters, 27 private affiliates, and 292 affiliated or community rebroadcasters. It had four commercial-free radio networks with 73 regional stations coast-to-coast in English and French. CBC also had two national TV networks (English and French) with 24 regional stations and 24 affiliated ones (Canadian Broadcasting Corporation, 2001). About 99% of the population has access to CBC's broadcast services (Auditor General, 2000, para 16). In addition, CBC had Radio Canada International, a shortwave broadcasting network operating in seven languages. In 2000–2001, the CBC's expenses totaled $1,396 million. Total funding by the federal government amounted to $956.9 million (including $794.1 million in the form of the Parliamentary appropriation for operating expenditures). Advertising revenues (from TV) and program sales generated $349.2 million while specialty services (notably "Newsworld") generated $107.7 million (Canadian Broadcasting Corporation 2001).
7 For a musical selection on radio to qualify as "Canadian" it must generally fulfill two of four conditions in the MAPL formula: M (Music): the music is composed entirely by a Canadian; A (Artist): the music is, or the lyrics are performed principally by a Canadian; P (Production): the musical selection consists of a live performance that is recorded wholly in Canada, or performed wholly in Canada and broadcast live in Canada; and L (Lyrics): The lyrics are written entirely by a Canadian. A Canadian is a Canadian citizen or landed immigrant (Stanbury 1998).
8 According to a newspaper report, Time-Warner's plans for the split-run edition of *Sports Illustrated* were approved by Investment Canada as an expansion of Time Canada Ltd. Also, Revenue Canada said in advance that there was no violation of Tariff Item 9958. See *Globe and Mail*, January 23, 1996, pp. B1, B8. The "logic" of protecting the ad revenues of Canadian magazines is that ads provide the money to pay for Canadian editorial content which is said to be an important part of Canadian culture which, in turn, is an important element of Canadians' "identity." Another way of explaining the protectionist policies is that they are the product of rent-seeking by the owner of Canadian magazines who do not want any competition from foreigners. Note that in 1977, the exemption in the 1965 legislation for *Time* and *Reader's Digest* was ended. *Time* then stopped publishing its split-run edition, but the US edition continued to be sold in Canada; *Reader's Digest* reorganized its Canadian operation so that it could continue to attract Canadian advertisers.
9 The role of rent-seeking in molding government decisions related to cultural industries is quite clearly illustrated in the move of Industry Canada to stop the establishment of Borders Canada. Borders Canada was established as an American and Canadian book retailing venture. Chapters President Larry Stevenson, sensing competition to his Canadian superstore book retailer, lobbied against the idea convincing Industry Canada to disallow the creation of the company.
10 The Diefenbaker Government in 1962 changed the regulations to eliminate all criteria related to race, religion or national origin. In 1967, the Pearson Government introduced a "points system" for immigrants focusing upon education, linguistic ability, and Canada's need for certain occupational skills. Generally, see Avery (1995), Green (1976), Green and Green (1995), Hawkins (1988), Knowles (1997), Kelley and Trebilcock (1998).
11 The number rose from 690,000 in 1985–89 to 1,179,000 in 1990–94 and was 1,017,000 in the period 1995–99.
12 The data from the 2001 Census was not available.
13 That is why Quebec pressed hard and recently obtained an agreement with the federal government which specifies that for a wide variety of fiscal and other purposes Quebec will be deemed to account for 25% of Canada's population even though it actually has less.

14 The concept of Canada as a "mosaic" preceded the official policy of multiculturalism. In his book, *The Vertical Mosaic*, sociologist John Porter (1965) emphasized the strength/persistence of social class and the power of elites (economic, political, military) which were quite closely tied to social status. See also the later work of Wallace Clement in the same vein. But note that in 1900, the focus was on assimilation by the immigrants arriving in vast numbers in Western Canada (see Berton 1984, p. 59).

15 Universal, single-payer, government-financed medical and hospital care (initiated by the federal government) was established in Canada in 1966. It now accounts for at least one-third of all expenditures by provincial governments (which now spend more on medicare than does the federal government).

References

Auditor General of Canada, *Canadian Broadcasting Corporation – Special Report*, Ottawa: Auditor General, June 29, 2000.
Aronson, A., Women's Magazines Go Global, *IPI Global Journalist*, 2, 2001, http://www.freemedia.at.ipreport2.01/ipigj2.01-8htm
Avery, D. H, *Reluctant Host: Canadian Responses to Immigrant Workers, 1896–1994*, Toronto: McClelland & Stewart 1995.
Baggs, J./Head, K./Ries, J., Free Trade, Firm Heterogeneity, and Canadian Productivity, paper presented at *the Canada-U.S. Economic Monetary Integration Conference* at the Kennedy School of Government, Harvard University, May 9–11, 2002.
Berton, P., *The Promised Land: Settling the West, 1896–1914*, Toronto: McClelland & Stewart 1984.
Bertrand, F., Our Collective Journey – Staying the Course for Better Canadian Content, Speech to the *Annual Convention of the Canadian Association of Broadcasters*, Calgary, Alberta, November 13, 2000, http://www.crtc.gc.caENG/NEWS/SPEECHES/2000.
Canada, *The State of Trade, 2001*, Ottawa: Department of Foreign Affairs and International Trade, Statistical Appendix 2001.
Canadian Broadcasting Corporation, *Annual Report, 2000–2001*, Ottawa: CBC/Radio-Canada, 2001.
Colville, D./Wylie, A., Notes for an Address to the Standing Committee on Canadian Heritage: Review of the Canadian Broadcasting System, Ottawa, November 21, 2001, http://www.crtc.gc.ca/eng/NEWS/SPEECHES/2001.
Copps, S., Speaking Notes for the Gala Dinner, International Meeting on Cultural Policy, Hull, Quebec, June 29, 1998, http://www.pch.gc.ca/culture/spch-disc/sc980484.htm.
Copps, S., *Connecting to the Canadian Experience: Diversity, Creativity and Choice*, Ottawa: Heritage Canada, November 1999.
Coyne, A., "The Con in CanCon," *National Post Online*, April 5, 2002.
Cultural Industries Sectoral Advisory Group on International Trade, *New Strategies for Culture and Trade, Canadian Culture in a Global World*, Ottawa: Department of Canadian Heritage, February, 1999, pp. 1–34.
Department of Canadian Heritage, News Release New Advertising Services Measure to Promote Canadian Culture, Toronto, July 29, 1998.
Department of Canadian Heritage, News Release, Canada and United States Sign Agreement on Periodicals – *Backgrounder*, Ottawa, June 4, 1999.
Department of Canadian Heritage, *Foreign Investment Policies in the Canadian Cultural Sector*, Ottawa: Trade and Investment Branch, Heritage Canada, October 2001.
Department of Canadian Heritage, Canadian Magazine Fund (CMF), 2002a, http://www.pch.gc.ca/culture/cult_ind/CMF/eindex.htm.
Department of Canadian Heritage, News Release: Sheila Copps Participates in Fifth Meeting of International Network on Cultural Policy in South Africa, Capetown, October 15, 2002b.

Department of Canadian Heritage, *What is Multiculturalism?*, 2003, http://www.canadianheritage.gc.ca/progs/multi/what-multi_e.cfm?nav=2.
Farhi, P./Rosenfeld M., American Pop Penetrates Worldwide, *Washington Post*, October 25, 1998, p. A1.
Friedman, T. L. *The Lexus and the Olive Tree: Understanding Globalization*, New York: Farrar, Strauss & Giroux 1998.
Fukuyama, F., Economic Globalization and Culture: A Discussion with Dr. Francis Fukuyama, *Merrill Lynch Forum: Globalization*, 1998, http://www.nl.com/woml/forum/global.htm.
Galloway, G., Widest linguistic diversity found in Toronto, *Globe and Mail*, December 11, 2002, p. A7.
Green, A. G. *Immigration and the Postwar Canadian Economy*, Toronto: Macmillan 1976.
Green, A. G./Green, D. A., Canadian Immigration Policy: The Effectiveness of the Point System and Other Instruments, *Canadian Journal of Economics*, 28, 4b, November 1995, pp. 1006–1041.
Harris, R. G., North American Economic Integration: Issues and Research Agenda, Discussion Paper No. 10, *Industry Canada Research Publications Program*, April, 2001 pp. 1–55.
Hawkins, F., *Canada and Immigration: Public Policy and Public Concern*, 2nd edition, Montreal/Kingston: McGill-Queen's University Press 1988.
Head, K./Ries J., Rationalization Effects of Tariff Reductions, *Journal of International Economics*, 47, 1999, pp. 295–320.
Helliwell, J. F., Do National Borders Matter for Quebec's Trade?, *Canadian Journal of Economics*, 29, 3, August 1996, pp. 507–522.
Heritage Canada, *12th Annual Report on the Operations of the Canadian Multiculturalism Act, 1999-2000*, Ottawa: Heritage Canada 2000.
Hofstede, G., Motivation, Leadership, and Organization: Do American Theories Apply?, *Organizational Dynamics*, Summer 1980, pp. 42–63.
Industry Canada, A Framework for Copyright Reform, Ottawa: Industry Canada, June 22, 2001, http://strategis.ic.gc.ca/SSG/rpolole.html.
Jamieson, F., Notes from Globalization as a Philosophical Issue, in Jamieson, F./Miyosi, M. (eds.), *The Culture of Globalization*, Durham and London: Duke University Press 1998, pp. 54–80.
Kelley, N./Trebilcock, M. J., *The Making of the Mosaic: A History of Canadian Immigration Policy*, Toronto: University of Toronto Press 1998.
Knowles, V. *Strangers at Our Gates: Canadian Immigration and Immigration Policy, 1540–1997*, rev'd ed., Toronto: Dundurn Press 1997.
Krugman, P., America the Scofflaw, *New York Times on the Web*, May 24, 2002, http://www.nytimes.com.
Little, B., Canada Still Lags U.S. Standard of Living, *Globe and Mail*, June 3, 2002, p. B6.
McCallum, J., National Borders Matter: Canada-U.S. Regional Trade Patterns, *American Economic Review*, June 1995, pp. 615–23.
Porter, J., *The Vertical Mosaic: An Analysis of Social Class and Power in Canada*, Toronto: University of Toronto Press 1965.
Rothkop, D., In Praise of Cultural Imperialism? Effects of Globalization on Culture, *Foreign Policy*, Issue 107, June 22, 1997, pp. 38–53.
Royal Commission on Bilingualism and Biculturalism, *Report*, Ottawa: Queen's Printer 1969.
Stanbury, W. T., Canadian Content Regulations: The Intrusive State at Work, *Fraser Forum, Special Issue*, Vancouver: Fraser Institute, August 1998, pp 1–90.
Statistics Canada, CANSIM II, Table 051-006, 2002a.
Statistics Canada, Detailed Mother Tongue, 2001 Census, Catalogue No. 97F007XCB01001, 2002b.
Statistics Canada, Immigrant population by place of birth and period of immigration, 1996 Census, Canada, 1996 Census, Nation Tables, Catalogue No. 93F0023XDB96005, 2003a, http://www.statcan.ca/English/Pgdb/demo25a.htm.
Statistics Canada, Population and Growth Components [1851–1996], 2003b, http://www.statcan.ca/English/Pgdb/demo03.htm.
Thomson, D. C. Jean Lesage and the Quiet Revolution, Toronto: Macmillan 1984.
UNESCO. *International Flows of Selected Cultural Goods, 1980–98*, New York: United Nations, 2000.
Waxman, S., Hollywood Attuned to World Markets, *Washington Post*, October 26, 1998, p. A1, http://www.washingtonpost.com/wp-srv/longterm/mia/part2.htm.
WTO Panel, Canada – Certain Measures Concerning Periodicals, March 14, 1997, WT-DS31/R, http://www.wto.org/English/tratop_e/dispa_e/distabase_e.htm.

**Management
International Review**
© Gabler Verlag 2004

Mamduh Hanafi/S. Ghon Rhee

The Wealth Effect of Foreign Investor Presence: Evidence from the Indonesian Market

Abstract

- The wealth effect of foreign investor presence on domestic investors remains an important policy issue to be considered when any country's capital market is opened to foreign investors.

- We investigated the wealth effect of foreign investor presence on the Indonesian domestic market before and after the announcement of lifting foreign stock ownership restrictions on September 4, 1997 in Indonesia.

Key Results

- The presence of foreign investors was associated with positive wealth effects as indicated by positive cumulative abnormal returns. The impact of this event, however, was modest and short-lived because of the Asian financial crisis when the announcement was made.

- The sources of wealth effects were largely limited to trading efficiency variables (rather than market liquidity) despite the adverse impact of the Asian financial crisis.

Authors

Mamduh Hanafi, Assistant Professor of Finance, The Gadjah Mada University of Indonesia, Bulaksumur, Yogyakarta, Indonesia.
S. Ghon Rhee, K. J. Distinguished Professor of International Finance and Banking, and Executive Director of the Asia-Pacific Financial Markets Research Center, College of Business Administration, The University of Hawaii at Manoa, Honolulu HI, USA.

Introduction

As of September 4, 1997, the Indonesian government eliminated a 49% foreign ownership restriction on Jakarta Stock Exchanges (JSX)-listed companies to discourage capital outflows from its financial system as the Asian financial crisis deepened. Under this new regulation, foreign investors were able to buy up to 100% of outstanding shares of non-financial companies. On January 28, 1998, the Indonesian government announced the removal of foreign ownership restrictions for financial companies as well. As a result, the Indonesian market was completely open to foreign investors.

This event provided a natural setting to study the effect of foreign investor presence (financial market liberalization) on domestic shareholders' wealth. Although this event involved the changing of foreign investment restrictions, we viewed it as the beginning of significant foreign investor presence in the Indonesian market. This event was similar to the change of foreign investment limits in the Singapore market examined by Lam (1997) and the announcement of liberalization studied by Henry (2000a, 2000b) and Kim and Singal (2000). While examining the wealth effects of financial market liberalization, this study should differ from past studies, however, in at least five aspects. First, Stulz and Wasserfallen (1995) studied the Swiss companies that changed foreign ownership restrictions voluntarily, hence the change was endogenous to the companies, while the Indonesian event was exogenous to all JSX-listed companies. Second, if policy makers liberalize the market when the economy is doing well, we may expect the positive wealth effect to be biased upward as we observed from Henry (2000a) and Kim and Singal (2000). Because the lifting of foreign ownership restrictions in September 1997 occurred in the midst of the Asian financial crisis, it should be interesting to observe whether or not the positive effect of foreign investor presence held up. Third, while Henry (2000a) and Kim and Singal (2000) used aggregate market data, we used the individual firm level data to investigate the effect of financial liberalization on the stock price behavior. The use of individual firm level data allowed us to investigate the cross-sectional determinants of abnormal stock returns resulting from foreign investor presence. Fourth, our study highlighted the differing effects of foreign investor presence on domestic stocks depending on their characterization in terms of efficiency and liquidity. This was not done in past studies. Fifth, this study examined the impact of significant foreign investors' presence on the stock price behavior, whereas a series of study by Bailey and Jagtiani (1994), Stulz and Wasserfallen (1995), Domowitz, Glen, and Madhavan (1997), and Lam (1997) focused on foreign investment restrictions or the violation of the law of one price as a result of segmented markets.

Our empirical findings indicated that the presence of foreign investors was associated with shareholder wealth-enhancing positive abnormal returns. The trading efficiency variables seemed to explain the abnormal returns better than the changes in market liquidity. Financial market liberalization conducted during a financial crisis still exhibited positive benefits, while the magnitude was modest.

We believe that the wealth effect of foreign investor presence on the domestic investors remains an important policy issue to be carefully examined. Very often, policy makers are reluctant in their country's globalization effort, especially when the capital markets have to be completely opened to foreign portfolio investments, because of the fear that foreign investors will take over the majority ownership of local businesses.

We organized this paper as follows. First, we discussed the institutional background of the Indonesian capital market. Then, we discussed our data, the methodology, and the major results. In the next section, we analyzed cross-sectional determinants of wealth effects generated by the significant presence of foreign investors. We offered some conclusions in the final section.

Institutional Background of the Indonesian Capital Market

The history of the Indonesian capital market dates back to its colonial era. The Dutch government established the first stock exchange in Batavia (now known as Jakarta, Indonesia's capital) in 1912. During the First World War, it was closed and then reopened in 1925. The Japanese occupation of Indonesia halted the exchange's operation. Seven years after Indonesian independence, the exchange was re-opened in 1952. The nationalization program in 1956 halted its trading again.

The modern JSX started in 1977 when President Suharto re-opened the exchange. The Badan Pelaksana Pasar Modal (BAPEPAM) or the Capital Market Executive Agency, served as the operator and regulator of the JSX market. During the early years of the JSX, BAPEPAM set a priority of promoting and protecting domestic investors. The policy of promoting domestic investors was designed for wealth distribution. Foreign companies or joint venture companies were among the first companies to go public under this policy. The government established a financial company called Danareksa that has been serving as a closed-end investment company. In this role, Danareksa helped implement the policy of promoting domestic investors' participation in the market. For investor protection, the government strongly discouraged speculation. Price movements were limited to four percent daily. Danareksa actively intervened in the market when the limits reached four percent. At this stage, the market was closed for foreign investors.

Such microstructure policy did not appeal much to potential market players. Macro economic policy did not help either. In the early 1980s, the Indonesian government introduced a series of banking deregulation measures. These reform measures created a stiff competition in the banking industry, leading to a higher interest rate to make investment in the stock market less attractive. From 1977 to 1988, there were only 24 listed companies. Most of these companies went public to satisfy the government's policy of promoting the welfare of domestic investors rather than raising equity capital. However, in the latter part of the 1980s, the Indonesian stock market responded positively to the government's deregulation packages aimed at promoting stock investment. In 1988, the government removed the four percent price limits, relaxed listing requirements and procedures for going public, and, most important of all, allowed foreign investors to buy up to 49% of outstanding shares of listed stocks. The government started to impose taxes on interest income in the same year making stock investment more attractive relative to savings deposit.

In the two years following deregulation, the number of companies that went public increased significantly from 24 to 67. Along with the growth of Indonesian economy, the JSX index started to move up significantly. Figure 1 showed the appreciation of the JSX index from 1985 to 1998. Table 1 presented the number of companies that went public and the amount of funds raised from 1977 to 1998.

With privatization in 1993, the JSX became a self-regulated organization owned by member brokerage firms. BAPEPAM, (now translated as the Capital

Figure 1 The Jakarta Stock Exchange Index (1985–1998)

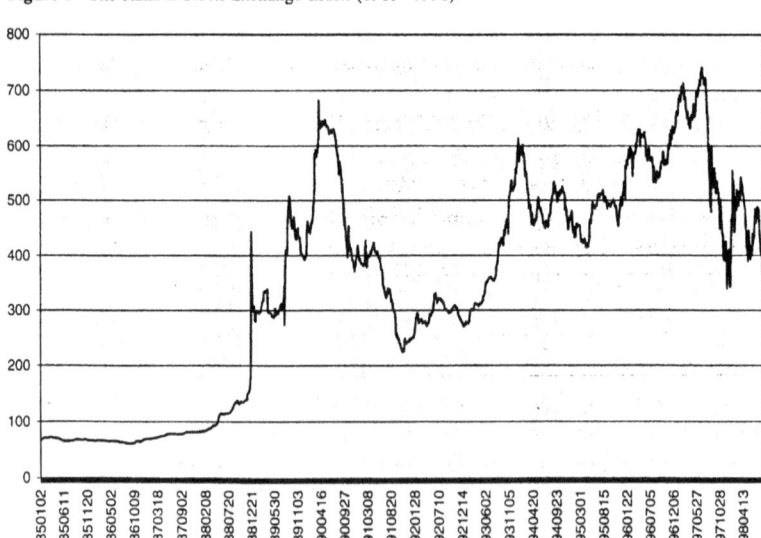

Wealth Impact of Foreign Investor Presence

Table 1. Listing Firms and Funds Raised in The Jakarta Stock Exchange (1977–1998)

Year	Issuer		Value (Rp Million)	
	Per-Year	Cumulative	Per-Year	Cumulative
1977	1	1	1,787.50	1,787.50
1978	0	1	–	1,787.50
1979	3	4	25,113.00	26,900.50
1980	2	6	8,527.50	35,428.00
1981	3	9	37,928.40	73,356.40
1982	5	14	20,262.60	93,619.00
1983	9	23	35,053.10	128,672.10
1984	1	24	320.50	128,992.60
1985	0	24	–	128,992.60
1986	0	24	407.10	129,399.70
1987	0	24	–	129,399.70
1988	1	25	44,309.10	173,708.00
1989	42	67	2,041,737.50	2,215,446.30
1990	65	132	5,221,651.60	7,437,097.90
1991	13	145	626,169.60	8,063,267.50
1992	17	162	743,665.00	8,806,932.50
1993	19	181	1,362,431.30	10,169,363.80
1994	50	231	4,804,494.00	14,973,857.80
1995	17	248	5,682,059.40	20,655,917.20
1996	19	267	2,662,207.30	23,318,124.50
1997	34	301	3,950,515.50	27,268,640.00
1998	3	304	68,125.00	27,336,765.00

This table provides the historical record of companies that went public to be listed on the Jakarta Stock Exchange (JSX) in 1977–1998 and the amount of funds raised from going public.
Source: Bapepam Indonesia

Market Supervisory Agency), shifted its role from managing and executing the exchange to supervising it. In 1995, the JSX introduced an automated trading system, called JATS (Jakarta Automated Trading System), to replace the manual trading system. The Indonesian market suffered a setback when the financial crisis hit Indonesia in October 1997.

The Indonesian market provided a 'partial' cycle of foreign ownership regulation. Until December 1987, it was practically closed to foreign investment. The government started to open its market gradually. During the next 10 years, the Indonesian government introduced four key measures to open up the Indonesian stock market: (i) the Minister of Finance decree of September 16, 1989 allowed foreign investors to buy up to 49% of outstanding shares of all listed non-financial companies, (ii) the Minister of Finance decree of October 30, 1992 allowed foreign investors to buy up to 49% of outstanding shares of listed financial companies, (iii) the Minister of Finance decree of September 1997 allowed foreign investors to buy up to 100% of listed non-financial companies, and (iv) the Minister of Finance decree of January 28, 1998 allowed foreign investors to buy up to 100% of listed financial companies. In this sequence of market liberalization, the September 1997 announcement represented the most important event that allows us to investigate the effect of significant foreign investor presence on the domestic stock price behavior.

Data, Methodology, and Major Findings

The Data

The daily price and volume data used in this study covered the period from May 1995 to August 1998. We focused on the regular board that was the most liquid market in Indonesia, accounting for about 83% [89%] of JSX's trading value [volume] during our study period.

Stock Price Reactions to Two Major Events

We used a modified market model to measure the price impact of foreign investor presence surrounding the event day of September 4, 1997 when foreign ownership restrictions were lifted. This modified market model was an improved variation of the standard event-study analysis for our tests because it accommodated the possibility of an exogenous shift in market model parameters, while providing us the same pattern and timing of abnormal returns as those that would have been obtained from a conventional event-study approach that did not allow an exogenous shift in the parameters (Binder 1985). Recent applications of similar types of modified market models can be found in Amihud, Mendelson, and Lauterbach (1997) and Berkman and Eleswarapu (1998).

$$R_{i,t} = \alpha_i + \beta_{1i}R_{m,t} + \beta_{2i}R_{m,t+1} + \beta_{3i}R_{w,t} + \beta_{4i}D(1)_t + \beta_{5i}D(2)_t + e_{i,t} \quad (1)$$

where,

$R_{i,t}$ = daily return on stock i on day t;
$R_{m,t}$ = daily return on the value-weighted JSX market index on day t;
$R_{w,t}$ = daily return on the US market portfolio (S&P 500 Index) return on day t;
$D(1)$ = indicator variable assigned with certain values (depending on the time-horizon prior to the event day) and zero otherwise;
$D(2)$ = indicator variable assigned with certain values (depending on the time-horizon subsequent to the event day) and zero otherwise; and
$e_{i,t}$ = random error terms.

Regressions were run for the period from t = −150 to t = +150. To address the problem of infrequent trading, we added lead and lag market return variables following Dimson (1979). Our preliminary investigation indicated that one period lead for market return provided the most consistent results as reported by Berkman and Eleswarapu (1998); hence, we used only one lead market return variable in both model specifications. Daily returns on the US market index were introduced to capture the worldwide impact on the Indonesian stock price behavior even though the S&P 500 Index was admittedly a crude proxy for the world market portfolio. Note that β_4 and β_5 measured pre- and post-event day cumulative abnormal returns over the event time-horizon. Five sets of event time-horizon were investigated to confirm the robustness of the results: (i) t = −1 to t = +1; (ii) t = −3 to t = +3; (iii) t = −5 to t = +5; (iv) t = −10 to t = +10; and (v) t = −20 to t = +20. Assigned values to indicator variables, D(1) and D(2), differed depending on the time-horizon selected. For example, we assigned a value of 1/4 to D(1) for event days from t = −3 to t = 0 and zero otherwise; and assigned a value of 1/3 to D(2) for event days from t = +1 to t = +3 and zero otherwise.

Table 2 summarized five sets of regression results. The most remarkable yet expected finding was that the impact of the Asian financial crisis was so intense that it seemed to overwhelm the wealth effects of market liberalization. The only exceptions were the shortest time-horizons from t = −1 to t = +1 and from t = −3 to t = +3. During the post-event period, one [three]-day abnormal returns were 0.043% and 0.049%, respectively, and significant in the two regressions with short time-horizons, while regressions for longer time-horizons exhibited negative abnormal returns after the announcement of market liberalization, indicating the dominance of the crisis-related market sentiment over the price behavior. It was possible that an information leakage could be associated with the government announcement. This was especially the case for the announcement of regulation because of the prolonged process of enactment (Binder 1985). In addition, since the government tended to introduce other reform measures simultaneously, Henry (2000a) pointed out the need to control for other liberalizations around the event date. In the case of information leakage, if we could identify the start of the leakage, then we might be able to isolate such effect. In view of possible confounding effects, we introduced 21-day (from t = −10 to t = +10) and 41-day (from t = −20 to t = +20) windows to measure abnormal returns. Interestingly but not surprisingly due to the Asian financial crisis, negative welfare effects were exhibited for these event windows of longer period. Contrasting the results of welfare effects observed for the event windows of short and long periods suggest that both the announcement of market liberalization and the Asian crisis simultaneously affected the results. Since we could not confirm whether the negative reaction of stock prices observed for longer event windows was attributed to the new

Table 2. Cumulative Abnormal Returns Around Event Day

	(1)	(2)	(3)	(4)	(5)
Intercept	-0.003	-0.003	-0.002	-0.020	-0.002
	(-4.73)***	(-4.36)***	(-3.83)***	(-3.34)***	(-2.38)**
$R_{m,t}$	0.008	0.008	0.008	0.008	0.008
	(33.79)***	(33.53)***	(36.19)***	(36.24)***	(35.91)***
$R_{m,t+1}$	0.0010	0.001	0.001	0.001	0.001
	(4.23)***	(5.05)***	(4.86)***	(4.50)***	(4.30)***
$R_{w,t}$	-0.0010	-0.001	-0.001	-0.001	-0.001
	(-1.77)*	(-1.87)*	(-1.82)*	(-1.69)*	(-1.50)
D(1)	0.015	-0.054	-0.091	-0.100	-0.227
	(1.02)	(-2.22)**	(-3.27)***	(-2.76)***	(-4.50)***
D(2)	0.043	0.049	-0.002	-0.061	-0.096
	(4.01)***	(2.70)***	(-0.08)	(-1.85)*	(-1.97)**
Number of Observations	12,586	12,586	12,586	12,586	12,586
Adjusted R-Square	0.10	0.10	0.10	0.10	0.10

This table presents five sets of regression results using the model: $R_{i,t} = \alpha_i + \beta_{1i}R_{m,t} + \beta_{2i}R_{m,t+1} + \beta_{3i}R_{w,t} + \beta_{4i}D(1)_t + \beta_{5i}D(2)_t + e_{i,t}$, where, $R_{i,t}$ = daily return on stock i on day t; $R_{m,t}$ = daily return on the value-weighted JSX market index on day t; $R_{w,t}$ = daily return on the US market portfolio (S&P 500 Index) return on day t; D(1) = indicator variable assigned with certain values (depending on the time-horizon prior to the event day) and zero otherwise; D(2) = indicator variable assigned with certain values (depending on the time-horizon subsequent to the event day) and zero otherwise; and $e_{i,t}$ = random error terms. Regressions are run for the period from t = -150 to t = +150. Five sets of event time-horizon are investigated to confirm the robustness of the results: (1) t = -1 to t = +1; (2) t = -3 to t = +3; (3) t = -5 to t = +5; (4) t = -10 to t = +10; and (5) t = -20 to t = +20. Assigned values to indicator variables, D(1) and D(2), differ depending on the time-horizon selected. For example, we assign a value of 1/4 to D(1) for event days from t = -3 to t = 0 and zero otherwise; and assign a value of 1/3 to D(2) for event days from t = +1 to t = +3 and zero otherwise. t-values are in parenthesis. ***, **, * mean statistical significance at 1%, 5%, 10% level respectively.

deregulation over foreign stock ownership or it was just manifestation of the adverse impact of the crisis itself, it became important to examine the sources of cumulative abnormal returns. The results were presented in the next section.

To sum up, the findings based on five regressions suggest that the foreign investor presence was associated with positive abnormal returns, while this positive wealth effects existed only for a short window of 1 to 3 days. This event highlighted the importance of the economic environment of market liberalization. This observation had one important policy implication. Countries experiencing financial crises should explore other reform measures rather than focusing on market liberalization per se. For example, Johnson et al. (2000) reported a strong association between corporate governance in emerging markets and the severity of the Asian financial crisis. Hence, the improvement in corporate governance might help combat the severity of the financial crisis more effectively than the lifting of foreign ownership restrictions.

The Determinants of Abnormal Returns in the Event Period

Since our focus was on the potential benefits and costs associated with foreign investor presence, we identified several variables that proxied for the benefits and costs of foreign investors. Specifically, we focused on efficiency and liquidity measures as a potential explanation for the abnormal returns.

Liquidity

We introduced three variables to measure liquidity in the pre- and post-event periods, respectively: (i) market-adjusted trading volume; (ii) market-adjusted trading value; and (iii) market depth. The pre-event period was from $t = -150$ to $t = -31$ and the post-event period was from $t = +31$ to $t = +150$ for each stock.

Market-Adjusted Trading Volume [Value]

To control for the market-wide impact, we calculated market-adjusted trading volume (value), which was trading volume (value) recorded for each stock deflated by market trading volume (value). This adjustment was particularly important for the event under study, since this event occurred during the crisis period. Market-adjusted volume was denoted by TRDVOL.

Market Depth

Market depth was calculated, following Amihud et al. (1997) and Chang et al. (1997):

$$\text{MKTDEP}_{i,t} = \sum \text{Volume}_{i,t} / \sum |R_{i,t}| \tag{2}$$

where

$\text{MKTDEP}_{i,t}$ = market depth of stock i on day t;
Volume = daily trading volume; and
$|R|$ = absolute value of daily return.

Market depth measured additional volume per one unit of price change. The greater the market depth, the higher the liquidity. This measure was consistent with Kyle (1985) who had defined market depth as the trading volume per unit of price change.

Efficiency Variables

To measure trading efficiency, we calculated the variance of daily returns (VARRET) and the variance of residual returns (RESVAR) estimated from the single-factor market model. We also used variances of residuals from the modified market model introduced earlier but the results remain unchanged. These variances were used as proxies for the level of trading noisiness in the pre- and post-event periods.

Foreign Ownership Restriction Variables

Of various variables suggested by the extant literature, we introduced two variables, following Bailey and Jagtiani (1994), to explain the behavior of the premium of the prices on the foreign board over the prices on the regular board. We included them in this study as control variables.

Size

This variable was used to proxy for information availability (Merton 1987). Every year we calculated size as the closing price at the end of the year times the number of shares outstanding at the end of the year. Then we averaged the numbers to obtain the size variable. It is well documented that foreign investors prefered large and well-known companies (Kang and Stulz 1997). An asset with a larger base of informed investors sold at higher price than that with a smaller base (Merton 1987). We would expect to have a positive association between size and abnormal returns for both events.

Trading Volume on Foreign Board

Bailey and Jagtiani (1994) suggested that trading volume on the foreign board could capture the degree of foreign investors' familiarity with domestic stocks. Prior to September 4, 1997 when the foreign ownership restriction of 49% was imposed, foreign investors had to buy shares from other foreign investors once the limits became binding. A foreign board was then created to facilitate trading of foreign owned shares among foreign investors. We predicted a positive association between this variable and the abnormal returns during the event period.

Relative Supply

Another interesting variable introduced by Bailey and Jagtiani (1994) was the relative supply measure, which was defined as:

$$\text{RS (Relative Supply)}_i = \frac{\text{Vol}_{i,\text{Foreign}}}{\text{Vol}_{\text{Foreign}}} - \frac{\text{Vol}_i}{\text{TotVol}} \qquad (3)$$

where subscript i referred to individual stock, $\text{Vol}_{\text{Foreign}}$ referred to trading volume on foreign board and TotVol denotes total volume of all stocks. This variable measured the degree of tightness of foreign demand relative to the supply of stocks. A low value implies a high degree of tightness in the demand for the stock relative to its supply. Investors are willing to pay a premium for a stock with this characteristic. We predicted a negative relation between relative supply and the abnormal returns, i.e., the tighter the demand for a stock, the larger the premium investors were willing to pay.

Descriptive Statistics of Liquidity and Efficiency Variables

Table 3 summarized descriptive statistics in the pre- and post-event periods. The decline in liquidity measures and the increase in trading noise from the pre- to post-event period were reported. For example, market-adjusted trading volume [value] declined from 7.63 [7.14] in the pre-event period to 5.92 [5.96] in the post-event period. This was not unexpected considering the financial crisis adversely affecting the market performance. Market depth also declined from 54,784 in the pre-event period to 39,964 in the post-event period, recording over a 25% rate of decline. A dramatic deterioration was indicated in the market efficiency variable as evidenced by the increase trading noise caused by the market turmoil during the Asian financial crisis.

Cross-sectional Regression: The Sources of Wealth Effects

To investigate the joint effect of efficiency and liquidity variables on the abnormal returns, we performed a cross-sectional regression. The dependent variable was measured by β_3 of the market model: $R_{i,t} = \alpha_i + \beta_{1i}R_{m,t} + \beta_{2i}R_{m,t+1} + \beta_{3i}D_t + e_{i,t}$ where the indicator variable D was assigned a value of 1/4 for day $t = -1, 0, +1,$ and $+2$, and zero otherwise. For liquidity variables (TRDVOL and MKTDEP) and daily returns (RET), their changes were defined as the differences between the pre- and the post-event period observations. For efficiency variables (RESVAR and VARRET), the changes were defined as the differences between the post- and the pre-event period observations. Under this specification, we expected to have negative coefficients for both efficiency and liquidity variables. Table 4 presents the results of the regression analysis.

Table 3. Descriptive Statistics of Liquidity and Efficiency Variables Around Event Day

	Mean	Minimum	Maximum	Standard Deviation	Num of Obs	t-value
Trading Volume (shares)						
Post	2,124,652	8	24,625,592	4,170,175	173	(6.702)***
Pre	1,462,964	13	12,040,720	2,705,255	171	(7.072)***
Difference	693,462	−19,484	11,184,271	4,590,266	167	(1.952)**
Trading Value (Rp)						
Post	2,254,533	6,512	64,553,420	6,507,212	173	(4.557)***
Pre	2,529,035	15,673	33,427,925	4,379,545	171	(7.551)***
Difference	−258,061	−32,764,527	49,498,224	6,953,435	167	(−0.479)
Market–Adjusted Trading Volume						
Post	5.92	0.01	84.35	13.54	162	(5.569)***
Pre	7.63	0.10	82.44	12.84	171	(7.769)***
Difference	−2.18	−80.57	69.99	16.68	156	(−1.636)*
Market–Adjusted Trading Value						
Post	5.96	0.01	145.69	17.91	162	(4.234)***
Pre	7.14	0.06	85.56	11.49	171	(8.127)***
Difference	−1.59	−82.51	140.25	18.52	156	(−1.071)
Market Depth (1,000)						
Post	39,964	125	634,162	85,749	173	(6.130)***
Pre	54,784	262	518,409	82,785	170	(8.628)***
Difference	−14,603	−488,718	513,274	93,164	166	(−2.019)**
Daily Residual Returns						
Post	−1.47E-15	−1.3359E-13	1.40E-13	3.64E-14	171	(−0.528)
Pre	−7.141E-16	−1.1828E-13	6.02E-14	2.41E-14	177	(−0.394)
Difference	−5.164E-16	−1.3578E-13	2.10E-13	4.46E-14	171	(−0.151)
Absolute Value of Daily Residual Returns						
Post	2.52E-14	0.00E+00	1.40E-13	2.63E-14	171	(12.535)***
Pre	1.73E-14	0.00E+00	1.18E-13	1.68E-14	177	(13.685)***
Difference	8.05E-15	−5.55E-14	1.33E-13	2.92E-14	171	(3.603)***
Variance of Daily Residual Returns						
Post	0.0084	0.0003	0.0387	0.0060	171	(18.295)***
Pre	0.0027	0.0002	0.0190	0.0024	177	(15.237)***
Difference	0.0058	−0.0114	0.0341	0.0059	171	(12.832)***
Variance of Daily Returns						
Post	0.0097	0.0003	0.0423	0.0065	173	(19.707)***
Pre	0.0031	0.0002	0.0191	0.0024	177	(17.007)***
Difference	0.0067	−0.0114	0.0369	0.0064	173	(13.629)***
Mean of Daily Returns						
Post	−0.0043	−0.0338	0.0220	0.0068	173	(−8.279)***
Pre	−0.0032	−0.0161	0.0201	0.0047	177	(−9.194)***
Difference	−0.0009	−0.0257	0.0309	0.0078	173	(−1.432)

Table 3 presents descriptive statistics of the liquidity and efficiency variables for the sample stocks before and after Event Two. Market-adjusted trading volume (value) is trading volume (value) recorded for each stock deflated by market trading volume (value). Market depth is defined as $MktDep_{i,t} = \sum Volume_{i,t} / \sum |R_{i,t}|$ where Volume = daily trading volume; and |R| = absolute value of daily return. Daily returns are obtained from the PACAP-Indonesia databases. Residual returns are measured from the one-factor market model. The pre-event period is from $t = -150$ to $t = -31$ and the post-event period is from $t = +31$ to $t = +150$. ***, **, and * mean significant at 1%, 5%, and 10%.

Table 4. The Cross-Sectional Determinants of Abnormal Returns Around The Announcement of Liberalization

	(1)	(2)	(3)	(4)	(5)	(6)	(7)	(8)
Intercept	0.06	0.08	0.05	0.07	0.07	0.08	0.09	0.11
	(4.812)***	(−4.246)***	(2.982)***	(4.240)***	(4.192)***	(2.001)*	(1.084)	(2.232)
ΔTRDVOL	5.19E-04	–	–	−2.78E-04	−2.78E-04	1.04E-03	–	−1.50E-03
	(0.426)			(−0.228)	(−0.227)	(0.301)		(−0.444)
ΔMKTDEP	9.01E-11	–	–	−7.15E-11	7.18E-11	−1.90E-10	–	−3.33E-10
	(0.452)			(−0.369)	(0.368)	(−0.252)		(−0.388)
ΔRESVAR	–	4.87E-03	−1.26E-04	−1.78E-04	−1.75E-04	–	−2.26E-04	−4.42E-04
		(4.221)***	(−4.221)***	(−0.808)	(−0.748)		(−0.449)	(−0.888)
ΔVARRET	–	−44.64	–	–	–	–	–	–
		(−4.221)**						
PRX-ΔVARRET	–	–	−44.642	−41.069	−41.06	–	−52.81	−50.02
			(−4.221)***	(−3.115)***	(−3.104)***		(−1.529)	(−1.609)
ΔRET	–	–	–	–	−0.07	–	–	–
					(−0.037)			
SIZE	–	–	–	–	–	3.45E-09	4.23E-09	1.61E-09
						(0.469)	(0.534)	(0.221)
VOLFBOARD	–	–	–	–	–	−0.689	−8.13E-01	−9.84E-01
						(−0.879)	(−0.941)	(−1.261)
RSUPPLY	–	–	–	–	–	0.35	0.81	1.11
						(0.276)	(0.924)	(0.816)
Number of Obs	154	170	170	154	154	34	35	34
Adjusted R–Sqr	−0.06	0.08	0.09	0.05	0.04	−0.15	−0.03	−0.06

The table presents regression coefficients of the cross-sectional determinants of the abnormal return during the announcement of financial liberalization on September 4, 1997. Abnormal return is estimated from coefficient regression of β_3 of the following model: $R_{i,t} = \alpha_i + \beta_{1i}R_{m,t} + \beta_{2i}R_{m,t+1} + \beta_{3i}D_t + e_{i,t}$. The indicator variable D is assigned a value of 1/4 for day $t = -1, 0, +1,$ and $+2$, and zero otherwise. The model is estimated from day -150 to day $+150$. For liquidity variables (TRDVOL and MKTDEP) and actual return (RET), their changes are the differences between the observations in the pre- and post-event periods. For efficiency variables (RESVAR and VARRET), the changes are the differences between the observations in the post- and pre-event periods. Size is the closing price at the end of year times outstanding shares at the end of year. A proxy for the changes in the variance of daily return (PRX-ΔVARRET$_i$) is obtained from the orthogonalization given high correlations between two efficiency variables (ΔRESVAR and ΔVARRET). Details of variable definitions are explained in the text. t-values are in parenthesis. ***, **, and * mean significant at 1%, 5%, and 10% level.

In regression (1) of Table 4, we used the changes in liquidity to explain the abnormal returns. Estimated coefficients for liquidity were insignificant. In regression (2), we used the changes in efficiency. The efficiency variables had significant coefficients, but with inconsistent signs between $\Delta RESVAR_i$ and $\Delta VARRET_i$. Given a high correlation between the two variables, we orthogonalized them by performing regression of $\Delta VARRET_i$ on $\Delta RESVAR_i$ to obtain a proxy for the changes in the variance of daily returns (PRX-$\Delta VARRET_i$).

In regression (3), significant coefficients with expected signs (negative coefficients) were observed for efficiency variables. The market seemed to negatively price noise increase in the post-event period. Regression (4) of table 4 included both the liquidity and the efficiency variables. We found that PRX-$\Delta VARRET_i$ had a significant negative coefficient. Regression (5) included return differences (ΔRET_i) along with the changes in the liquidity and the efficiency. We found a significant negative coefficient for PRX-$\Delta VARRET_i$. Regression (6), (7), and (8) included variables found to be the determinants of the premium of prices on the foreign board over prices on the regular board. The power of PRX-$\Delta VARRET_i$ disappeared. The smaller sample size might explain the weak results found in regression (6), (7), and (8). Size had an expected sign, while trading volume on the foreign board and the degree of demand tightness showed unexpected signs. None of these coefficients was significant at the conventional level. We have also used positive abnormal returns for the time-horizon from $t = -1$ to $t = +1$ as the dependent variable in this cross-sectional regressions. The results are similar to those summarized in Table 4.

Conclusion

This study investigated the effect of market liberalization on domestic asset prices and the sources of asset price revaluation resulting from liberalization. We found that the announcement of liberalization was associated with modest positive abnormal returns only for the 3-day window, whereas longer-term windows failed to provide any significant abnormal returns. Further examination of the sources of abnormal returns indicated that the efficiency variables explained the abnormal returns better than did the liquidity variables. Specifically, the market seemed to negatively price noise increase in the post-event period. Liberalization in the crisis period could not minimize the noise associated with the crisis period as shown by increases of noise level in the post-event period. The setting of liberalization (boom, normal, and crisis periods), therefore, had varying effects on the domestic stock price behavior.

References

Amihud, Y./Mendelson, H./Lauterbach, B., Market Microstructure and Securities Values: Evidence from the Tel Aviv Stock Exchange, *Journal of Financial Economics*, 45, 1997, pp. 365-390.
Bailey, W./Jagtiani, J., Foreign Ownership Restrictions and Stock Price in the Thai Capital Market, *Journal of Financial Economics*, 42, 1994, pp. 57-87.
Berkman, H./Eleswarapu, V. R., Short-Term Traders and Liquidity: A Test Using Bombay Stock Exchange Data, *Journal of Financial Economics*, 47, 1998, pp. 339-355.
Binder, J. J., Measuring the Effects of Regulation with Stock Price Data, *The Rand Journal of Economics*, 16, 2, 1985, pp. 167-174.
Chang, R. C./Huang, N. K./Shu, S. Z./Rhee, S. G., The Effects of Trading Methods on Volatility and Liquidity: Evidence from the Taiwan Stock Exchange, *Journal of Business Finance & Accounting*, 26, 1999, pp. 137-170.
Dimson, E., Risk Measurement When Shares Are Subject to Infrequent Trading, *Journal of Financial Economics*, 7, 1979, pp. 197-226.
Domowitz, I./Glen, J./Madhavan, A., Market Segmentation and Stock Prices: Evidence from An Emerging Market, *Journal of Finance*, 52, 1997, pp. 1059-1085.
Henry, P. B., Stock Market Liberalization, Economic Reform, and Emerging Market Equity Prices, *Journal of Finance*, 55, 2000a, pp. 529-564.
Henry, P. B., Do Stock Market Liberalizations Cause Investment Booms? *Journal of Financial Economics*, 58, 2000b, pp. 301-334.
Johnson, S./Boone, P./Breach, A./Friedman, E., Corporate Governance in the Asian Financial Crisis, *Journal of Financial Economics*, 58, 2000, pp. 141-186.
Kang, J./Stulz, R. M., Why Is There a Home Bias? An Analysis of Foreign Portfolio Equity Ownership in Japan, *Journal of Financial Economics*, 46, 1997, pp. 3-28.
Kim, E. H./Singal, V., Stock Market Openings: Experience of Emerging Economies, *Journal of Business*, 73, 2000, pp. 25-66.
Kyle, A. S., Continuous auctions and insider trading, *Econometrica*, 53, 1985, pp. 1315-1335.
Lam, S., Control Versus Firm Value: The Impact of Restrictions on Foreign Share Ownership, *Financial Management*, 26, 1997, pp. 48-61.
Merton, R. C., A Simple Model of Capital Market Equilibrium with Incomplete Information, *Journal of Finance*, 42, 1987, pp. 483-510.
Stulz, R. M./Wasserfallen, W., Foreign Equity Investment Restrictions, Capital Flight, and Shareholder Wealth Maximization: Theory and Evidence, *Review of Financial Studies*, 8, 1995, pp. 1019-1057.

mir *Edition*

Andreas Wald

Network Structures and Network Effects in Organizations

A Network Analysis in Multinational Corporations

2003, XVIII, 238 pages, pb., € 49,90 (approx. US $ 49,90)
ISBN 3-409-12395-4

Network structures have been praised as the organizational form of today's multinational corporation. Building on conceptual work on network organizations, a quantitative network analysis of formal and informal organizational structures is performed in this study. It is tested whether network structures can be identified empirically. Moreover, the effects of organizational structures on strategic decision making in two multinational corporations are analyzed. A theoretical framework is provided by an exchange model and by social capital theory.
The book is addressed to scholars of international management and organizational studies.

Betriebswirtschaftlicher Verlag Dr. Th. Gabler GmbH, Abraham-Lincoln-Str. 46, 65189 Wiesbaden

Management
International Review
© Gabler Verlag 2004

EDITORIAL OBJECTIVES

MANAGEMENT INTERNATIONAL REVIEW presents insights and analyses which reflect basic and topical advances in the key areas of International Management. Its target audience includes scholars and executives in business and administration.

EDITORIAL POLICY

MANAGEMENT INTERNATIONAL REVIEW is a refereed journal which aims at the advancement and dissemination of international applied research in the fields of Management and Business. The scope of the journal comprises International Business, Transnational Corporations, Intercultural Management, Strategic Management, and Business Policy.

MANAGEMENT INTERNATIONAL REVIEW stresses the interaction between theory and practice of management by way of publishing articles, research notes, reports and comments which concentrate on the application of existing and potential research for business and other organizations. Papers are invited and given priority which are based on rigorous methodology, suggest models capable to solve practical problems. Also papers are welcome which advise as to whether and to what extent models can be translated and applied by the practising manager. Work which has passed the practical test of successful application is of special interest to MIR. It is hoped that besides its academic objectives the journal will serve some useful purpose for the practical world, and also help bridging the gap between academic and business management.

PUBLISHING · SUBSCRIPTION · ADVERTISEMENTS

Published quarterly, fixed annual subscription rate for foreign countries: Individual subscription 114 Euro (approx. US $ 129.–), institutional subscription 228 Euro (approx. US $ 258.–), single copy 62 Euro – (approx. US $ 64.–). Fixed annual subscription rate for Germany: Individual subscription 104 Euro –, institutional subscription 218 Euro. Payment on receipt of invoice. Subscriptions are entered on a calendar basis only (Jan.–Dec.). Cancellations must be filed by referring to the subscription number six weeks before closing date (subscription invoice); there will be no confirmation. There may be 1 to 4 supplementary issues per year. Each supplementary issue will be sent to subscribers with a separate invoice allowing 25% deduction on the regular price. Subscribers have the right to return the issue within one month to the distribution company. – Subscription office: VVA, post-box 7777, D-33310 Gütersloh, Germany, Tel. 0049/(0)5241-801968/802891, Fax 80 96 20. Distribution: Kristiane Alesch, Tel. 0049/(0)611/7878-359. Advertising office: Thomas Werner, Tel. 0049/(0)611/7878-138. Editorial Department: Susanne Kramer, Tel. 0049/(0) 611/7878-234, e-mail: Susanne.Kramer@gabler.de. Annelie Meisenheimer, Tel. 0049/(0)611/7878-232. Production: Frieder Kumm, Tel. 0049/(0)611/7878-175, Fax 7878-400. Internet: Publisher http://www.gabler.de; Editor http://www.uni-hohenheim.de./~mir; Managing Director Dr. Hans-Dieter Haenel; Publishing Director Dr. Heinz Weinheimer; Senior Publishing Editor Claudia Splittgerber; Sales Manager Gabriel Göttlinger; Production Manager Reinhard van den Hövel. Produced by Druckhaus „Thomas Müntzer" GmbH, Bad Langensalza – Contributions published in this journal are protected by copyright.

© Betriebswirtschaftlicher Verlag Dr. Th. Gabler/GWV Fachverlage GmbH, Wiesbaden 2004. Gabler Verlag is a company of Springer Science+Business Media.

No part of this publication may be reproduced, stored in a retrieval system or transmitted in any form or by any means: electronic, magnetic tape, mechanical, photocopying, recording or otherwise, without permission in writing from the publisher. There is no liability for manuscripts and review literature which were submitted without invitation.

ISSN 0938-8249

Have you already visited our **mir** homepage?

If not, then it is high time you did!

http://www.uni-hohenheim.de/~mir

ISBN 3-409-12644-9
VVA 126/02644

GPSR Compliance

The European Union's (EU) General Product Safety Regulation (GPSR) is a set of rules that requires consumer products to be safe and our obligations to ensure this.

If you have any concerns about our products, you can contact us on

ProductSafety@springernature.com

In case Publisher is established outside the EU, the EU authorized representative is:

Springer Nature Customer Service Center GmbH
Europaplatz 3
69115 Heidelberg, Germany

www.ingramcontent.com/pod-product-compliance
Lightning Source LLC
LaVergne TN
LVHW011940070526
838202LV00054B/4734